KU-216-566

A World Without Email

A World Without Email

Also by Cal Newport

The Time-Block Planner

Digital Minimalism

Deep Work

So Good They Can't Ignore You

How to Be a High School Superstar

How to Become a Straight-A Student

How to Win at College

A World Without Email

Reimagining Work in an Age of Communication Overload

Cal Newport

Portfolio / Penguin

PORTFOLIO / PENGUIN
An imprint of Penguin Random House LLC
penguinrandomhouse.com

Copyright © 2021 by Calvin C. Newport
Penguin supports copyright. Copyright fuels creativity, encourages diverse voices,
promotes free speech, and creates a vibrant culture. Thank you for buying an authorized
edition of this book and for complying with copyright laws by not reproducing, scanning,
or distributing any part of it in any form without permission. You are supporting writers
and allowing Penguin to continue to publish books for every reader.

Most Portfolio books are available at a discount when purchased in quantity for sales
promotions or corporate use. Special editions, which include personalized covers, excerpts,
and corporate imprints, can be created when purchased in large quantities. For more
information, please call (212) 572-2232 or email specialmarkets@penguinrandomhouse
.com. Your local bookstore can also assist with discounted bulk purchases using the
Penguin Random House corporate Business-to-Business program. For assistance in
locating a participating retailer, email B2B@penguinrandomhouse.com.

ISBN 9780525536550 (hardcover)
ISBN 9780593332603 (international edition)
ISBN 9780525536574 (ebook)

Printed in the United States of America

Book design by Daniel Lagin

To Max, Asa, and Josh:

May your future not be dominated by inboxes

Contents

Contents

Introduction

The Hyperactive Hive Mind

In late 2010, Nish Acharya arrived in Washington, DC, ready to work. President Barack Obama had appointed Acharya to be his director of innovation and entrepreneurship, and a senior adviser to the secretary of commerce. Acharya was asked to coordinate with twenty-six different federal agencies and over five hundred universities to dispense $100 million in funding, meaning that he was about to become the prototypical DC power player: smartphone always in hand, messages flying back and forth at all hours. But then the network broke.

On a Tuesday morning, just a couple of months into his new role, Acharya received an email from his CTO explaining that they had to temporarily shut down their office's network due to a computer virus. "We all expected that this would be fixed in a couple of days," Acharya told me when I later interviewed him about the incident. But this prediction proved wildly optimistic. The following week, an undersecretary of commerce convened a meeting. She explained that they suspected the virus infecting their network had come from a foreign power, and that

Homeland Security was recommending that the network stay down while they traced the attack. Just to be safe, they were also going to destroy all the computers, laptops, printers—anything with a chip—in the office.

One of the biggest impacts of this network shutdown was that the office lost the ability to send or receive emails. For security purposes, it was difficult for them to use personal email addresses to perform their government work, and bureaucratic hurdles kept them from setting up temporary accounts using other agencies' networks. Acharya and his team were effectively cut off from the frenetic ping-pong of digital chatter that defines most high-level work within the federal government. The blackout lasted six weeks. With a touch of gallows humor, they took to calling the fateful day when it all began "Dark Tuesday."

Not surprisingly, the sudden and unexpected loss of email made certain parts of Acharya's work "quite hellish." Because the rest of the government continued to rely heavily on this tool, he often worried about missing important meetings or requests. "There was an existing information pipeline," he explained, "and I was out of the loop." Another hardship was logistics. Acharya's job required him to set up many meetings, and this task was substantially more annoying without the ability to coordinate over email.

Perhaps less expected, however, was that Acharya's work didn't grind to a halt during these six weeks. He instead began to notice that he was actually getting *better* at his job. Lacking the ability to simply send a quick email when he had a question, he took to leaving his office to meet with people in person. Because these appointments were a pain to arrange, he scheduled longer blocks of time, allowing him to really get to know the people he was meeting and understand the nuances of their issues. As Acharya explained, these extended sessions proved "very valuable" for a new political appointee trying to learn the subtle dynamics of the federal government.

The lack of an inbox to check between these meetings opened up cognitive downtime—what Acharya took to calling "whitespace"—to dive more deeply into the research literature and legislation relevant to the topics handled by his office. This slower and more thoughtful approach to thinking yielded a pair of breakthrough ideas that ended up setting the agenda for Acharya's agency for the entire year that followed. "In the Washington political environment, no one gives themselves that space," he told me. "It's all neurotic looking at your phone, checking email—it hurts ingenuity."

As I talked to Acharya about Dark Tuesday and its aftermath, it occurred to me that many of the hardships that made the blackout "hellish" seemed solvable. Acharya admitted, for example, that his concern about being out of the loop was largely alleviated by the simple habit of calling the White House each day to learn if there were any meetings he needed to know about. Presumably, a dedicated assistant or junior team member could handle this call. The other issue was the annoyance of scheduling meetings, but this could also be handled by an assistant or some sort of automated scheduling system. It seemed, in other words, that it might be possible to preserve the profound benefits of the email blackout while avoiding many of the accompanying annoyances. "What would you think of this way of working?" I asked after explaining my proposed fixes. The phone line went silent for a moment. I had pitched an idea so preposterous—permanently working without email—that Acharya's mind had temporarily frozen.

———

Acharya's reaction was not surprising. A widely accepted premise of modern knowledge work is that email saved us: transforming stodgy, old-fashioned offices, filled with secretaries scribbling phone messages and paper memos delivered from mail carts, into something sleeker and more efficient. According to this premise, if you feel overwhelmed by tools like email or instant messenger, it's because your personal habits are sloppy: you need to batch your inbox checks, and turn off your notifications, and write clearer subject lines! If inbox overload gets really bad, then maybe your organization as a whole needs to tweak their "norms" around issues like response time expectations. The underlying value of the constant electronic communication that defines modern work, however, is never questioned, as this would be hopelessly reactionary and nostalgic, like pining for the lost days of horse transport or the romance of candlelight.

From this perspective, Acharya's Dark Tuesday experience was a disaster. But what if we have this exactly backward? What if email didn't save knowledge work but instead accidentally traded minor conveniences for a major drag on real productivity (not frantic busyness, but actual results), leading to *slower* economic growth over the past two decades? What if our problems with these tools don't come from easily fixable bad habits and loose norms, but instead from the way they dramatically and unexpectedly changed the very nature of how we work? What if Dark Tuesday, in other words, was not a disaster, but instead a preview of how the most innovative executives and entrepreneurs will be organizing their work in the very near future?

I've been obsessed with studying how email broke work for at least the past half decade. An important inflection point in this journey was in 2016, when I published a book titled *Deep Work*, which went on to become a surprise hit. This book argued that the knowledge sector was undervaluing concentration. While the ability to rapidly communicate using digital messages is useful, the frequent disruptions created by this behavior also make it hard to focus, which has a bigger impact on our ability to produce valuable output than we may have realized. I didn't spend much time in *Deep Work* trying to understand how we ended up drowning in our inboxes, or suggesting systemic changes. I thought this problem was largely one of insufficient information. Once organizations realized the importance of focus, I reasoned, they could easily correct their operations to make it a priority.

I discovered that I was overly optimistic. As I toured the country talking about my book, meeting with both executives and employees, and writing more about these topics on my blog, as well as in the pages of publications like *The New York Times* and *The New Yorker*, I encountered a grimmer and more nuanced understanding of the current state of the knowledge sector. Constant communication is not something that gets in the way of real work; it has instead become totally intertwined in how this work actually gets done—preventing easy efforts to reduce distractions through better habits or short-lived management stunts like email-free Fridays. Real improvement, it became clear, would require fundamental change to how we organize our professional efforts. It also became clear that these changes can't come too soon: whereas email overload emerged as a fashionable annoyance in the early 2000s, it has recently advanced into a much more serious problem, reaching a saturation point for many in which their actual productive output gets squeezed into the early morning, or evenings and weekends, while their workdays devolve into Sisyphean battles against their inboxes—a uniquely misery-inducing approach to getting things done.

This book is my attempt to tackle this crisis. To pull together—for the first time—everything we now know about how we ended up in a culture of constant communication, and the effects it's having on both our productivity and our mental health, as well as to explore our most compelling visions for what alternative forms of work might look like. The idea of a world without email was radical enough to catch Nish Acharya off guard. But I've come to believe it's not only possible, but actually inevitable, and my goal with this book is to provide a blueprint for this coming revolution. Before I can better summarize what to expect in the pages ahead, we must start with a clearer understanding of the problem we currently face.

———

As email spread through the professional world in the 1980s and 1990s it introduced something novel: low-friction communication at scale. With this new tool, the cost in terms of time and social capital to communicate with anyone related to your job plummeted from significant to almost nothing. As the writer Chris Anderson notes in his 2009 book, *Free*, the dynamics of reducing a cost to zero can be "deeply mysterious,"[1] which helps explain why few predicted the changes unleashed by this arrival of free communication. We didn't just shift our existing volume of voicemails, faxes, and memos to this new, more convenient electronic medium; we completely transformed the underlying *workflow* that determines how our daily efforts unfold. We began to talk back and forth much more than we ever had before, smoothing out the once coarse sequence of discrete work activities that defined our day into a more continuous spread of ongoing chatter, blending with and softening the edges of what we used to think of as our actual work.

One study estimates that by 2019 the average worker was sending and receiving 126 business emails per day, which works out to about one message every four minutes.[2] A software company called RescueTime recently measured this behavior directly using time-tracking software and calculated that its users were checking email or instant messenger tools like Slack once every six minutes on average.[3] A team from the University of California, Irvine, ran a similar experiment, tracking the computer behavior of forty employees at a large company over twelve workdays. They found that the workers checked their inboxes an average of seventy-seven times a day, with the heaviest user checking more than four hundred times daily.[4] A survey conducted by Adobe revealed that knowledge workers self-report spending more than three hours a day sending and receiving business email.[5]

The issue, then, is not the tool but the new way of working it introduced. To help us better understand this new workflow, I'll give it a name and definition:

The Hyperactive Hive Mind

A workflow centered around ongoing conversation fueled by unstructured and unscheduled messages delivered through digital communication tools like email and instant messenger services.

The hyperactive hive mind workflow has become ubiquitous in the knowledge sector. Whether you're a computer programmer, marketing consultant, manager, newspaper editor, or professor, your day is now largely structured around tending your organization's ongoing hive mind conversation. It's this workflow that causes us to spend over a third of our working hours in our inbox, checking for new messages every six minutes. We're used to this now, but when viewed in the context of even recent history, it represents a shift in our work culture that's so radical it would be absurd to allow it to escape closer scrutiny.

To be fair, the hyperactive hive mind is not obviously a bad idea. Among the benefits of this workflow is the fact that it's simple and incredibly adaptive. As one researcher explained to me, part of email's appeal was that this one easy tool could be applied to almost every type of knowledge work—a much smaller learning curve than needing to master a separate bespoke digital system for each type of work. Unstructured conversation is also an effective method for identifying unexpected challenges and quickly coordinating responses.

But as I'll argue in part 1 of this book, the hyperactive hive mind workflow enabled by email—although natural—has turned out to be spectacularly ineffective. The explanation for this failure can be found in our psychology. Beyond the very small scale (say, two or three people), this style of unstructured collaboration simply doesn't mesh well with the way the human brain has evolved to operate. If your organization depends on the hive mind, then you cannot neglect your inbox or chat channels for long without slowing down the entire operation. This constant interaction with the hive mind, however, requires that you frequently switch your attention from your work to talking about work, and then back again. As I'll detail, pioneering research in psychology and neuroscience reveals that these context switches, even if brief, induce a heavy cost in terms of mental energy—reducing cognitive performance and creating a sense of exhaustion and reduced efficacy. In the moment, the ability to quickly delegate tasks or solicit feedback might seem like an act of streamlining, but as I'll show, in the long run, it's likely *reducing* productivity, requiring more time and more expenses to get the same total amount of work accomplished.

In this first part of the book, I'll also detail how the social element of the hive mind workflow clashes with the social circuits in our brains. Rationally, you know that the six hundred unread messages in your inbox are not crucial, and you remind yourself that the senders of these messages have better things to do than wait expectantly, staring at their screens and cursing the latency of your response. But a deeper part of your brain, evolved to tend the careful dance of social dynamics that has allowed our species to thrive so spectacularly since the Paleolithic, remains concerned by what it perceives to be neglected social obligations. As far as these social circuits are concerned, members of your tribe are trying to get your attention and you're ignoring them: an event that registers as an emergency. The result of this constant state of unease is a low-grade background hum of anxiety that many inbox-bound knowledge workers have come to assume is unavoidable, but is actually an artifact of this unfortunate mismatch between our modern tools and ancient brains.

The obvious question is why we would ever adopt a workflow that comes with so many negative features. As I explain at the end of part 1, the story behind the rise of the hyperactive hive mind is complicated. No one really *decided* that it was a good idea; it instead arose, in some sense, of its own volition. Our belief that frenetic communication is somehow synonymous with work is largely a backfilled narrative we tell ourselves to make sense of sudden changes driven by complex dynamics.

Understanding the arbitrariness behind how we currently work, perhaps more than anything else, should motivate us to seek better options. This is exactly the goal I take on in part 2 of the book. In this second part, I introduce a framework I call *attention capital theory* that argues for creating workflows built around processes specifically designed to help us get the most out of our human brains while minimizing unnecessary miseries. This might sound obvious, but it actually contradicts the standard way of thinking about knowledge work management. As I'll show, driven by the ideas of the immensely influential business thinker Peter Drucker, we tend to think of knowledge workers as autonomous black boxes—ignoring the details of how they get their work done and focusing instead on providing them with clear objectives and motivational leadership. This is a mistake. There is massive potential productivity currently latent in the knowledge sector. To unlock it will require much more systematic thinking about how best to organize the fundamental objective of getting a collection of human brains hooked together in networks to produce the most possible value in the most sustainable way. Hint: the right answer is unlikely to involve checking email once every six minutes.

The bulk of part 2 explores a collection of principles for applying attention capital theory to rebuild the workflows that drive organizational, team, and individual work in this direction—moving us away from the hyperactive hive mind and toward more structured approaches that avoid the problems of constant communication detailed in part 1. Some of the ideas supporting these principles come from cutting-edge examples of organizations experimenting with novel workflows that minimize unscheduled communication. Other ideas are drawn from the practices that enabled complex knowledge organizations to function effectively in an age before digital networks.

The principles described in part 2 don't insist that you banish messaging technologies like email and instant messenger. These tools remain a very useful way to communicate, and it would be reactionary to return to older and less convenient technologies just to make a point. But these principles will push you to reduce digital messaging from a constant presence to something that occurs more occasionally. The world without email referenced in the title of this book, therefore, is not a place in which protocols like SMTP and POP3 are banished. It is, however, a place where you spend most of your day actually working on hard things instead of talking about this work, or endlessly bouncing small tasks back and forth in messages.

This advice is designed to apply to many audiences. This includes business leaders looking to overhaul their company's operation, teams looking to function more efficiently, solo entrepreneurs and freelancers looking to maximize their value production, and even individual employees looking to get more out of their individual communication habits by viewing them from the perspective of attention capital. Accordingly, my examples span from the large scale, such as CEOs making drastic changes to their company's culture, to the small scale, such as my own experiments with using systems borrowed from software development to move my academic administrative tasks out of my inbox and into a more organized format.

Not every suggestion in part 2 applies to every situation. If you're an employee of a company that still worships at the altar of the hyperactive hive mind, for example, there are only so many changes you can make on your own without infuriating your coworkers. Some care will therefore be needed in picking and choosing the strategies you implement. (I attempt to help you in this selection by highlighting examples of how the various principles have applied in the individual context.) Similarly, if you're a start-up entrepreneur, you're better able to experiment with radical new work processes than if you're the CEO of a large company.

But I firmly believe that any individual or organization who starts to think critically about the hyperactive hive mind workflow, then systematically replaces elements of it with processes that are more compatible with the realities of the human brain, will generate a substantial competitive edge. The future of work is increasingly cognitive. This means that the sooner we take seriously how human brains actually function, and seek out strategies that best complement these realities, the sooner we'll realize that the hyperactive hive mind, though convenient, is a disastrously ineffective way to organize our efforts.

This book, therefore, should not be understood as reactionary or anti-technology. To the contrary, its message is profoundly future-oriented. It recognizes that if we want to extract the full potential of digital networks in professional settings, we must continually and aggressively try to optimize how we use them. Attacking the flaws of the hyperactive hive mind is decidedly not an act of Luddism—if anything, the true obstruction to progress is giving in to the simplistic comforts of this blunt workflow at the expense of further refinement.

In this formulation, a world without email is not a step backward but a step forward into an exciting technological future we're only just beginning to understand. Knowledge work does not yet have its Henry Ford, but workflow innovations with impact on the same scale as the assembly line are inevitable. I can't predict all the details of this future, but I'm convinced it will not involve checking an inbox every six minutes. This world without email is coming, and I hope this book will get you as excited about its potential as I am.

Part 1

The Case Against Email

Chapter 1

Email Reduces Productivity

The Hidden Costs of the Hyperactive Hive Mind

When I first met Sean, he told me a familiar story about communication in his workplace. Sean was the cofounder of a small technology firm that designed internal-facing applications for large organizations. His company had seven employees working out of a London office, and they were, as Sean described it, enthusiastic practitioners of the hyperactive hive mind workflow. "We used to have Gmail opened constantly," he told me. "Everything was handled in email." Sean would start sending and receiving messages immediately on waking up and continue into the night. One employee even asked Sean to stop sending emails so late, as the knowledge of messages from the boss piling up while he slept was stressing him out.

Then the hyperactivity shifted into a new gear. "There was all this hype about Slack, so we decided to try it," Sean remembered. The rate of back-and-forth communication intensified, especially after a demanding client was provided access to their channels, allowing them to check in and ask questions whenever they felt like it: "Constant interruptions, every day." Sean could feel the whiplash attention swings from messages to work to messages and back again wearing down his ability to think clearly. He grew to despise his phone's notification pings. "I hated it—the sound still gives me the shivers," he said. Sean worried that the mental grind of managing all this communication was reducing his company's effectiveness. "I would work until one a.m. every night," he said, "because that was the only time I felt free from distractions." He also began to doubt that all this incessant chatter was mission critical. When he ran a review of his team's Slack usage, he found that the most popular feature was a plug-in that inserts animated GIFs into the chat conversations. Sean reached a new low when two of his project supervisors suddenly quit. "They were burnt out."

Sean's frustrated sense that all this digital back-and-forth is making us less productive turns out to be a common sentiment. In the fall of 2019, as part of the research for this book, I invited my readers to participate in a survey about the role of email (and related tools like Slack) in their professional lives. More than 1,500 people responded, and many of them echoed Sean's frustration—not with the tools themselves, which are self-evidently efficient ways to communicate, but with the hyperactive hive mind–style workflows they enable.

One thread of these responses concerned the sheer volume of communication generated by this workflow. "Every day it's a barrage of emails regarding scheduling, deadlines, and they're not used very effectively," wrote a lawyer named Art. George, also a lawyer, described his inbox as containing "an avalanche of messages" in which important things get lost.

Another thread focused on the inefficiency of stretching out conversations into endless back-and-forth messaging. "The asynchronous nature is both a blessing and a curse," wrote a financial analyst named Rebecca. "It is a blessing in that I can ask a question or delegate a task without having to find the person. It is a curse in that there is an implicit expectation that we are checking email all the time and will respond quickly." An IT project manager similarly complained: "Simple conversations (that could have been dealt with within a matter of hours) can end up beginning a drawn-out email thread being read by an ever-increasing list of recipients." A public services administrator noted that moving these interactions to digital messages also makes them "overly formal" and "less creative or on-point." As she elaborated: "A project or task that could be relatively simply completed with a group working together in person becomes far more complicated by trying to manage all of the back-and-forth communication via email."

Another common argument for email diminishing productivity centered on its ability to increase the amount of irrelevant information it suddenly forces you to process. "I'm frustrated that I receive so many updates . . . that have nothing to do with my position," wrote a teacher named Jay. "People now confuse answering emails with real work," wrote an editor named Stephanie. "There is a performative dimension to writing emails and cc'ing everybody, like 'Look at all the work I'm doing.' It's annoying." As an HR consultant named Andrea put it: "In at least 50% of messages you still have open questions. . . . You get the feeling that the person just shot off an email without caring about how I could answer it."

As in Sean's story, instant messenger tools like Slack weren't let off the hook by my respondents, as they were described by many readers as simply email with faster response expectations. "Slack is just a string of messages. It invites people to post almost without limitations," wrote an executive coach named Mark. "It's awful."

The above stories, of course, are anecdotal. But as I'll elaborate in the following pages, when you turn your attention to the relevant research literature, it becomes clear that the problems the respondents hinted at are even worse than most probably realize. Email might have made certain specific actions much more efficient, but as the science will make clear, the hyperactive hive mind workflow this technology enabled has been a disaster for overall productivity.

Constant, Constant Multitasking Craziness

In the late 1990s, Gloria Mark enjoyed an enviable professional setup. Mark's research focused on a field known as computer-supported collaborative work (CSCW), which, as the name suggests, looks at ways that emerging technology can help people work together more productively. Though CSCW had been around since at least the 1970s, when it began with a focus on dry topics like management information systems and process automation, it received a jolt of energy in the 1990s as computer networks and the internet enabled innovative new approaches to work.

At this time, Mark was a researcher at the German National Research Center for Information Technology in Bonn, where she could, as she told me, "work on whatever I wanted." Practically, this translated to her "going deep" on a small number of projects at a time, most of which focused on novel collaboration software. Among other projects, Mark worked on a hypermedia system named DOLPHIN, meant to make meetings more effective, and a digital document-handling system named PoliTeam, meant to simplify paperwork within a government ministry. As was the custom in Germany, lunch was the main meal of the day. As

Mark explained, she would enjoy long meals with her colleagues followed by long walks around the campus—they called these "rounds"—to digest their food and work through interesting thoughts. "It was beautiful," she told me. "The campus had a castle on it."

In 1999, Mark decided it was time to return to her native United States. Both she and her husband had secured academic jobs at the University of California, Irvine, so they packed up, said goodbye to the long stretches of deep work interspersed with leisurely meals and afternoon rounds by the castle, and headed west. Arriving in an American academic job, Mark was immediately struck by how *busy* everyone seemed. "I had a very difficult time focusing," she said. "I had all of these projects to work on." The long lunches she enjoyed in Germany became a distant memory. "I barely had time to grab a sandwich or salad for lunch," she said, "and when I returned, I could see my colleagues in their offices doing the same thing, eating in front of their computer screens." Curious to figure out how general these work habits had become, Mark persuaded a local knowledge sector company to allow her research team to shadow a group of fourteen employees over three workdays, looking over their shoulders and precisely recording how they spent their time. The result was a now famous paper—or infamous, depending on your perspective—presented at a 2004 computer-human interaction conference, with a provocative title that quotes a research subject's description of her typical workday: "Constant, Constant, Multitasking Craziness."[1]

"Our study confirms what many of our colleagues and ourselves have been informally observing for some time: that information work is very fragmented," Mark and her co-author, Victor González, write in the paper's discussion section. "What surprised us was exactly how fragmented the work is." The core finding of the paper is that once you eliminate formally scheduled meetings, the employees they followed

shifted their attention to a new task *once every three minutes* on average. Mark's experience of suddenly being pulled in many different
directions when she arrived in California was not unique to her—it
instead seemed a more universal property beginning to emerge in knowledge work.

When I asked Mark what caused this fragmentation, she replied
quickly: "Email." She came to this conclusion, in part, by diving back
into the relevant literature. Since at least the 1960s, researchers have been
measuring how managers spend their time in the workplace. Though
the different categories they tracked have changed over the years, there
are two key types of effort that show up consistently: "scheduled meetings" and "desk work." Mark pulled out the findings on these two categories from a series of papers beginning in 1965 and ending with a
2006 follow-up to her original multitasking craziness study.

When Mark tabulated these results into a single data table, a clear
trend emerged. From 1965 to 1984, the employees studied spent around
20 percent of their day engaged in desk work and around 40 percent in
scheduled meetings. In the studies since 2002, these percentages roughly
swap. What explains this change? As Mark points out, in the gap between the 1984 and 2002 studies, "email became widespread."[2]

When email arrived in the modern workplace, people no longer
needed to sit in the same room as their colleagues to discuss their work,
as they could now simply trade electronic messages when convenient.
Because email counts as "desk work" in these studies, we see time spent
on desk work grow as time spent in scheduled meetings falls. Unlike
scheduled meetings, however, conversations held through email unfold
asynchronously—there's usually a gap between when a message is sent
and ultimately read—meaning that the compacted interactions that
once defined synchronous meetings are now spread out into a shattered

rhythm of quick checks of inboxes throughout the day. In Mark and González's study, the average scheduled meeting took close to forty-two minutes. By contrast, the average time spent in an email inbox before switching to something else was only two minutes and twenty-two seconds. Interaction now occurs in small chunks, fragmenting the other efforts that make up the typical knowledge worker's day.

It's here, therefore, in these nondescript data tables from CSCW papers published over a decade ago, that we find some of the first empirical evidence for the hyperactive hive mind hypothesis I outlined in this book's introduction. We shouldn't, however, place too much emphasis on just a single study. Fortunately for our purposes, around the time Gloria Mark began studying how communication technologies were transforming knowledge work, other researchers began asking similar questions.

A 2011 paper appearing in the journal *Organization Studies* replicated Mark and González's pioneering work by shadowing a group of fourteen employees in an Australian telecommunications firm. The researchers found that, on average, the employees they followed divided their workday into eighty-eight distinct "episodes," sixty of which were dedicated to communication.[3] As they summarize: "These data . . . seem to lend support to the notion that knowledge workers experience very fragmented workdays." In 2016, in another paper co-authored by Gloria Mark, her team used tracking software to monitor the habits of employees in a research division at a large corporation and found that they checked email, on average, over seventy-seven times per day.[4]

Papers measuring the average number of email messages sent and received per day also show a trend toward increasing communication: from fifty emails per day in 2005,[5] to sixty-nine in 2006,[6] to ninety-two by 2011.[7] A recent report by a technology research firm called the

Radicati Group projected that in 2019, the year when I started writing this chapter, the average business user would send and receive 126 messages per day.[8]

Combined, this research carefully documents both the rise and the reality of the hyperactive hive mind workflow in the knowledge sector over the past fifteen years. But the studies cited provide only small snapshots of our current predicament, with the typical experiment observing at most a couple dozen employees for just a handful of days. For a more comprehensive picture of what's going on in the standard networked office, we'll turn to a small productivity software firm called RescueTime, which in recent years, with the help of a pair of dedicated data scientists, has been quietly producing a remarkable data set that allows an unprecedented look into the details of the communication habits of contemporary knowledge workers.

The core product of RescueTime is its eponymous time-tracking tool, which runs in the background on your devices and records how much time you spend using various applications and websites. The company's origin story begins in 2006, when a group of web application developers became fed up with the experience of working hard all day and then feeling like they didn't have much actual output to show for it. Curious to figure out where their time was going, they cobbled together some scripts to monitor their behavior. As Robby Macdonell, the current CEO, explained to me, their experiment became popular in their social circles: "We were hearing from more and more people who wished they could see what their application use actually looked like." In the winter of 2008, the idea was accepted by the prestigious Y Combinator incubator, and the company was born.

The primary purpose of RescueTime is to provide individual users with detailed feedback on their behavior so they can find ways to be more productive. Because the tool is a web application, however, all this data is stored in central servers, which makes it possible to aggregate and analyze the time use habits of tens of thousands of users. After a few false starts, RescueTime got serious about getting these analyses right. In 2016 they hired a pair of full-time data scientists, who transformed the data into the right format to study trends and properly protect privacy, and then got to work trying to understand how these modern, productivity-minded knowledge workers were actually spending their time. The results were staggering.

A report from the summer of 2018 analyzed anonymized behavior data from over fifty thousand active users of the tracking software.[9] It reveals that half these users were checking communication applications like email and Slack every six minutes or less. Indeed, the most common average checking time was *once every minute*, with more than a third of people checking their inbox every three minutes or less. Keep in mind that these averages are likely inflated because they include periods like lunch breaks and one-on-one meetings in which the subjects were presumably away from their computer screens. (Gloria Mark's study, by comparison, didn't count time spent in formal meetings when calculating the subjects' average attention-switching times.)

To help understand the true scarcity of uninterrupted time, the RescueTime data scientists also calculated the *longest* interval that each user worked with no inbox checks or instant messaging. For half the users studied, this longest uninterrupted interval was no more than forty minutes, with the most common length clocking in at a meager twenty minutes. More than two thirds of the users never experienced an hour or more of uninterrupted time during the period studied.

To make these observations more concrete, Madison Lukaczyk, one of the data scientists involved in this report, published a chart capturing one full week of her own communication tool usage data. During all the hours Lukaczyk spent working over this seven-day period, there are only eight blocks of thirty minutes or more that didn't include communication checks—averaging out to slightly more than one such modestly sized undistracted block per day. (And this is someone who makes a living studying technological distractions!)

In a related report, the RescueTime data scientists sought to connect this communication to productivity by restricting their attention to the time spent in activities that the users self-reported as "productive."[10] For each user, they split this productive time into five-minute buckets and then isolated the buckets that *did not* include a check of an email inbox or instant messenger application. These isolated buckets roughly approximate undistracted productive work. The average user studied had only fifteen such uninterrupted buckets, adding up to no more than an hour and fifteen minutes total of undistracted productive work per day. To be clear, this is not an hour and fifteen minutes *in a row*, but instead the total amount of undistracted productive work conducted throughout the entire day.

The implication of the RescueTime data set is striking: the modern knowledge worker is almost never more than a few minutes away from sending or receiving some sort of electronic communication. To say we check email too often is an understatement; the reality is that we're using these tools *constantly*.

———

The only thing missing from the data sets we've just discussed is a sense of what's in all these emails that we're sending so constantly throughout the day. To help fill this gap in our knowledge, I asked the 1,500 people who took my reader survey to choose a recent representative workday and categorize the emails they received during that day. I provided seven categories: planning (setting up meetings, arranging calls, etc.), informational (which I defined as not requiring a response), administrative, work discussion, client communication, personal, and miscellaneous.

I was curious to learn which types of emails were dominating my readers' work. To my surprise, the answer turned out to be *all types*. The average number of planning, administrative, work discussion, client communication, and miscellaneous emails received were all between eight and ten per day, with the average number of personal emails being slightly less. The only outlier was informational emails, which numbered eighteen per day on average.

Pulling together these various observations provides us with a clear and disturbing portrait of interaction in the modern office setting. It's no longer accurate to think of communication tools as occasionally interrupting work; the more realistic model is one in which knowledge workers essentially partition their attention into two parallel tracks: one executing work tasks and the other managing an always-present, ongoing, and overloaded electronic conversation about these tasks. The authors of the 2011 Australian study underscore this point: "Our findings lead us to conclude that such a distinction [between primary work and communication interruptions] does not hold in an environment suffused with communication media, which constantly call for employees' attention." Not only are we communicating all the time, but, as detailed in my reader survey responses, the number of different types of things we're communicating about is also large. The modern knowledge work organization truly does operate like a hive mind—a collective intelligence of many different brains tethered electronically into a dynamic ebb and flow of information and concurrent conversations.

It's important to emphasize that this *parallel track* approach to knowledge work, though perhaps shocking in its severity, is not obviously a bad thing. One could argue, for example, that this ongoing communication is efficient because it eliminates the overhead required to schedule formal meetings, and it allows people to receive exactly the information they need, exactly when they need it. Writing in 1994, at the beginning of the digital communication revolution, the late sociologist Deirdre Boden made a compelling form of this argument by analogizing these increasingly frenetic messaging habits to the "just in time" processes that had recently proved massively profitable in manufacturing and big-box retail.[11] One could also argue that the large number of different types of things we communicate about in a given day is also adaptive: a higher throughput approach to work that was made possible only by highly efficient messaging tools.

As I'll argue next, however, this optimism is flawed. The abstract value of the hyperactive hive mind workflow quickly dissipates when we're forced to confront the concrete reality of how our ancient brains—evolved in a context far removed from electronic networks and low-friction messaging—actually function when asked to rapidly switch between many different targets of attention.

The Sequential Brain in a Parallel World

We take for granted our ability to pay attention. As foundational results in neuroscience reveal, part of what distinguishes us from our primate ancestors is the ability of our prefrontal cortex to operate as a kind of traffic cop for our attention, amplifying signals from brain networks associated with our current object of focus while suppressing signals from everywhere else.[12] Other animals can do this with respect to immediate stimuli, such as the deer alertly raising its head when it hears a branch crack, but only humans can decide to focus on something not actually happening around them at the moment, like planning a mammoth hunt or composing a strategy memo.

From the perspective of a frenzied knowledge worker, a serious shortcoming of this process is that the prefrontal cortex can service only one attention target at a time. As Adam Gazzaley and Larry Rosen bluntly summarize in their 2016 book, *The Distracted Mind*: "Our brains do not parallel process information."[13] As a result, when you attempt to maintain multiple ongoing electronic conversations while also working on a primary task like writing a report or coding a computer program, your prefrontal cortex must continually jump back and forth between different goals, each requiring the amplification and suppression of different brain networks. Not surprisingly, this *network switching* is not an instantaneous process; it requires both time and cognitive resources. When you try to do it rapidly, things get messy.

The fact that switching our attention slows down our mental processing has been observed since at least the early twentieth century, long before anyone understood how the prefrontal cortex was actually executing these changes. One of the first papers documenting this phenomenon was published by Arthur Jersild in 1927. It introduced what became a basic experimental structure for investigating the costs of attention switching: give the subject two different tasks, measure how long it takes them to do each task in isolation, and then see how much they slow down when they have to alternate back and forth between the tasks.[14]

For example, one of Jersild's experiments presented the subjects with a column of two-digit numbers. One task was to add 6 to each number and the other was to subtract 3. If you asked the subjects to perform just one task repetitively, like adding 6 to every number in the list, they finished much faster than if you asked them to alternate between adding and subtracting.[15] When Jersild made the tasks more complex, by asking the subjects to now add seventeen and subtract thirteen, the difference in completion times got even larger, indicating that more involved tasks require more involved switching.

In the decades following Jersild's classical work, numerous other studies modified the details but came to substantially the same result: network switching slows down the mind. The goal of these papers, however, was to better understand how the brain operated. It wasn't until 2009 that scientists began to take seriously the question of how these switching costs might impact actual workplace performance. It was then that a newly minted assistant professor named Sophie Leroy published an organizational behavior paper that pulled together these threads. The title of the paper presents a blunt question that captures much of what had started going wrong with the hyperactive hive mind approach to collaboration: *Why is it so hard to do my work?*[16]

As with Gloria Mark, Leroy's interest in the psychology of knowledge work was inspired by personal experience. When she began her doctoral studies at NYU in 2001, she had just left a multi-year stint as a New York–based brand consultant, where she had witnessed firsthand the increasingly fragmented nature of the knowledge sector. "We had so much work," she told me, "people were constantly switching between targets [of their attention]." At the time, the academic specialty of organizational behavior hadn't yet considered the psychological impacts of all these interruptions. Leroy decided to change this.

Her study worked as follows. Subjects were given five minutes to complete a tricky word puzzle. Some subjects were provided a version of the puzzle that could be easily completed during this time, and others were provided a version that *couldn't* actually be solved, ensuring that the task would remain uncompleted after the five minutes were up. In addition, some subjects were given time pressure, including a visible countdown clock and a reminder every sixty seconds of how much time remained, while others were given no such cues and told that they should have no trouble finishing the puzzle in time.

This setup provided four possible combinations of the complete/ incomplete and pressure/no pressure conditions to test. For each such combination, after the first five minutes, Leroy surprised the subjects by having them complete a standard psychological exercise called a lexical decision task that was designed to quantify exactly how much the word puzzle remained on their mind—a measure she called *attention residue*. Leroy found that under low time pressure, whether or not the subject completed the task didn't make a difference to the amount of attention residue: in both cases, concepts related to the puzzle remained more on the subjects' minds than neutral concepts.

Under high time pressure, if the subject didn't complete the task, similar amounts of attention residue were measured. The only outlier was high time pressure and a completed task: under this combination, attention residue was reduced. As Leroy hypothesizes, when a task is confined to a well-defined block of time and fully completed during this block, it's easier to move on, mentally speaking, when you're done. (Unfortunately for our purposes, when switching back and forth from email inboxes or instant messenger channels, we rarely experience well-defined time limits for our tasks or a sense of completion before switching again.)

Next, Leroy replicated these conditions, except this time, when the first task was complete, instead of measuring attention residue the subjects moved directly to a second task meant to mimic the demands of normal work: reading and evaluating résumés for a hypothetical job opening. The subjects' performance on this task was measured by how many details they could remember from the résumés after reviewing them for five minutes. The connection between attention residue and performance on this second task was clear. The three conditions that resulted in high attention residue all produced roughly the same performance on the résumé evaluation task, and this performance was notably lower than under the low attention residue condition. The more the first task remained on the subject's mind, the worse they did on the subsequent task.

"Every time you switch your attention from one task to another, you're basically asking your brain to switch all of these cognitive resources," Leroy explained to me when I asked her about this work. "Unfortunately, we aren't very good at doing this." She summarizes the current context in which knowledge workers operate as a state of "divided attention," in which the mind rarely gets closure before switching tasks, creating a muddle of competing activations and inhibitions that all add up to reduce our performance. In other words, Leroy identified a clear answer to the question that titles her paper. Why is it so hard to do our work? Because our brains were never designed to maintain parallel tracks of attention.

Email Is Not a Job

I have a friend who is both a management consultant and a business advice book aficionado (he runs a self-improvement reading group at his firm). Naturally, when we get together, we like to talk shop about work habits and productivity. Early in the process of my work on this book, we went for a hike on a trail in Rock Creek Park, near his home in Washington, DC, and I outlined my concerns about email and how we might do better. He was incredulous—quickly listing reasons why frequent email use provides more benefit than harm in his role as someone who manages a team of other consultants. His reaction seemed convincing, so after our hike, I rushed to jot down his points in my notebook.

His argument centered on communication efficiency. Email, he explained, allows him to "quickly coordinate with diverse groups of people to make progress on things." He told me that when someone on his team got stuck, a short message from him could get them unstuck, so taking long breaks from his inbox could significantly reduce his team's effectiveness. He saw himself like an orchestra conductor, keeping everyone's actions coordinated—his presence in the middle of this frenetic scrum was where he believed he was most valuable.

Many people feel the same way as my friend. They acknowledge that some jobs might benefit from significantly less interruption, but not theirs. When confronted with the research summarized earlier in this chapter, they'd probably accept that constant attention switching is reducing their cognitive capacity in the moment, but they would then conclude that this is not a problem, as it's more important for them to be responsive to their team or clients than to be maximally sharp. As my friend told me that day in Rock Creek Park: "Not everyone does deep work all the time."

The implication of this final quip is that there's a small group of professions that specifically value uninterrupted hard thinking—writers, programmers, scientists—but for most positions, being in the thick of things is a major part of the job. We can find a classic example of this split in Paul Graham's often cited 2009 essay, "Maker's Schedule, Manager's Schedule."[17] In this piece, Graham notes that for a manager, meetings are a big part of what they do during the day, while for a maker, a single meeting can be "a disaster," as it breaks up their ability to work continuously on a difficult problem. Whether or not they've read Graham's essay, many knowledge workers, like my consultant friend, have internalized its underlying thesis that non-distracted work is relevant to only a small number of jobs.

I've come to believe that this partition is too crude. For many different knowledge work positions—if not *most*—the ability to slow down, tackle things sequentially, and give each task uninterrupted attention is crucial, even if the role doesn't regularly require hours of continuous deep thinking. The flip side of this claim is that for most positions, the hyperactive hive mind workflow, which derails attempts at clear cognition, makes you less productive. It's obvious that constant attention switching is bad for Graham's makers, but as I'll now show, it can be just as bad for his managers.

People in managerial roles are right to emphasize the importance of constant communication to their job—*as it exists right now*. If your team currently operates using the hyperactive hive mind workflow, then it's crucial to monitor your communication channels closely. In the hive mind, managers are often at the center of a web of ad hoc connections—if they step back, the whole clunking contraption grinds to a halt. But given all the different ways we could work, is this hyperactive messaging really the *best* way to manage teams, or departments, or even whole organizations? Whenever someone insists the answer is "yes," I can't help but think about a legendary figure whose approach to leadership undermines this belief.

George Marshall was the US Army chief of staff during World War II, meaning that he essentially ran the entire war effort. His name might not be as well known as Dwight Eisenhower (whom Marshall hand-selected for advancement), but those who were involved in the war credit Marshall as a key figure—if not *the* key figure—in coordinating the Allies' triumph. "Millions of Americans gave their country outstanding service," Harry Truman once said, "[but] General of the Army George C. Marshall gave it victory."[18] In 1943, Marshall was *Time* magazine's Man of the Year, not long before being named the country's first five-star general.[19]

I'm mentioning Marshall here because of an illuminating case study I stumbled across, written by an army lieutenant colonel in the early 1990s, that brings together multiple sources to describe *how* Marshall organized the War Department and led it to victory.[20] The key point that jumps out as you read these notes is that even though Marshall managed more people, had a larger budget, and faced more complexity, more urgency, and higher stakes than just about any manager in the history of management, he rejected the attraction of an always-on, hyperactive hive mind approach to his work.

When Marshall became army chief of staff, he encountered an organizational structure in which he had 30 major and 350 minor commands under his control, with over sixty officers who had direct access to him. Marshall described the setup as "bureaucratic" and "red-tape-ridden." There was no way he could win the war while trying to manage the deluge of issues, small and large, this setup would generate—he would drown in memos and urgent phone calls. So he acted. With "ruthless" efficiency, Marshall took advantage of President Franklin Roosevelt's recently granted wartime powers to radically restructure the War Department.

Numerous agencies and commands were consolidated into three main divisions, each run by a general. Marshall reduced a bloated staff of over three hundred personnel, operations, and logistics officers down to only twelve. Some major divisions were eliminated altogether. As the report summarizes:

[The reorganization] provided a smaller, more efficient staff and cut paperwork to a minimum. In addition, it set up clear lines of authority. Lastly, it freed Marshall from the details of training and supply. Marshall delegated responsibility to others while he freed himself to concentrate on the war's strategy and major operations abroad.

Those who retained access to Marshall were provided a clear structure for their interactions, turning briefing the general into an exercise in controlled efficiency. You were instructed to enter his office and sit down without saluting (to save time). At Marshall's signal, you would begin your brief while he listened with "absolute concentration." If he discovered a flaw or something missing, he would become angry that you hadn't noticed and resolved the issue before wasting his time. When you finished, he'd ask for your recommendation, deliberate briefly, then make a decision. He then delegated taking action on the decision back to you.

Perhaps Marshall's most striking habit was his insistence on leaving the office each day at 5:30 p.m. In an age before cell phones and email, Marshall didn't put in a second shift late into the night once he got home. Having experienced burnout earlier in his career, he felt it was important to relax in the evening. "A man who worked himself to tatters on minor details had no ability to handle the more vital issues of war," he once said.

Marshall focused his energy as a manager on making key decisions that would impact the outcome of the war. This was a task for which he was uniquely suited. He then trusted his team to execute these decisions without involving him in the details. As Eisenhower recalls Marshall telling him: "[The War Department] is filled with able men who analyze the problems well but feel compelled always to bring them to me for final solution. I must have assistants who will solve their own problems and tell me later what they have done."

It seems clear that Marshall would have rejected the claim that it's more important for managers to be responsive than thoughtful. The report on Marshall's leadership style emphasizes on multiple occasions the general's commitment to concentration, especially when it came to making key decisions, when he would exhibit "thinking at a fantastic speed, and with unmatched powers of analysis." The report also emphasizes the attention Marshall invested in "reflection" and big picture planning—trying to stay a step ahead of the complicated landscape of problems presented by global warfare.

Marshall was more effective at his job because of his ability to focus on important issues—giving each full attention before moving on to the next. If he had instead accepted the status quo of the War Department operation, with sixty officers pulling him into their decision making and hundreds of commands looking for his approval on routine activity, he would have fallen into the frantic and predictably busy whirlwind familiar to most managers, and this almost certainly would have harmed his performance. Indeed, if something like a hyperactive hive mind workflow had persisted in the 1940s War Department, we might have even lost the war.

Let's put aside for a moment whether or not you as a manager feel like you have the authority to effect Marshall-style changes to how your team operates, as this is among the issues I tackle in the second part of the book. (Hint: you probably have more latitude than you imagine when it comes to reducing your role in monitoring minutiae.) The key lesson I want to extract from Marshall's story is that management is about more than responsiveness. Indeed, as detailed earlier in this chapter, a dedication to responsiveness will likely degrade your ability to make smart decisions and plan for future challenges—the core of Marshall's success—and in many situations make you worse at the big picture goals of management. In the short term, running your team on a hive mind workflow might seem flexible and convenient, but in the long term, your progress toward what's important will be slowed.

We can find contemporary support for this claim in an academic paper titled "Boxed In by Your Inbox," published in 2019 in *The Journal of Applied Psychology*, which used multiple daily surveys to study the impact of email on the effectiveness of a group of forty-eight managers in various industries.[21] One of the paper's authors summarized their findings as follows: "When managers are the ones trying to recover from email interruptions, they fail to meet their goals, they neglect manager-responsibilities and their subordinates don't have the leadership behavior they need to thrive." As the number of these messages increases, the manager becomes more likely to fall back on "tactical" behaviors to maintain a feeling of short-term productivity—tackling small tasks and responding to queries—while avoiding the bigger picture, George Marshall–style "leadership" behaviors that help an organization make progress toward its goals. As the paper concludes: "Our research suggests the pitfalls of e-mail demands may have been underestimated—in addition to its impact on leaders' own behavior, the reductions in effective leader behaviors likely trickle down to adversely affect unwitting followers."

Armed with these insights, let's return to my friend's trailside quip: "Not everyone does deep work all the time." Notice that this claim applies to Marshall: outside of long flights or train rides, he rarely sat for hours at a time thinking big thoughts about one thing. But he also avoided falling into a responsiveness trap. He didn't run around putting out fires; he instead systematically worked through issues that really mattered, giving each the attention it deserved before moving on to the next. As I'll now argue, managers aren't the only knowledge workers for whom clear thinking is crucial.

———

Let's shift our attention from *managers* to *minders*, the latter being my term for the many different roles that provide administrative or logistical support in knowledge work organizations. Even more so than managers, minder positions seem like an obvious case where responsiveness should be a key part of the job description. But is this true?

To use an example familiar to my professional world, consider an administrator who provides support to professors in an academic department. This admin likely operates in a hyperactive hive mind workflow, where urgent emails arrive haphazardly throughout the day. If you polled the professors in this hypothetical department, they would likely argue that this workflow is a good thing, as the admin's ability to respond quickly to queries is central to their usefulness!

On closer examination, however, a distinction emerges between communicating about tasks and actually executing them. In fact, these two activities are often in conflict. One minder role that long ago identified this conflict was IT support. As desktop computers spread through offices in the 1980s and 1990s, they brought with them the need for a new type of employee within these organizations: information technology professionals to fix the computers when they broke. As these systems got more complicated, the demands on IT departments became more insistent—with frustrated users calling and emailing with new urgent problems or to check on previously reported issues. A catch-22 emerged: if the IT staff put off responding to these calls and emails, the employees they supported would be irate, but if they dedicated themselves to being fully responsive, they wouldn't have the uninterrupted time needed to actually resolve the issues.

To solve this problem, these departments began to cobble together custom software tools that became known as ticketing systems. Loosely inspired by the old model of physical help desks, where you would be handed a ticket in exchange for the piece of broken machinery you brought in for repair, these systems automated most of the communication tasks related to submitting, monitoring, and solving IT problems.[22]

In their modern incarnations, these systems work roughly as follows. If you have a problem, you send an email to an address like helpdesk@company.com. The ticketing software monitors this address, and when it sees your query, it extracts the problem and your contact information, assigns it a unique number, and submits this data as a "ticket" in the system. At the same time, it replies to your email, letting you know the issue has been received and giving you instructions on how to check its status.

Inside the ticketing system, the problem is categorized and typically assigned a priority—this might be automatic or require some triage by a staff member who monitors incoming issues. If you're a member of the IT team using the system, when you log in, you're shown only the tickets that apply to your specialty and you can select the most urgent to work on. At this point, you focus on the selected issue until you finish or reach a natural stopping point where further help might be required. Only once done do you return to your queue to select the next ticket to tackle. As progress is made, updates are sent automatically to the person who originally submitted the issue, and other staff members can monitor your progress and chime in with help when you get stuck.

Ticketing systems have become big business because they've consistently been shown to reduce IT staffing costs, as focused technicians solve problems faster. They also increase satisfaction, as they provide structure and clarity to the process of resolving technical issues. The premise on which this effectiveness is built is that communicating about tasks often gets in the way of executing them—the more you can off-load this communication from the cognitive space of your staff, the more effective they become at actually getting things done.

Which brings us back to our example of the department admin. Though this trade-off between communication and execution is now well understood in the IT setting, it's still largely ignored in other minder positions. Our hypothetical admin, therefore, like an early IT profes-sional, finds himself overwhelmed by messages, fearing that if he steps away from any of his ongoing email threads with harried professors he'll invite frustration. The resulting hyperactive hive mind communi-cation then reduces his ability to think clearly about the often subtle and complicated issues he's trying to resolve for the professors in the first place.

To make this more concrete: The same week I was writing the first draft of this chapter, for example, I sent my own department's admin a note about a postdoc I was hiring using a research grant. The postdoc had originally been scheduled to start at the end of the summer, but due to visa issues, he needed to delay his start until January. This was a simple message to write, but its implications were subtle, involving HR, budgets, and office space allocations, among other impacts. Putting to-gether a plan to properly react to this start date shift would require some careful thought, but I couldn't help reflecting that the space for such thinking is hard to find when dealing with my request is interrupted by the many other unexpected emails likely demanding our admin's attention that same morning.

Too often, we think of those with minder roles as automatons, who spend their days cranking through tasks, one after another, as they arrive as input through inboxes and chat channels. But this perspective condescendingly dismisses the cognitively demanding nature of this work. Fixing my postdoc start date issue is no less complicated than pulling together a smart strategy memo or sharp section of computer code. It follows that embedding minders into a concentration-eroding hyperactive hive mind workflow, though superficially convenient in the moment to those who interact with them, reduces their ability to do their job well. As we learned from the example of IT ticketing systems, if we can somehow create space between communication and execution, people in these roles would find the tasks before them more easily dispatched.

This discussion of minders is important because this professional role is about as far as you can get from Paul Graham's vision of makers dedicating entire afternoons to solving a single challenging problem, and yet, even for the much more varied and administrative obligations of minders, the hyperactive hive mind still ends up causing problems. To conclude this investigation on the hive mind and effectiveness, however, we'll veer sharply back toward the focused end of the spectrum and look closer at what's actually at stake when constant communication invades the world of people who create valuable things with their minds.

As I learned after publishing my 2016 book, *Deep Work*, people enjoy hearing stories about intensely creative types retreating into undisrupted seclusion to produce brilliant work. One fan favorite is the habits of Maya Angelou, who revealed in a 1983 interview that when she wrote, she was up by five thirty, soon after which she retreated to a hotel room to work without distraction. "[It's] a tiny mean room with just a bed, and sometimes, if I can find it, a face basin," she explained. "I keep a dictionary, a Bible, a deck of cards and a bottle of sherry in the room."[23] Ensconced in this isolation, she wrote until around two in the afternoon, unless the writing was flowing well, in which case she kept going until the energy diminished. When she was done, she read over what she'd written, cleared her head, took a shower, then had a drink with her husband before dinner.

When people encounter stories like Maya Angelou's, they're quick to accept that uninterrupted concentration supports difficult creative endeavors. When we shift these endeavors into the office setting, however, where retreating to a seedy hotel with a bottle of sherry would likely be frowned upon by even the most dedicated productivity hacker, the importance of the connection between focus and value begins to dissipate.

Not long ago, for example, I heard from an engineer who wrote technical white papers for a Silicon Valley start-up. These papers were complicated to pull together but important for the company's marketing efforts. As the engineer explained to me, he was having a hard time executing his job because the start-up embraced a hyperactive hive mind workflow. "If you didn't respond quickly to a Slack message," he said, "you were, ironically, considered to be slacking off."

Inspired by some of my writing on these issues, the engineer set up a meeting with his CEO. He summarized the research on how attention switching reduces cognitive performance and explained his concerns about constant interruptions hurting his work. He also acknowledged that retreating into complete, Angelou-style isolation would also create problems, as other people on his team needed to interact with him on a regular basis. He asked the CEO's advice on how to maximize the value he produced for the company. "As soon as I asked this question," he told me, "it was clear that it would be absurd to suggest that I should spend all of my time [in a state of responsiveness] just because it made certain things easier."

They agreed that he should spend four hours a day—50 percent of his work hours—in a distraction-free state, and the other 50 percent plugged into the hive mind workflow. To implement this goal, they set aside a two-hour chunk each morning and a two-hour chunk each afternoon during which the engineer was considered unreachable. The CEO explained this new setup to the engineer's team. "It took them about a week to get used to it, then it was no longer a problem," he told me. As a result, the engineer's productivity significantly increased—with few negative impacts. The real surprise in all this was the fact that until the engineer forced the issue, no one had ever stopped to wonder about whether the way they were working was actually working.

Nish Acharya's story from this book's introduction provides another example of a position where it's accepted that focused thought is important, but the workflows put in place make these efforts nearly impossible. It wasn't until Acharya's email servers were temporarily taken away that he got the "whitespace" needed to actually figure out his team's strategy. Journalists suffer from a similar mismatch. Not long ago, I was chatting with a well-known reporter who had started his own media company. He lamented that he was "required" to constantly check Twitter to make sure he wasn't missing breaking news—a behavior that impeded his ability to efficiently write good stories. I pointed out that his office was full of young, tech-savvy interns looking to get their foot in the door of his profession. "Wouldn't it make more sense to have one of them monitor Twitter and call you if something important was happening?" I asked. The thought had never occurred to him—he just assumed some degree of distraction was the cost of doing business.

Most people accept the premise that the hyperactive hive mind workflow reduces the productivity of makers. At the same time, however, this workflow is really convenient. Accordingly, so long as the benefits of focus are left vague, this trade-off might seem like a wash, where a little lost productivity is compensated with some gained managerial flexibility. But when we get specific about what exactly can be gained when makers are extracted from hyperactive communication, this trade-off can suddenly resolve itself to be massively lopsided. As with the white paper–writing engineer or Acharya when it comes to makers, moving away from the hive mind workflow isn't about tweaking productivity habits, but instead about significant boosts to effectiveness. When these advantages are made clear, it becomes harder to justify their loss simply for the added convenience of responsiveness.

Beyond the Hive Mind

I opened the chapter with the story of Sean, whose team was burnt out by the demands of the hyperactive hive mind. He was suspicious that all this communication was somehow dragging down their productivity. As we now know, he was right—this workflow conflicts with the human brain in ways that make most knowledge work tasks more difficult to complete. Unlike many who share similar suspicions, however, he decided to do something about it.

As Sean told me, the sudden departure of his two project supervisors rattled him. "This forced me to take a step back and ask what we're actually doing," he said. "To ask, is this communicating doing more harm than good?" Sean and his cofounder decided to make some radical changes. They shut down their Slack servers for good and relegated email to a tool used mainly to coordinate with entities outside the company. Intrigued by this claim, I put Sean on the spot during one of our phone interviews and asked him to open his email inbox while we spoke and tell me what was in it. He was happy to oblige: it contained a message from the firm's accountant, a support ticket from a web hosting company they use for some of their projects, a few invoices from contractors, and a message from a freelancer they were working with on a new project. There was no internal-facing communication and nothing requiring an urgent reply. Sean used to send messages until 1:00 a.m. every day. Now, as he reported, "on a normal day I check email once." Some days he doesn't get around to checking his inbox at all.

Email and Slack served important purposes in Sean's company: they're how his team coordinated and how they interacted with their clients. If Sean had eliminated these tools without replacing the functions they served with alternative processes, his company would have fallen apart. Following the types of principles explored later in this book, however, he did put alternatives in place and they seemed to work fine.

Sean divided the day into a morning block and an afternoon block. At the beginning of each block, his team gathers in person, with the occasional remote worker joining using videoconferencing software, to discuss the upcoming block. "Each person covers three points: what they did yesterday, what they are doing today, and what issues they're having or blocks they're experiencing," Sean told me. "It lasts fifteen minutes max." Then everyone does something that has become exceedingly rare in our current age of connectivity: they simply work, for several hours in a row, with no inboxes to check or chat channels to monitor, until the block is over.

On the client side, the company now includes a section in their contract that spells out exactly how they will (and implicitly will not) interact with the client. For most clients, this means a regular phone call to provide updates and answer questions that is immediately followed up with a written document that captures everything discussed. Sean's cofounder, who manages these relationships, was terrified that their clients would be irate to learn that their access was being reduced. This fear was unfounded—the clients turned out to appreciate the clear expectations. "They are absolutely much happier," Sean said.[24]

I wanted to share the changes Sean made because, as I've learned from discussing this topic over the years, many will continue to defend the hyperactive hive mind workflow, even after evidence of its harm is presented. Their counterargument hinges on the claim that this workflow is somehow fundamental. That is, they'll concede that all this communication might slow down our brains, but they can't imagine any other reasonable way to get work done. Sean demonstrates that once you know what pain you're trying to avoid and what benefits you're trying to amplify, other approaches emerge.

Part 2 will dive deeper into the principles for designing these alternatives, but before we move on to the world beyond the hive mind, we must first confront an equally important argument against this approach to work: not only does it make us less productive; it also makes us miserable—a reality that has massive consequences for both individual well-being and organizational stability. It's to this claim that we now turn our (hopefully not too divided) attention.

Chapter 2

Email Makes Us Miserable

An Epidemic of Silent Suffering

In early 2017, a new French labor law went into effect that attempted to preserve a so-called "right to disconnect." According to the law, French companies with fifty employees or more are required to negotiate specific policies about email after work hours, with the goal of significantly reducing the time workers spend in their inbox in the evening or over the weekend. Myriam El Khomri, the minister of labor, justified the new law in part as a necessary step to reduce burnout. Regardless of whether or not you believe such business activities should be subject to government regulation, the fact that the French felt the need to pass this law in the first place points to a more universal problem that expands well beyond the borders of a particular country: email is making us miserable.[1]

We can make this claim more concrete by turning to the relevant research literature. In a 2016 paper co-authored by Gloria Mark, whom we met in the last chapter, a research team hooked up forty knowledge workers to wireless heart rate monitors for twelve workdays. They recorded the subjects' heart rate variability, a common technique for measuring mental stress. They also monitored the workers' computer use, allowing them to correlate email checks with stress levels. What they found would not surprise the French: "The longer one spends on email in [a given] hour the higher is one's stress for that hour."[2]

In a follow-up study conducted in 2019, a team once again led by Mark placed thermal cameras below each subject's computer monitor, allowing them to measure the telltale heat that blooms across the face indicating psychological distress. They discovered that batching your inbox checks—a commonly suggested "solution" to improving your experience with email—is not necessarily a panacea. In fact, for those who score high in the common personality trait of neuroticism, batching emails actually makes you *more* stressed (perhaps due to worry about all the urgent messages you're ignoring). The researchers also found that when stressed, people answer emails faster, but not better—a text analysis program called the Linguistic Inquiry and Word Count reveals that these anxious emails are more likely to contain words that express anger.[3] "While email use certainly saves people time and effort in communicating," the authors of the 2016 study conclude, "it also comes at a cost." Their recommendation? "[We] suggest that organizations make a concerted effort to cut down on email traffic."[4]

Other researchers have found similar connections between email and unhappiness. A different 2019 study, appearing in *The International Archives of Occupational and Environmental Health*, looked at long-term trends in the self-reported health of a group of nearly five thousand Swedish workers. The researchers found that repeated exposure to "high information and communication technology demands" (translation: a need to be constantly connected) was associated with "suboptimal" health outcomes. This trend persisted even after they adjusted the statistics for many potentially confounding factors, including age, sex, socioeconomic status, health behavior, BMI, job strain, and social support.[5]

Another way to measure the harm caused by email is to see what happens when you reduce its presence. This is exactly what Harvard Business School professor Leslie Perlow explored in an experiment conducted with consultants from Boston Consulting Group. After Perlow introduced a technique called *predictable time off* (PTO), in which team members were provided set times each week when they could completely disconnect from email and the phone (with the full support of their colleagues), the consultants became markedly happier. Before PTO was introduced, only 27 percent of the consultants reported that they were excited to start work in the morning. After the reduction in communication, this number jumped to over 50 percent. Similarly, the percentage of consultants satisfied with their job jumped from under 50 percent to over 70 percent. Contrary to expectations, this mild reduction in electronic accessibility didn't make the consultants feel less productive; it instead increased the percentage of those who felt like they were "efficient and effective" by over twenty points.[6] As reported in her 2012 book on this research, *Sleeping with Your Smartphone*, these results, when first encountered, left Perlow puzzled about why a culture of constant connectivity was ever adopted in the first place.[7]

Of course, we don't really need data to capture something that so many of us feel intuitively. As mentioned in the last chapter, I conducted a survey of over 1,500 of my readers to find out more about their relationship with tools like email. I was surprised by the strong and emotionally charged words people used when asked to describe their feelings toward this technology:

- ☐ "It's slow and very *frustrating*. . . . I often feel like email is impersonal and a waste of time."
- ☐ "I *hate* that I can never be 'off.'"
- ☐ "It creates *anxiety*."
- ☐ "I'm *frazzled*—just keeping up."
- ☐ "With email, I'm a lot more *isolated* in my workday . . . and I don't like that."
- ☐ "You get *haunted* when everything is very busy."
- ☐ "I feel an almost uncontrollable need to stop what I'm doing to check email. . . . It makes me very *depressed*, *anxious*, and *frustrated*."

I suspect that people's language would be much more neutral if we asked them about other workplace technologies, like, say, their word processor or the coffee maker. There's something uniquely deranging about digital messaging. The critic John Freeman effectively summarizes our relationship with email when he notes that with it, "we become task-oriented, tetchy, terrible at listening as we try to keep up with the computer."[8] Media theorist Douglas Rushkoff is also onto something when he laments: "We compete to process more emails . . . as if more to do on the computer meant something good. . . . Instead of working inside the machine, as we did before, we must *become* the machine."[9] We depend on email, but we also kind of hate it.

This reality is important for practical reasons. When employees are miserable they perform worse. They're also more likely, as the French labor minister warned, to burn out, leading to increased healthcare costs and expensive employee turnover. Case in point: Leslie Perlow found that predictable time off from email increased the percentage of employees planning to stay at the firm "for the long term" from 40 percent to 58 percent. Miserable employees, in other words, are bad for the bottom line.

The reality that email makes us unhappy, however, also has an implication that's more philosophical than pragmatic. McKinsey estimates that there are over 230 million knowledge workers worldwide,[10] which includes, according to the Federal Reserve, more than a third of the US workforce.[11] If this massive population is being made miserable by a forced devotion to inboxes and chat channels, then this adds up to a whole lot of global misery! From a utilitarian perspective, this level of suffering cannot be ignored—especially if there's something we might be able to do to alleviate it.

The previous chapter was about the impact of the hyperactive hive mind on human productivity. This chapter is more about its impact on the human soul. My goal in the pages ahead is to understand *why* this workflow makes us so unhappy. As I'll argue, this reality is not some incidental side effect that can be cured with clever inbox filters or better company norms; it's instead fundamental to the various ways in which this highly artificial workflow conflicts with how our human brains naturally operate.

Email Scrambles Our Ancient Social Drives

The Mbendjele BaYaka people are made up of hunter-gatherer tribes scattered through the forests of the Republic of Congo and the Central African Republic. They live in camps called langos, containing, typically, somewhere between ten and sixty individuals. Each nuclear family in the camp lives in its own hut, known as a fuma. The Mbendjele BaYaka lack food storage technology, which makes food sharing a crucial activity for tribal survival. As a result, like many previously studied hunter-gatherer tribes, they're highly cooperative.

From a scientific perspective, the Mbendjele BaYaka are interesting because they help us understand the social dynamics of hunter-gatherer tribes. These dynamics remain relevant, as we spent the entirety of our history before the Neolithic Revolution living in such arrangements. We can therefore hope that by studying these tribes (with suitable caution[12]) we might learn something about how our species is hardwired through evolutionary pressures to interact with one another. And by doing so, we might perhaps improve our understanding of why our modern inboxes stress out our ancient minds.

In a 2016 study, published in *Nature Scientific Reports*, a group of researchers from University College London studied three different Mbendjele BaYaka camps in the Likoula and Sangha regions of the Congo's Ndoki Forest.[13] Their goal was to measure each individual's "relational wealth," a technical term for what we might call popularity within the tribe. To do so, they deployed an established technique called the honey stick gift game, in which participants are each given three honey sticks—a highly prized food—and asked to distribute them among other tribe members. By measuring how many honey sticks each participant ends up receiving, the researchers can approximate their relative standing in the tribe.

They discovered striking differences in how this relational wealth was distributed, with some tribe members receiving many more honey sticks than others. More important, these differences correlated strongly with factors such as body mass index and female fertility, which, in a hunter-gatherer tribe, play a major role in determining whether you succeed in passing your genes to the next generation. Many prior studies have documented what the researchers call "psychological and physiological reinforcement mechanisms encouraging the formation and maintenance of social relationships." This work helps explain why these mechanisms evolved in the first place: in the types of social settings that defined our Paleolithic past, being popular increased the chance your lineage survived.

A natural next step is to ask *how* someone becomes popular in a hunter-gatherer tribe. A follow-up study of the Mbendjele BaYaka, published in 2017 in the same journal, provides some insight into this question.[14] In this work, the researchers persuaded 132 adults in a BaYaka camp to wear small wireless sensors around their necks for a week. These devices captured and logged one-on-one interactions between subjects, deploying short-range signals every two minutes to record who was near who.

The researchers then used these voluminous logs of interactions to create what's known as a *social graph*. The process here is straightforward. Imagine that you start with a large blank sheet of paper, pinned to a wall. You first draw a circle for every subject who wore a sensor, scattering them evenly across the page. Now, for every interaction event in your log, you draw a line between the circles that represents the two subjects interacting. If a line between them already exists, you can thicken it slightly. When you're done processing all the interactions, you're left with a spaghetti pile mess of lines of varying thickness connecting the circles on the paper. Some circles, like busy transit hubs, emanate thick lines in all directions, while others are only sparsely connected; some collections of circles may have very few lines between them, while others are deeply interconnected.

To a normal human observer, these social graphs seem like a

complicated jumble. But to scientists in the burgeoning academic field that has become known as network science, these graphs, once coded into digital bits and fed into computers to be analyzed by algorithms, can provide deep insight into the social dynamics of the groups they describe. Which is exactly why the authors of the 2017 research paper went through the trouble of persuading the Mbendjele BaYaka to wear wireless sensors.

They found that by studying the social graph generated by these logs, they could accurately predict the number of living offspring of the BaYaka mothers involved in the study. The more robust[15] their connection into the network, the higher their reproductive success. As learned in the previous study, in a hunter-gatherer tribe, popularity makes a difference in genetic fitness—more popular tribe members got more food and support, making them healthier and therefore more likely to have healthy children. The new study found that this popularity was captured by the record of one-on-one conversations: those who managed these direct interactions properly thrived, while those who didn't struggled to pass on their genes.

One-on-one conversations are *crucial* to the Mbendjele BaYaka. It is therefore a small leap of evolution-inspired theorizing to expect that we are all hardwired to treat such socializing with great psychological urgency—if you neglect interactions with those around you, they'll give their metaphorical honey sticks to someone else. This leap seems small in part because it describes something we already so clearly feel. The drive to interact with others is one of the strongest motivational forces humans experience. Indeed, as the psychologist Matthew Lieberman explains in his 2013 book, *Social: Why Our Brains Are Wired to Connect*, the social networks in our brains are connected to our pain systems, creating the intense heartbreak we feel when someone close to us dies, or the total desolation we experience when isolated from human interaction for too much time. "These social adaptations are central to making us the most successful species on earth," Lieberman writes.[16]

Long before scientists probed the underlying structures of our sociality, we were already quite aware and reflective about our crushing need to properly manage interactions. The Torah explicitly forbids rechilut (gossip): "Thou shalt not go up and down as a talebearer among thy people; neither shalt thou stand against the blood of thy neighbor: I am the LORD,"[17] a biblical recognition of the power latent in the information moving through a group's social graph. Shakespeare also identified friendship as central to the human experience when he wrote Richard II's famous lament: "I live with bread like you, feel want, / Taste grief, need friends: subjected thus, / How can you say to me, I am a king?"[18]

Which brings us back to email. The flip side of a deep evolutionary obsession with one-on-one interaction, as with most hardwired drives, is a corresponding feeling of distress when it's thwarted. Much in the same way our attraction to food is coupled with the gnawing sensation of hunger in its absence, our instinct to connect is accompanied by an anxious unease when we neglect these interactions. This matters in the office because, as we've documented, an unfortunate side effect of the hyperactive hive mind workflow is that it constantly exposes you to exactly this form of distress. This frenetic approach to professional collaboration generates messages faster than you can keep up—you finish one response only to find three more have arrived in the interim—and while you're at home at night, or over the weekend, or on vacation, you cannot escape the awareness that the missives in your inbox are piling ever thicker in your absence. Not surprisingly, reports of these forms of stress were common in the responses to my reader survey:

☐ "I have a constant sense of having missed something."

☐ "Psychologically, I can't leave emails unread, no matter how insignificant."

☐ "I feel like things are piling up, and then I'm becoming stressed."

☐ "My inbox stresses me out because I know how much effort it takes to PROPERLY communicate via email."

At this point, however, you might complain that there's a big difference between neglecting an email and neglecting a fellow hunter-gatherer tribe member. The worst-case consequence of the former is that you might annoy Bob in accounting, while the worst case for the latter is that you starve to death. In fact, your company might even have crystal clear norms about how long it is acceptable to wait before responding to email, meaning that Bob is probably absolutely fine with your delayed reply. The problem, of course, is that deeply embedded human drives are not known for responding to rationality.

When you skip a meal, telling your rumbling stomach that food is coming later in the day, and therefore it has no reason to fear starvation, doesn't alleviate the powerful sensation of hunger. Similarly, explaining to your brain that the neglected interactions in your overfilled inbox have little to do with your survival doesn't seem to prevent a corresponding sense of background anxiety. To your entrenched social circuitry, evolved over millennia of food shortages mitigated through strategic alliances, these unanswered messages become the psychological equivalent of ignoring a tribe member who might later prove key to surviving the next drought. From this perspective, the crowded email inbox is not just frustrating—it's a matter of life or death.

We can actually measure this triumph of the ancient social drives over the rational modern brain in the laboratory. In one particularly devious study, published in 2015 in *The Journal of Computer-Mediated Communication*, researchers figured out how to discreetly assess our psychological response to thwarted digital connection.[19] Subjects were brought into a room to work on word puzzles. They were told that as part of the experiment, the researcher also wanted to test out a wireless blood pressure monitor. After the subject worked on the puzzle for a few minutes, the researcher returned to the room and explained that the subject's smartphone was creating "interference" with the wireless signal, so they needed to move the phone to a table twelve feet away— still within earshot, but out of reach. After the subject worked on the puzzle for a few more minutes, the researcher covertly called the subject's phone. At this point, the subject was trying to solve the word puzzle while hearing their phone ringing from across the room, but was prevented from answering it due to a previous warning from the researcher that it was important not to get up "for any reason."

Throughout this entire charade, the wireless monitor was tracking the subject's physiological state by measuring blood pressure and heart rate, allowing the researchers to observe the effect of the phone separation. The results were predictable. During the period when the phone was ringing across the room, indicators of stress and anxiety jumped higher. Similarly, self-reported stress rose and self-reported pleasantness fell. Performance on the word puzzle also decreased during the period of unanswered ringing.

Rationally speaking, the subjects knew that missing a call was not a crisis, as people miss calls all the time, and they were clearly engaged in something more important in the moment. Indeed, in many cases, the subject's phone had already been set to Do Not Disturb mode, which the researchers surreptitiously turned off as they moved the phone across the room. This means that the subjects had already *planned* on missing any calls or messages that arrived during the experiment. But this rational understanding was no match for the underlying evolutionary pressures which ingrain the idea that ignoring a potential connection is *really bad*! The subjects were bathed in anxiety, even though their rational minds, if asked, would admit that there was nothing going on in that laboratory that was actually worth worrying about.

The missed connections that necessarily accompany the hyperactive hive mind sound these same Paleolithic alarm bells—regardless of our best attempts to convince ourselves that this unanswered communication isn't critical. This effect is so strong that when Arianna Huffington's company Thrive Global explored how to free its employees from this anxiety while on vacation (when the knowledge of piling messages becomes particularly acute), it ended up deploying an extreme solution known as Thrive Away: if you send an email to a colleague who's on vacation, you receive a note informing you that your message has been automatically deleted—you can resend it when they return.

In theory, a simple vacation autoresponder should be sufficient—as it tells people sending you a message not to expect a reply until you return—but logic is subservient in this situation. No matter what the expectations, the awareness that there are messages waiting for you somewhere triggers anxiety, ruining the potential relaxation of your time off. The only cure is to prevent the messages from arriving altogether. "The key is not just that the tool is creating a wall between you and your email," explained Huffington. "It's that it frees you from the mounting anxiety of having a mounting pile of emails waiting for you on your return—the stress of which mitigates the benefits of disconnecting in the first place."[20]

A tool like Thrive Away might temporarily alleviate the social stress of the hyperactive hive mind, but we cannot ignore the fifty or so weeks a year when we're not on vacation. As long as we remain committed to a workflow based on constant, ad hoc messaging, our Paleolithic brain will remain in a state of low-grade anxiety.

Email Communication Is Frustratingly Ineffective

The wild olive baboons of the Mpala Research Centre in Kenya, like most types of baboons, live in highly social troops that remain remarkably stable even as they travel long distances each day in search of forage. For the scientists who study these animals, a key question is figuring out how they reach a consensus on which direction to move. Answering this question is complicated because these troops can grow as large as one hundred individuals, and deducing how they make their movement decisions would require the simultaneous observation of most of them—a challenge described by a well-known researcher in this field as one of "daunting dimensions."[21]

Not long ago, however, an international group of biologists, anthropologists, and zoologists, led by Ariana Strandburg-Peshkin of Princeton University, set out to overcome these obstacles.[22] Their secret weapon: high-resolution, custom-designed GPS collars that record precise locations at a rate of one per second. The team was able to get the collars on close to 85 percent of the animals in the population, yielding a detailed look at the exact movements of the troop throughout the day. Armed with advanced data-mining algorithms and statistical analysis, the researchers were able to extract the process by which these baboons seem to make their decisions about which direction to move—a process, it turns out, that's fundamentally spatial.

When preparing to migrate, the baboons in the troop carefully watch one another's movements, looking in particular for *initiators* who begin to head away from the group in some fixed direction. How they respond to these initiators depends a lot on how they're arranged in space. If the angle between two initiators is more than ninety degrees, meaning they are leaving the group in quite different directions, then the remaining baboons will commit their loyalty to one, reinforcing that proposal. On the other hand, if two initiators head off in similar directions, the remaining baboons will tend to compromise by committing to a direction that's somewhere in between. If too many initiators are active at the same time, the remaining baboons are more likely to stay where they are, slowing down the decision-making process until the options converge. Once a given initiator attracts enough followers, the whole troop will follow.

To apply these ideas to the problems of email, let's shift our attention from wild olive baboons to their close primate cousins: us. Instead of studying how baboons decide which direction to forage in the forests of Kenya, consider instead a scenario in which a team of knowledge workers is evaluating business plans. In shifting from the forest to the office, we've also shifted the decision-making process from one embodied in the physical world to one that's likely purely writing-based, as most such decisions unfold through electronic messaging in the era of the hyperactive hive mind.

Before we applaud our modern approach as superior, however, it should give us some pause to remember that written language is at most only five thousand years old,[23] which is minuscule with respect to evolutionary timescales. The ancient collaboration processes etched into our neural circuits over millions of years of evolution, and hinted at by the behaviors of our primate cousins, must still be present, and presumably expecting something quite different from our interactions than simply exchanging written words over computer screens. This mismatch between how we're wired to communicate and how we're coerced into communicating by modern technology creates a deeply human sense of frustration.

Around the same time that researchers were fitting GPS collars to baboons, an MIT professor named Alex Pentland was fitting an even more sophisticated package of sensors to a group of business executives gathered around a conference table on MIT's campus. These sensors, called sociometers, are roughly the size of a deck of cards and are worn around the neck. They include an accelerometer to track the subject's movement, a microphone to record their speech, a wireless Bluetooth chip to determine who is nearby, and finally, an infrared sensor to detect whether or not the subject is looking another subject in the face while interacting.[24]

The executives would each present a business plan to the group. Their goal was to then work together to agree on which plan was best. A standard technique to study such collaboration is to transcribe all the words that are spoken, but the reason why Pentland went through the trouble of outfitting the subjects with advanced sensors is that he had become convinced that this *linguistic* channel of information captured only a small part of what would be important for understanding the interaction underway in that conference room. Flowing concurrently alongside the words being said was an unconscious social channel, made up of subtle physical cues in body language and voice tone that painted a richer picture of how decisions were being reached in that room. These "ancient primate signaling mechanisms" had been previously studied in apes, but Pentland's sociometers were designed to prove that these mechanisms still play a major role in human collaboration.[25]

There are many signals that work on this social channel. As Pentland explains in his book on the topic, *Honest Signals: How They Shape Our World*, this information is processed largely unconsciously, often using lower-level circuits in our nervous system, which is why it evades our perceived experience. Its impact, however, shouldn't be underestimated. "These social signals are not just a back channel or complement to our conscious language," Pentland writes. "They form a separate communication network that powerfully influences our behavior."[26]

One such signal delivered through this unconscious network is called, aptly enough, *influence*. It describes the degree to which one person can cause another to match their speaking pattern. This information, which is processed in our brain through subcortical structures centered on the tectum, provides a fast and accurate snapshot of power dynamics in a given room. Another such signal is *activity*, which describes a person's physical movements during a conversation. Shifting in your seat, leaning forward, demonstrative gesticulating—these behaviors, which are mediated largely through the autonomic nervous system ("an extremely old neural structure"), provide a surprisingly accurate reading of the true intentions of an individual in the interaction.[27]

We know these signals are important because, as Pentland demonstrates in his research, by measuring them using his sociometers he can accurately predict outcomes of face-to-face scenarios such as dating, salary negotiations, and job interviews without any reference to the actual words spoken. Indeed, returning to the study of the business executives in the MIT conference room, Pentland later presented written versions of the plans to a new group and asked each group member to decide on their own which was best. Their decisions were significantly different from those reached by the group that heard the pitches in person. "The executives [in the group setting] thought they were evaluating the plans based on rational measures," Pentland explains, "[but] another part of their brain was registering other crucial information, such as: How much does this person believe in this idea? How confident are they when speaking? How determined are they to make it work?"[28] The executives who simply read the plans didn't realize how much they were missing. Both groups reviewed the same pitches, but they were working with vastly different information.

When we shifted toward the hyperactive hive mind workflow in the 1990s and early 2000s, we believed we were just taking the conversations that were happening in conference rooms and on phone lines and shifting them onto a new messaging medium, leaving the content of these interactions largely unchanged. As research like Alex Pentland's emphasizes, however, this prioritization of abstract written communication over in-person communication disregarded the immensely complex and finely tuned social circuits that our species evolved to optimize our ability to work cooperatively. By embracing email, we inadvertently crippled the systems that make us so good at working together. "Memos and emails simply don't work the same way that face-to-face communications work," Pentland bluntly concludes.[29] It's no wonder that our inboxes so often leave us with an unspecified and gnawing sense of annoyance.

This annoyance is heightened by the fact that we often overestimate our correspondents' ability to understand our messages. In a now classic experiment that appeared in her 1990 doctoral dissertation, a Stanford psychology student named Elizabeth Newton paired up research subjects, who sat across from each other at a table. She asked one person to tap out a well-known song using their knuckles on the table, while the other subject had to guess the song. The tappers estimated that about 50 percent of the listeners would figure out the song. In reality, fewer than 3 percent succeeded in naming the rhythmic tune.[30]

As Newton argued, when the tapper is knocking on the table, they hear in their head all the accompaniment for the song—the singing, the instruments—and have a hard time putting themselves into the mental state of the listener, who has access to none of that information and is instead left grappling with a puzzling jumble of sporadic knocks. Social psychologists call this effect *egocentrism*, and as a research team led by Justin Kruger of NYU set out to demonstrate in a surprisingly entertaining 2005 paper, appearing in *The Journal of Personality and Social Psychology*, it plays a big role in explaining why email drives us crazy.[31]

Kruger and his collaborators started by studying sarcasm. In their first experiment, they gave a group of participants a list of topics. For each topic, they were asked to write two sentences: one normal and one sarcastic. They then emailed their sentences to participants in another group, who were tasked with identifying which sentences were meant to be sarcastic. "As expected, the participants were overconfident," the paper explains. The sentence writers predicted that the readers would essentially get every choice right. In reality, they failed nearly 20 percent of the time.

In a follow-up experiment, half the sentence writers got to record themselves reading their sentences on a tape recorder, while the other half still emailed their creations. Perhaps not surprisingly, hearing sentences on a recording made it easier to determine whether or not they were sarcastic. What *was* surprising was that the sentence writers predicted there would be no difference: they believed the recipients would have an equally easy time detecting sarcasm in written and recorded sentences.

To test the claim that *egocentrism* was the source of the participants' overconfidence, the researchers turned their attention to humor. They now provided each sender with a short humorous passage. In particular, they drew from humorist Jack Handey's *Deep Thoughts*: absurdist mini monologues delivered as scrolling text, read by a deadpan narrator and set against a relaxing backdrop. These appeared as a regular feature on *Saturday Night Live* during the 1990s and early 2000s. To make this experiment more concrete (and to provide me an excuse to replicate the funniest passage I've ever read in a peer-reviewed article), here's an example *Deep Thought* that was actually used by the researchers:

> I guess of all my uncles, I liked Uncle Caveman the best. We called him Uncle Caveman because he lived in a cave, and because sometimes he'd eat one of us. Later on we found out he was a bear.

To test egocentrism, the researchers randomly divided the senders into two groups. Each participant in the first group was simply provided a *Deep Thought* to send via email. Those in the second group were shown a clip of the thought being delivered on *Saturday Night Live*, with the oh-so-perfect calming music, the deadpan narrator, and the shocked laughter from the audience. After watching the clip, this group also emailed just the text. In both cases, the senders were asked how funny they thought the passage was and to estimate how funny the recipients would find it.

"Participants in the videotape condition thought that the [*Deep Thoughts*] were funnier than did participants in the control condition," the paper reveals, "and the same was true of participants' predictions of the recipients' evaluation of the jokes." Seeing the video clip provided the minds of the participants with a richer accompaniment to play alongside the text they were typing into the email. Like Elizabeth Newton's song tappers hearing the music in their head, the videotape group couldn't shake the funny visuals and laughing crowd when trying to judge how well their email would be understood. The richer the sender's subjective experience of what she's trying to communicate, the bigger the gap grows between her understanding and that of her correspondent—evidence that egocentrism is at the core of the measured overconfidence.

The conclusion of this work is that emails are commonly misunderstood because of the "inherent difficulty of moving beyond one's subjective experience of a stimulus and imagining how the stimulus might be evaluated by someone who does not share one's privileged perspective." To make matters even worse, the researchers found that the recipients of these ambiguous messages were as overconfident as the senders. They were confident that they were correctly detecting sarcasm or identifying humor, even when they weren't doing well at all. This last observation applies a particularly devious twist to our understanding of email's many confusions. It's not just that we're less clear than we think, but we're often completely misunderstood. You were *sure* that you were sending a nice note, while your receiver is equally *sure* you were delivering a pointed critique. When you build an entire workflow on exactly this type of ambiguous and misunderstood communication—a workflow that bypasses all the rich, non-linguistic social tools that researchers like Alex Pentland documented as being fundamental to successful human interaction—you shouldn't be surprised that work messaging is making us miserable.

We don't need research studies, however, to emphasize something that many of us already experience on a daily basis. In her book *Reclaiming Conversation*, MIT social scientist Sherry Turkle catalogs stories of the issues caused when workplaces shift more of their interaction to written text. One such case study focuses on the trials of a technology director named Victor, who manages a team at a large financial services firm. "Typically, things get into trouble when too much has been done by email," Victor tells Turkle. He keeps having to convince his team that when problems arise with a client, they need to talk to them in person. "This is not something they would come to themselves," he explains. "I'm usually facing someone who wants to send twenty-nine emails to fix a problem." His solution is simpler: "Go talk to them." As Victor elaborates, his younger colleagues see electronic communication as a "universal language" that provides a more efficient way to interact. Increasingly, Victor sees his role as convincing them that this couldn't be further from the truth: email is not a universal form of interaction, he keeps trying to explain; it is instead an impoverished simulacrum of the types of complex and nuanced behaviors that through most of human history defined our communication. We all increasingly feel the effects of this mismatch.[32]

Email Creates More Work

In 2012, a research team led by Gloria Mark published one of my favorite studies on the impact of email.[33] Their experiment was brilliant in its simplicity: they selected thirteen employees at a large scientific research firm and had them stop using email for five workdays. The researchers didn't make elaborate contingency plans or develop alternative workflows in advance of the experiment: they simply shut down the subjects' email addresses and sat back to watch what happened.

Though the study includes many interesting results, I want to focus on an observation that was not reported in the published paper but was instead brought to my attention more recently in a conversation with Gloria Mark. As she explained to me, one of the subjects was a research scientist who needed to spend around two hours each day setting up a laboratory for an experiment. He reported that he was frequently frustrated because his boss had the habit of sending him emails during this preparation period, asking him questions or delegating work. This required the scientist to stop what he was doing to attend to his boss's wishes—significantly slowing down the lab setup. The reason Mark remembers this scientist's plight was because during the five days when he was without email, his boss stopped bothering him during his lab setup. What makes this observation remarkable is that the boss's office was only *two doors* down the hall. The small amount of extra difficulty required to walk a few steps and poke his head through the door was enough to prevent the boss from handing off extra work to the scientist. "He was thrilled," Mark remembers.

This vignette of the frustrated scientist and his distracting boss underscores an important cost of email that we often miss. Tools like email almost completely eliminate the effort required—in terms of both time and social capital—to ask a question or delegate a task. Viewed objectively, this seems like a good thing: less effort equals more efficiency. As I'll show, however, the side effect of this transformation is that knowledge workers began to ask more questions and delegate more tasks than ever before, leading to a state of perpetual overload that's driving us toward despair.

—————

One way to examine our changing workloads is to look at the systems we use to keep track of them. As productivity guru David Allen argues in his canonical 2001 bestseller, *Getting Things Done*, the period in which email spread was defined by significant changes in time management approaches. As late as the 1980s, the "essence of being organized" involved keeping a pocket-sized Day-Timer (a paper calendar) and making a daily to-do list to help figure out how to spend the time in between appointments. Especially organized workers would use prioritization schemes, such as Alan Lakein's ABC Method or Stephen Covey's Four Quadrants, to help determine the order in which to complete the handful of tasks they identified as important for the day.

"The traditional approaches to time management and personal

organization were useful in their time," Allen notes. But as the 1980s gave way to the 1990s, the idea that your day could be captured by a short list of coded tasks became quaint. "More and more people's jobs are made up of dozens or even hundreds of e-mails a day, with no latitude left to ignore a single request, complaint or order," Allen writes. "There are few people who can . . . maintain some predetermined list of to-dos that the first . . . interruption from their boss won't totally *undo*."[34]

Allen rose to fame within time management circles at the same time that the hyperactive hive mind rose toward ubiquity. He sold over 1.5 million copies of his book in large part because he was one of the first business thinkers to take seriously how much this new workflow was increasing the *amount* of work dumped on our plates. He told his newly overwhelmed readers that they needed to capture every last one of these obligations into a "trusted system," where they could be clarified and organized—providing the foundation for a frenetic work style in which you attempt to execute existing items faster than new ones arrive.

Getting-things-done rookies are often shocked by the length of their task lists. As Allen recalls, in his consulting work, he soon found he needed two full uninterrupted days to help executives go through and clarify everything they were supposed to be doing. The process of simply listing tasks for which they were responsible often took "six hours or more."[35] Gone are the days of the "productive" executive consulting his Day-Timer, then carefully listing out the six things he hoped to accomplish. In the modern world, knowledge workers now feel under siege by obligations.

The relevant research literature also helps clarify this sense of overload. In their original 2004 study on attention fragmentation, Victor M. González and Gloria Mark partitioned the efforts of the employees they observed into distinct *working spheres*, each representing a different project or objective. They found that on average their subjects worked on ten different spheres per day, spending less than twelve minutes on one before switching to another.[36] A follow-up study in 2005 found the observed employees touching on eleven to twelve different working spheres per day on average.[37] The large number of different spheres these subjects tackled in a given day, combined with the reality that each sphere demands the accomplishment of many smaller tasks and presumably dozens of emails, provides a harried portrayal of modern knowledge work. "At night, I often wake in a panic about all the things I need to do or didn't get done," writes journalist Brigid Schulte in *Overwhelmed,* her 2014 book on this busyness epidemic. "I worry that I'll face my death and realize that my life got lost in this frantic flotsam of daily stuff."[38]

This brings us back to my original contention that we can blame email—or more accurately, the hyperactive hive mind workflow it enabled—for much of this shift toward overload. One piece of evidence for this claim is timing. This rise in busyness seems to have occurred somewhere between the late 1980s and the early 2000s: the same period when email spread throughout the working world. Another piece of evidence comes from the experts themselves. David Allen and Gloria Mark, among other relevant commentators, specifically connect email with our current state of frenetic activity.

We can also identify a plausible mechanism that helps explain how email might have increased our workload. I opened this section with the story of the frustrated scientist fending off requests from his boss. When the scientist's email was temporarily removed, the boss stopped handing off the extra requests, even though his office was only two doors down from the scientist's laboratory. Simply adding a small amount of *friction* significantly reduced the requests coming the scientist's way.

For many knowledge workers, this story probably makes sense—how many of the quick asks for someone else's time and attention that you dash off over email during a normal day would you still make if you had to instead walk down the hallway and interrupt someone's work?

This effect implies there's something irrational lurking in this system we use to allocate cognitive resources in the workplace. If slightly increasing friction drastically reduces the requests made on your time and attention, then most of these requests are not vital to your organization's operation in the first place; they are instead a side effect of the artificially low resistance created by digital communication tools. The idea that eliminating friction can cause problems might sound unusual, as we're used to thinking about more efficiency producing more effectiveness, but among engineers like me, this concept is commonly understood. Too little friction can lead to feedback loops that spiral out of control, as happens when a microphone gets too close to a speaker and the self-amplification recursively explodes into a deafening screech.

Something like the workload equivalent of the microphone screech is happening in modern knowledge work. When the friction involved in asking someone to do something was removed, the number of these requests spiraled out of control. I frantically try to grab other people's time and attention to make up for the time and attention they've already grabbed from me. Soon everyone is like Brigid Schulte, up late at night, drowning in the "frantic flotsam of daily stuff."

What would happen to this "stuff" if some friction was reintroduced to the system (as in Gloria Mark's email freedom experiment)? My guess is that a lot of these urgent tasks would simply disappear: the vital question I dashed off in a quick Slack message suddenly becomes less vital when asking it requires me to go interrupt what you're doing and confront that look of annoyance on your face. I might drop it or just handle it myself. Many other tasks would probably get consolidated into more reasonable chunks. What used to unfold over a few dozen ad hoc messages might become a larger discussion at a regular status meeting. This is slightly more annoying in the moment, as you now have to keep track of things you need help with until the next meeting, but everyone ends up much less distracted.

Friction also motivates the development of more intelligent processes. Imagine that I frequently need you to sign a certain type of requisition form. With low-friction communication tools like email, I might simply shoot you copies of the forms to sign whenever I need them, as this gets the responsibility off my plate with minimal effort. Without email, however, the pain of having to come physically find you for every signature will motivate me to develop a better system, such as one where I put these forms in your mailbox on Friday morning and you promise to sign them and have them back to me by Monday morning. This system is much better for you, as it frees you from yet another source of unscheduled requests for your time and attention, but it was unlikely to emerge in a setting where just firing off the forms electronically generated essentially zero cost.

To summarize, we often overestimate the rational nature of our workloads. If a task is on our plate, we believe, it's because it's important—part of the job. But as I've just argued, both the type and quantity of the efforts that make up our day can be strongly influenced by less rational factors, such as the relative cost of asks for someone else's time and attention. When we made communication free, we accidentally triggered a massive increase in our relative workloads. There's nothing fundamental about these newly increased workloads; they're instead an unintended side effect—a source of stress and anxiety that we can diminish if we're willing to step away from the frenetic back-and-forth that defines the hyperactive hive mind workflow.

Clarifying the Misery Mechanisms

Most knowledge workers intuitively feel a sense of unhappiness ema-
nating from their overflowing inboxes. The reason this reality hasn't
catalyzed a revolt, however, is that it's often portrayed as unavoidable—
the sine qua non of work in a hyper-connected, high-tech age. As a 2018
article from the *MIT Sloan Management Review* explains: "The 'keep
everybody busy' theory remains alive and well . . . in knowledge work."[39]
(The article elaborates that the manufacturing sector, by contrast, figured out in the 1980s that relentless busyness was not an optimal way
to run things.)

   In this chapter, I attempted to push back against this generalized
fatalism by detailing three specific ways in which the hyperactive hive
mind workflow makes us unhappy: the psychological anxiety of an inbox that fills up faster than we can empty it, the frustrating ineffective-
ness of text-only communication, and the out-of-control overload that
results when friction is eliminated from office interactions. When we
isolate these sources of unease, they no longer seem unavoidable; rather,
they are unfortunate and largely unexpected clashes between the specific ways we work and the natural operation of our brains. The solution
is not to shrug our shoulders, but instead to pursue the obvious fix:
replace the hyperactive hive mind with alternative workflows that still
get things done, but sidestep the worst of these misery-inducing side
effects. A world without email, as we'll explore in part 2, is largely a
happier world. We have one last stop, however, before we begin this
discussion of what works better. The challenge we take up in the next
and final chapter of part 1 is trying to understand how we ended up
wedded to such an unproductive and misery-inducing approach to work
in the first place.

Chapter 3

Email Has a Mind of Its Own

The Rise of Email

Why did email become so popular? One clue can be found in an unlikely place: hidden behind the walls of the Central Intelligence Agency's original headquarters building in Langley, Virginia. Here you'll
find more than thirty miles of four-inch steel tubing, installed in the
early 1960s, as part of an elaborate, vacuum-powered intra-office mail
system. Messages, sealed in fiberglass containers, rocketed at thirty feet
a second among approximately 150 stations spread over eight floors.
Senders specified each capsule's destination by manipulating brass rings
at its base; electromechanical widgets in the tubes read those settings
and routed the capsule. At its peak, the system delivered 7,500 messages each day.[1]

According to oral histories maintained by the CIA, employees were
saddened when, in the late 1980s, during an expansion of the headquarters, this steampunk messaging system was shut down. Some of

them reminisced about the comforting *thunk, thunk* of the capsules arriving at a station; others worried that internal office communication would become unacceptably slow, or that runners would wear themselves out delivering messages on foot. The agency's archives contain a photograph of a pin that reads "Save the Tubes."

Why would the CIA invest the significant amount of resources required to build and maintain such an unwieldy system? By the mid-twentieth century, much more common and inexpensive methods for office communication had already become standard. When this headquarters was built, for example, internal telephone exchanges had been around for decades. Isn't it unnecessary to send you a note through a pneumatic tube network when I could just as easily call you directly using the telephone on my desk?

But the telephone was no panacea. It represents an example of what communication specialists call *synchronous messaging*, which requires all parties in the interaction to participate at the same time. If you're not at your desk when I dial your extension, or if your line is busy, then the attempted interaction is a bust. In a small organization, tracking people down on the phone might be manageable, but as the nineteenth century gave way to the twentieth, single-room countinghouses and small managerial suites tucked in the backs of factories gave way to huge edifices, like the CIA headquarters, that could house thousands of white-collar employees under the same roof. At this scale, the overhead of arranging synchronous communication becomes onerous, leading to drawn-out games of secretarial phone tag and piles of missed-call message slips.

An alternative form of interaction that avoids the overhead problem is *asynchronous messaging*, which doesn't require a receiver to be present when a message is sent. The intra-office mail cart is a classic example of this communication type. If I want to send you a note, I can drop it in my outgoing mail tray when it's convenient for me, and once it's delivered to your incoming mail tray, you can pick it up and read it when convenient for you—all with no coordination between us required. The problem with the mail cart, of course, is that it's slow. It might take the better part of a day for my note to actually make it from my outbox to a sorting station, then on to a cart on your floor, where eventually it will be pushed past your desk and manually delivered. This might be fine for conveying static information, but it's clearly an impractical means to efficiently coordinate or share time-sensitive news.

What the rise of the large office really needed—a productivity silver bullet of sorts—was some way to combine the *speed* of synchronous communication with the *low overhead* of asynchronous communication. Which brings us back to the CIA. This is exactly what they were trying to achieve with their pneumatic tube system. Their electromechanically routed, vacuum-driven capsules were the equivalent of a turbocharged mail cart: I can now asynchronously deliver you a message within minutes instead of hours. It's not surprising, therefore, that the CIA employees were saddened to see the tube system shut down when the headquarters was expanded in the 1980s. But this sadness didn't last long, as this same period marked the arrival of a newer, cheaper, even faster method for practical asynchronous messaging: electronic mail.[2]

––––––

Most organizations lacked the resources to build a system similar to the CIA's tubes, so for them, the arrival of email was the first time they could enjoy high-speed asynchrony. We're so familiar with this capability today that we take it for granted, but during the 1980s and 1990s, when it began to spread widely, its impact was profound.

We can find nice snapshots of email's rapid ascendency in the archives of *The New York Times* from this period. One of the paper's earliest mentions of this technology in a business context is in a 1987 article that places the word *e-mail* in quotation marks throughout.[3] "Although 'e-mail,' as it is called, has not spread as rapidly as its proponents predicted," it explains, "it has established itself as a niche market, and it has a small but increasing following in the corporate world." As the article clarifies, professional email at this point still required a special application that would dial into a server to establish a connection, allowing you to send and receive messages before disconnecting. If you needed to reference the information from a message later, a laborious process was required to save it to a disk. Given the complexity of this technology at this early stage, the article's caution about its importance is understandable. But this soon changed.

Appearing just a few years later is another instructive article—this time without quotation marks around *e-mail*.[4] The article describes the embrace of this technology within the entertainment industry. In 1989, we learn, Mike Simpson, the cohead of the powerful motion picture department at the William Morris Agency, connected three hundred computers in their Beverly Hills and New York offices with an early computer network technology offered by Steve Jobs's post-Apple start-up, NeXT, Inc. "A cornerstone of our business is the quicker you get information, the quicker you can use it," Simpson says. "E-mail has already given us an edge."

The article contains other examples of early admiration for email's potential. "It's fast information, replaces telephone calls, is environmentally correct and allows more people to know things at the same time," explains one agent. Another talks about his experience shifting to the rival Creative Artists Agency, where, to his "horror," he discovered that they were still delivering paper notes with runners. He insisted his new colleagues adopt email. We also learn that at Disney, Jeffrey Katzenberg set up a private email network connecting twenty high-level executives. "We had to love e-mail because Jeffrey loves it," explains the vice president of feature publicity at Disney, before helpfully clarifying: "You communicate by computer instead of by phone."

Email was still new enough in 1992 that not everyone understood its potential. "E-mail is fun, but it's a toy," says a story analyst at Columbia Pictures, providing a quote he probably now wishes he could take back. He then adds: "E-mail encourages people to chatter and say things that don't need to be said." The article also notes that at this point, most motion picture studios still depended on a primitive communication device called the Amtel, a combination of screen and keyboard that was used to send short text messages. (A common use of the Amtel in Hollywood was to allow assistants to inform executives, without interrupting their closed-door meetings, about who was holding on various phone lines.)

In a 1989 article, the venerable technology writer John Markoff provides more insight into the dynamics that helped accelerate email's growth.[5] "Electronic mail, which has taken a secondary position to the facsimile machine through the personal computer boom of the 1980's," he writes, "is finally coming into its own." As Markoff's piece clarifies, in the late 1980s, email was largely used to connect employees within the same company. In 1989, under pressure from the Aerospace Industries Association (a group of fifty aerospace companies with over six hundred thousand total employees), the main email network providers "grudgingly" agreed to interconnect their networks using an early email protocol called X.400, allowing users from one network, for the first time, to communicate with users from another.

Markoff presciently argues that once email becomes global, it will largely eliminate the need for fax machines and therefore spread rapidly. He wasn't the only one to see this potential. In the article, Markoff quotes Steve Jobs—identified as "Steven P. Jobs"—providing what turned out to be an accurate prediction: "In the 1990's, personal computing will transform personal communication roughly by the same magnitude that, in the 1980's, spreadsheets transformed business analysis and desktop publishing."

The case studies in Markoff's long piece paint a picture of a technology on the rise. "We found that electronic mail dramatically improved the way in which we communicated," explains a hospital executive. "It took off and permeated our organization." Markoff later elaborates: "In large and small offices throughout the country, [email] is being seized on as a means of communication more efficient than the telephone."

By 1992, the *Times* reported that email had become a $130-million-a-year business, projected to be a $500 million business by mid-decade as many big software companies, including IBM and Microsoft, began preparing to enter the market.[6] A couple of years later, email's dominance was unquestioned. "Ever since the Lotus 1-2-3 spreadsheet was anointed a decade ago as the first killer app . . . people have been asking, 'What's the next killer app?'" writes Peter Lewis in a 1994 article. "In my mind, there is no doubt: electronic mail is the killer app for the 1990s."[7]

As portrayed by these articles, the speed with which email spread through the business sector is astounding. In 1987, it's a clunky tool useful to only a "niche market." By 1994, it's the "killer app" of the decade and the foundation of a half-billion-dollar software industry. That's about as close to an overnight transformation as you're likely to find in the history of commercial technology adoption.

We shouldn't be surprised that this tool spread so fast. As I established, it solved a real problem—the need for high-speed asynchronous communication—and did so in a manner that was relatively inexpensive and easy to master.[8] But it's important to remember that there's nothing fundamental about email as a tool that demands that we use it constantly. One could imagine an alternative history in which email simplified existing communication that used to occur over voicemail and memos, but office work otherwise remained the same as it had been in the mid-1980s. You can enjoy the practical benefits of email, in other words, without having to also embrace the hyperactive hive mind workflow. So why did this frenetic behavior become universal in the aftermath of email's arrival, even though, as argued in the preceding chapters, it makes us less productive and more miserable? When you look closer at this question, a nuanced and fascinating collection of answers emerges, all of which point to a surprising conclusion: maybe the way we work today is much more arbitrary than we realize.

What Does Technology Want?

Adrian Stone's first job after graduating from college in the early 1980s was at the IBM headquarters in Armonk, New York. At the time, internal communication at IBM relied heavily on scribbling notes. As Stone recalls in a 2014 essay he wrote about this period, if you wanted to talk to someone, you might try calling, but because this often failed, the default approach was to walk to their cubicle and leave a note for them to read later. "Once they read their little note, they got a chance to be 'it' and play the game in reverse," Stone wrote. "This could go on for days."[9]

This is an important reminder that the world before email was no prelapsarian paradise. Communicating in big organizations during this period was a real pain, and email, when it came on the scene, offered a simple solution. So it's no surprise that as IBM began to network its operations in the 1980s, it was quick to deploy an internal email service.

One of Stone's first tasks at the company was to help these efforts by investigating how much IBM employees at the Armonk headquarters were currently communicating through voicemail, memos, scribbled notes, and so on. They assumed most of this communication would shift to email, and they wanted to provision a sufficiently large mainframe to handle the load. (As Stone explained to me, these machines were expensive at the time—"We're talking prices in the millions"—so it was important to identify exactly how much processing power you really needed.)

Stone soon put together an estimate for a server that could easily handle all the analog communication already occurring in the office. The system was configured and deployed, and once activated, it was a hit among employees; too much of a hit, as it turned out. Within a few days, they "blew" the server due to overload. As Stone told me, they experienced five to six times *more* traffic than he had estimated, meaning that almost immediately after email was introduced at IBM, the volume of internal communication exploded.

A closer examination revealed that not only did people send many more messages than they did in the pre-email era; they also began cc'ing these messages to many more people. "Pre-email, simple communication was largely person-to-person," Stone told me. After email, these same conversations now unfolded over long back-and-forth threads including many different people. "Thus—in a mere week or so—was gained and blown the potential productivity gain of email," he joked.

This story is important because it highlights a dynamic between people and technology that's often overlooked. We like to believe that we deploy tools rationally to solve specific problems. But cases like IBM's server meltdown complicate this story line. No group of managers at IBM decided that massively increasing internal communication would improve productivity, and the individuals suddenly trapped in this deluge of messages weren't happy about it. As Adrian Stone recalls, the intention of the system was simply to move the communication that already existed in the office to a more efficient medium—to take what people were already doing and make it easier. So who ultimately decided that everyone should instead start interacting five to six times more than normal? To some who study this question closely, the answer is radical: it was the technology itself.

If you talk with a scholar of the history of technology, you'll likely discover a fascination with a seemingly unlikely topic: the rise of medieval feudalism in the early Carolingian Empire. Historians trace the origins of this style of government to the reign of Charles Martel, grandfather to Charlemagne. In the eighth century CE, Martel kick-started feudalism by confiscating Church lands and redistributing them to his vassals.

Why did Martel begin grabbing Church lands? This question was answered in a magisterial tract published in 1887 by the German historian Heinrich Brunner, who argued that granting land to loyal subjects was necessary for Martel to maintain horse-mounted warriors for his army.[10] In later periods of history, rulers might simply tax their subjects and use the revenue to fund their military, but in the early medieval period, land was the primary source of capital. If you wanted someone to maintain a mounted warrior for your army, they needed land to do so. Brunner marshaled historic documents to demonstrate persuasively that this maintenance of knights in shining armor was one of the main motivations for Martel's setting up fiefdoms throughout his kingdom.

As is often the case with history, this answer leads to another question: Why did Martel feel the sudden need to raise a massive cavalry force? Brunner proposed a simple answer. When the Franks under Martel faced a Muslim army from Spain, near Poitiers in 732, Martel's forces were largely fighting on foot, while the Muslim soldiers were largely mounted. According to Brunner's theory, Martel quickly realized his disadvantage. Almost immediately after this conflict—indeed, later that same year—he began his sudden confiscation of Church lands. As historian Lynn White Jr. summarizes: "Thus, Brunner concluded, the crisis which generated feudalism, the event which explains its almost explosive development toward the middle of the eighth century, was the Arab incursion." This theory proved resilient in the decades after it was proposed, standing up, according to White, "remarkably well against assaults from all directions."[11]

But then in the mid-twentieth century, Brunner's theory took a blow. New scholarship revealed that Brunner's date for the pivotal Battle of Poitiers was wrong; it actually took place a year *after* Martel began grabbing Church lands. "We are faced, in the reigns of Martel [and his successors], with an extraordinary drama which lacks motivation," writes White.[12] The idea that feudalism was instigated by the need to support mounted warriors remained an accepted hypothesis, but the reason for this shift toward cavalry was suddenly once again shrouded in mystery. That is, until White, at the time a middle-aged history professor at UCLA, came across a "rambling" footnote, written by a scholar of German antiquities in 1923, that concludes with the following offhanded claim: "The new age is heralded in the eighth century by excavations of stirrups."[13]

The footnote implied that the force that drove Charles Martel to develop feudalism was the arrival in western Europe of a basic technology: the horse stirrup. In his now classic 1962 book that fills out this hypothesis, *Medieval Technology and Social Change*, White meticulously draws from both archaeology and linguistics to show that the introduction of the stirrup does indeed explain well Martel's sudden shift toward mounted troops.[14]

Before the stirrup, a warrior on a horse had to wield his spear or sword with "the strength of shoulder and biceps."[15] The stirrup enabled a "vastly more effective mode of attack." By bracing a lance between his upper arm and body, a rider leaning forward in metal stirrups could deliver a blow with the combined force of his weight and the weight of his stallion. The difference between these two attacks was monumental. In the eighth century, the warrior with a lance and stirrups on a horse was a form of "shock warfare" devastating to opponents. In a medieval version of the nuclear arms race that would follow more than a millennium later, Charles Martel realized that the advantage provided by the stirrup was so "immense" that he had to do whatever it took to get it before his enemies did—even if that meant upending centuries of tradition and creating a brand-new form of government.

In Lynn White Jr.'s study of the stirrup we find a classic example of a technology introduced for a simple reason (to make riding horses easier) leading to vast and complicated consequences never imagined by its inventors (the rise of medieval feudalism). In the second half of the twentieth century, many scholars in the field of the philosophy of technology began to research similar case studies of unintended consequences. Over time, this idea that tools can sometimes drive human behavior became known as *technological determinism*.

The literature on this philosophy is filled with fascinating examples. One of the better-known determinist books is Neil Postman's 1985 classic, *Amusing Ourselves to Death*. In this short treatise, Postman argues that the format through which mass media is delivered can impact the way a culture thinks about the world. (If this reminds you of

Marshall McLuhan's famed claim that "the medium is the message," you won't be surprised to learn that Postman studied under McLuhan.)

Postman uses this concept to argue, among other points, that the impact of the printing press is deeper than we realize. The standard narrative about this invention is that mass-produced pamphlets and books allowed information to spread faster and farther, speeding up the evolution of knowledge that culminated in the Age of Reason. Postman replies that the influence of the resulting "typographic" culture did more than just speed up information flow; it changed the way our brains processed our world. "Print put forward a definition of intelligence that gave priority to the objective, rational use of the mind," he writes, "and at the same time encouraged forms of public discourse with serious, logically ordered content."[16] It was this new way of thinking—not just newly available information—that suddenly made intellectual innovations such as Enlightenment philosophy and the scientific method natural next steps. Gutenberg, in other words, thought he was setting information free, but in reality, he was changing fundamentally what information we treated as important.

A more modern example of technological determinism is the introduction of the Like button to Facebook. As revealed by contemporaneous blog posts written by the design team, the original purpose of this feature was to clean up the comments below users' posts. Facebook engineers noticed that many such comments were simple positive exclamations, like "cool" or "nice." They figured that if those could instead be captured by clicking Like, the comments that remained would be more substantive. The goal of this tweak, in other words, was a modest improvement, but they soon noticed an unexpected side effect: users began spending more time on the service.

As became clear in retrospect, incoming Likes provide users with an uneven stream of *social approval indicators*—bits of evidence that other people are thinking about you. The idea that every tap of the Facebook app might give you new information about these indicators hijacked ancient social drives in the human brain and made the platform suddenly significantly more appealing. Whereas people used to log on to Facebook occasionally to see what their friends were up to, they were now more likely to check in constantly throughout the day to see how much approval their latest posts had generated. Soon every other major platform introduced similar approval indicator streams—favorites, retweets, auto-tagging photos, streaks—as part of a technological contest played out on the field of what became known as attention engineering, a battle that left in its wake a small number of massively powerful technology platform monopolies and a weary populace exhausted by a life increasingly dominated by handheld glowing screens. All this because of a small number of engineers who desired to make social media comments less cluttered.[17]

A key property of technological determinism is that the innovation in question alters our behavior in ways that were neither intended nor predicted by those first adopting the tool. This idea might make you uncomfortable, as it seems to impart some notion of autonomy to inanimate objects—as if the technology itself is deciding how it should be used. You wouldn't be alone in your unease: there are many scholars today who steer well clear of determinist analysis, which in recent years has fallen out of fashion in academic circles currently more enamored with theories that understand tools as vectors of social power. But the longer I study the intersection of technology and office culture, the more I'm convinced that in this particular setting, the determinists have something useful to teach us.

To make this case, let's first strip this philosophy of its spooky undertones of self-aware tools. When examined closer, the unintended consequences in technological determinism case studies almost always have pragmatic causes. New tools open up some new options for behavior while closing off others. When these changes then interact with our inscrutable human brains and the complex social systems in which we operate, the results can be both significant and unpredictable. The technologies in question in these studies are not literally deciding how humans should behave, but their effects can be so surprising and sudden to those involved that a story line of tools determining behavior seems as valid as any for describing what's going on. (The technology scholar Doug Hill uses the term *de facto autonomy* to describe this effect.)

If you're careful, you can often look backward after a new tool has created profound change and decode some of the forces at play. In the case of the horse stirrup, for example, scholars have done exactly this work by excavating the specific context in which Charles Martel encountered the stirrup—what was going on in his political world, what experience he had previously with mounted warfare, and so on. In retrospect, the idea that the stirrup would spark feudalism makes sense. But no one planned or predicted it in advance.

This brings us back to email. The case study of Adrian Stone and IBM is pure technological determinism: a tool introduced for a simple purpose (to make existing communication practices more efficient) had an unexpected result (a shift toward the hyperactive hive mind style of collaboration). The speed of this transformation, which required less than a week to get rolling, underscores how powerful these forces can be once unleashed.

Determinist dynamics similar to what Adrian Stone observed at IBM went on to unfold in offices around the world as email spread throughout the 1990s, ushering in a general embrace of the hyperactive hive mind without anyone ever stopping to ask whether this radical new way of working made any sense. We chose to use email because it was a rational solution to the need for practical asynchronous communication in large offices. The hyperactive hive mind, in some sense, subsequently chose us once this tool had spread, at which point we seemed to have all looked up from our newly empowered inboxes, shrugged, and quipped: "I guess this is how we work now."

Stumbling into the Hive Mind

The horse stirrup enabled a new type of shock troop that the Carolingian Empire couldn't survive without. This led to land grabs, which in turn upended the very nature of government, and thus we get from the introduction of a narrowly useful bit of metal and leather to full-blown feudalism. I just argued that more than a millennium later, the introduction of another narrowly useful innovation, electronic messaging, led the modern office to embrace the hyperactive hive mind workflow. To justify this claim, let's look closer at the types of underlying complex forces that plausibly might have driven us from the rational adoption of email to the less rational embrace of the hive mind approach to work. There are at least three of these hive mind drivers that likely played a role in this unintentional transformation of the office.

Hive Mind Driver #1: The Hidden Costs of Asynchrony

As argued earlier, email helped solve a practical problem generated by the growing size of offices: the need for efficient asynchronous communication—that is, a fast way to send messages back and forth without requiring the sender and receiver to be communicating at the same time. Instead of having to play phone tag with a colleague from the other side of your office building, you can replace this real-time conversation with a short message, delivered when convenient for you, and then read when convenient for the recipient.

To many, this asynchronous approach to communication seemed strictly more efficient. One technology commenter I came across in my research compares synchronous communication—the type that requires actual conversation—to an outdated office technology like the fax machine: it's a relic, he writes, that "will puzzle your grandkids" when they look back on how people used to work.[18]

The problem, of course, is that email didn't live up to its billing as a productivity silver bullet. The quick phone call, it turns out, cannot always be replaced with a single quick message, but instead often requires dozens of ambiguous digital notes passed back and forth to replicate the interactive nature of conversation. If you multiply the many formerly real-time exchanges now handled through multitudinous messaging, you get a long way toward understanding why the average knowledge worker sends and receives 126 emails per day.[19]

Not everyone, however, was surprised by the added complexity of drawn-out communication. As email was taking over the modern office, scholars in the theory of distributed systems—the subfield of computer science that I study in my academic research—were also examining the trade-offs between synchrony and asynchrony. As it happens, the conclusion they reached was exactly the opposite of the prevailing consensus in the workplace.

The synchrony-versus-asynchrony issue is fundamental to the history of computer science. For the first couple of decades of the digital revolution, programs were designed to run on individual machines. Later, with the development of computer networks, programs were written to be deployed on multiple machines that operated together over a network, creating what are called *distributed systems*. Figuring out how to coordinate the machines that made up these systems forced computer scientists to confront the pros and cons of different communication modes.

If you connect a collection of computing machines on a network, their communication, by default, will be asynchronous. Machine A sends a message to Machine B, hoping that it will eventually be delivered and processed, but Machine A doesn't know for sure how long it will be until Machine B reads the message. This uncertainty could be due to many factors, such as the fact that different machines run at different speeds (if Machine B is also running many other unrelated processes, it might take a while until it gets around to checking its queue of incoming messages), unpredictable network delays, and equipment failures.

Writing distributed system algorithms that could handle this asynchrony turned out to be much harder than many engineers originally believed. A striking computer science discovery from this period, for example, is the difficulty of the so-called *consensus problem*. Imagine that each machine in a distributed system starts an operation, such as entering a transaction into a database, with an initial preference to either proceed or abort. The goal is for these machines to reach a consensus—either all agreeing to proceed or all agreeing to abort.

The simplest solution is for each machine to gather the preferences of its peers and then apply some fixed rule—for example, counting the votes to determine a winner—to decide which preference to adopt. If all the machines gather the same set of votes, they will all adopt the same decision. The problem is that some of the machines might crash before they vote. If that happens, the rest of the group will end up waiting forever to hear from peers that are no longer operating. Because delays are unpredictable in an asynchronous system, the waiting peers don't know when they should give up and move on with the votes they've already gathered.

At first, to the engineers who studied this problem, it seemed obvious that instead of waiting to learn the preference of every machine, one could just wait to hear from most of them. Imagine, for example, the following rule: if I hear from most machines, and they all want to proceed, then I'll decide to proceed; otherwise I'll default to abort, just to be safe. At first glance, this rule seems like it should lead to a consensus, so long as only a small number of machines die. And yet, to the surprise of many people in the field, in a 1985 paper, three computer scientists—Michael Fischer, Nancy Lynch (my doctoral adviser), and Michael Paterson—proved, through a virtuosic display of mathematical logic, that in an asynchronous system, *no* distributed algorithm could guarantee that a consensus would always be reached, even if it was sure that at most a single computer might crash.[20]

The details of this result are technical,[21] but its impact on distributed systems was obvious. It made it clear that asynchronous communication complicates attempts to coordinate, and therefore, it's almost always worth the extra cost required to introduce more synchrony. In the context of distributed systems, the added synchrony explored in the aftermath of this famous 1985 paper took several forms. One heavy-handed solution, used in some early fly-by-wire systems and fault-tolerant credit card transaction processing machines, was to connect the machines on a common electrical circuit, allowing them to operate at the same lockstep pace. This approach eliminates unpredictable communication delays and allows your application to immediately detect if a machine has crashed.

Because these circuits were sometimes complicated to implement, software approaches to adding synchrony also became popular. By leveraging knowledge about message delays and processor speeds, it turns out that it's possible to write programs that structure communication into well-behaved rounds, or simulate reliable machines that can help synchronize the actual unreliable machines participating in the system.

This fight against asynchrony ended up playing a crucial role in the rise of the internet age, enabling, among other innovations, the software driving the huge data centers run by such companies as Amazon, Facebook, and Google. In 2013, Leslie Lamport, a major figure in the field of distributed systems, was given the A. M. Turing Award—the highest distinction in computer science—for his work on algorithms that help synchronize distributed systems.[22]

What's striking about these technical results on asynchrony versus synchrony is how much they diverge from the conclusions of the business thinkers tackling these same issues in the workplace. As we've learned, managers in office settings fixated on eliminating the overhead of synchronous communication—the annoyance of phone tag or taking the elevator to a different floor to chat with someone in person. They believed that eliminating this overhead using tools like email would make collaboration more efficient. Computer scientists, meanwhile, came to the opposite conclusion. Investigating asynchronous communication from the perspective of algorithm theory, they discovered that spreading out communication with unpredictable delays introduced tricky new complexities. While the business world came to see synchrony as an obstacle to overcome, computer theorists began to realize that it was fundamental for effective collaboration.

People are different from computers, but many of the forces that complicate the design of asynchronous distributed systems loosely apply to humans attempting to collaborate in the office. Synchrony might be expensive to arrange—both in the office setting and in computer systems—but trying to coordinate in its absence is also expensive. This reality summarizes well what many experienced as office communication shifted to email: they traded the pain of phone tag, scribbled notes, and endless meetings for the pain of a surprisingly large volume of ambiguous electronic messages passed back and forth throughout the day. As the engineers discovered when they tried to coax their networked computers into reaching a consensus, asynchrony is not just synchrony spread out; it instead introduces its own difficulties. A problem that might have been solvable in a few minutes of real-time interaction in a meeting room or on the phone might now generate dozens of messages, and even then might still fail to converge on a satisfactory conclusion. It's possible, in other words, that once you move your workplace toward this style of communication, the *hyperactive* property of the hyperactive hive mind workflow becomes unavoidable.

Hive Mind Driver #2: The Cycle of Responsiveness

Harvard Business School professor Leslie Perlow is an expert in the culture of constant connectivity that dominates the modern workplace. As she recounts in her 2012 book, *Sleeping with Your Smartphone*, the severity of this problem was brought to her attention by a series of surveys she conducted between 2006 and 2012—the period in which the hive mind workflow shifted into a new gear of hyperactivity as smartphones became common. These surveys targeted over 2,500 managers and professionals who held what Perlow describes as "high-pressure, demanding jobs."[23] She asked respondents about their work habits: how many hours they worked per week, how often they checked their work accounts outside work, whether they slept with their phones nearby. The results were stark: these professionals were almost always "on."

What makes Perlow's work particularly relevant to our discussion is that she then went deeper, talking with her research subjects to better understand *how* they ended up in this state of constant communication. What she uncovered was a social feedback loop gone awry—a process she named the *cycle of responsiveness*. The cycle begins with legitimate demands on your time. Perhaps it's 2010, you've just started using a smartphone, and you realize it's now possible to answer client questions that arrive after work hours or respond quickly to colleagues in different time zones. These clients and colleagues now learn that you're available at these new times and begin to send more requests and expect faster responses. Faced with this increased influx, you check your phone more often so you can keep up with the incoming messages. But now the expectations for your availability and responsiveness increase further, and you feel pressured to respond even quicker. As Perlow summarizes:

> And thus the cycle spins: teammates, superiors and subordinates continue to make more requests, and conscientious employees accept these marginal increases in demands on their time, while their expectations of each other (and themselves) rise accordingly.[24]

This is a nice example of technological determinism at work. None of these teammates, superiors, and subordinates *like* the culture of constant connection that this cycle produces. None of them ever suggested it, or made a conscious decision to adopt it. Indeed, when Perlow later persuaded teams at Boston Consulting Group to schedule protected time away from communication devices, the team members described their efficiency and effectiveness as increasing.[25] She further proposed an email server configured such that messages sent after work hours would be automatically held and delivered the next morning (a special flag could be set to bypass this restriction for actual urgent communication). This change might sound simple, but by short-circuiting the cycle of responsiveness, its impact could be profound.

The important lesson from Perlow's work is the haphazard and unplanned manner in which an entirely new way of communicating emerged. The media theorist Douglas Rushkoff uses the term "collaborative pacing" to describe this tendency for groups of humans to converge toward strict patterns of behavior without ever actually explicitly deciding that the new behaviors make sense.[26] I notice you're responding a little quicker to my message, so I begin to do the same. Others follow suit; the pattern of responsiveness emerges, then becomes a new default. The consultants Perlow studied didn't choose the cycle of responsiveness; in some sense, email chose it for them.

Hive Mind Driver #3: The Caveman at the Computer Screen

In a paper published in 2018 in the journal *Quaternary*, Tel Aviv University archaeologists Aviad Agam and Ran Barkai review the available "archaeological, ethnographic and ethno-historical records" to summarize our current understanding of how early humans, starting in the Lower Paleolithic, hunted elephants and mammoths.[27] This paper includes four striking charcoal drawings illustrating the authors' best guesses about how these hunts might have transpired.

The first drawing shows a group of seven Paleolithic hunters charging a rearing elephant, each throwing spears toward vulnerable organs. The second and third show lone hunters attempting to surprise an elephant by stealth, landing a critical spear stab before the animal realizes what is happening. In one case, the hunter attacks from below, stabbing up through the belly; in the other, the hunter hides in a tree and stabs downward as the elephant passes. In the fourth drawing, a group of six hunters rush to finish off with spears an elephant that has fallen into a pitfall trap.

For our purposes, it's important to notice the small size of the groups engaged in each of these hunting scenarios. Throughout our species's deep history, this evidence suggests, when we hunted mega-fauna we did so either alone or in small groups. This reality likely also holds for the other activities—hunting small game, foraging—that made up the "work" that dominates our evolutionary history. It doesn't re-quire a large leap of speculative evolutionary psychology to arrive at the reasonable conclusion that *Homo sapiens* are well adapted to small-group collaboration.

To connect this observation of our deep past to our current discus-sion of email, consider the dynamics of these collaborations. If you're part of a small group of Paleolithic hunters stealthily approaching an elephant, your communication would be ad hoc and unstructured as you adjust on the fly to the unfolding situation (imagine the following dialogue delivered in some now lost caveman dialect):

"Careful . . . watch out for those sticks, which might crack and spook the elephant. . . ."

"Wait, circle around that way. . . ."

"Slowly now, its ears are perking up. . . ."

Even when we leave deep history and return to our more recent pre-industrial past, for the vast majority of people, the vast majority of their experience working with others would still involve small groups— from the farmer and his kids navigating a plow to the blacksmith work-ing closely with his apprentice at the forge. As with the Paleolithic hunters, the most natural way for small groups to coordinate is in a free-form manner. It follows that the mode of collaboration most instinctually embedded in both our genetics and our cultural memory shares the main characteristics of the hyperactive hive mind workflow. We shouldn't be surprised, therefore, that when the introduction of low-friction messaging tools like email made similarly unstructured communication possible in the modern large office scenario, we were drawn to this mode of interaction.

The problem, of course, is that the hyperactive hive mind deployed in an office differs from the hive mind collaboration of a Stone Age elephant hunt in one key property: the office connects many more people. Unstructured coordination is great for a group of six hunters but becomes disastrously ineffective when you connect many dozens, if not hundreds, of employees in a large organization. We know this in part because of the robust research literature studying the optimal group size for working together and solving professional problems. "The size question has been asked since the dawn of social psychology," explains Jennifer Mueller, a management professor at Wharton.[28]

One of the first studies in this area was the now famous work of a nineteenth-century French agricultural engineer, Maximilien Ringelmann, who demonstrated that when you dedicate more people to the task of pulling a rope, the average force exerted by each individual decreases—leading to diminishing returns as group sizes grow. Though the physical task of rope pulling is not that relevant to the modern knowledge sector, Ringelmann's work proved influential, as it introduced the general idea that increasing the size of a team doesn't necessarily increase its effectiveness in direct proportion.

In the modern era, many management professors have built on this observation by studying what happens to the effectiveness of workplace collaboration when you increase team sizes. A 2006 review article published by Wharton summarizes many such research papers. Though there's no specific team size that consistently emerges as optimal, essentially every result falls into a narrow range of roughly four to twelve people—exactly as we observed all the way back with the Paleolithic elephant hunters.

There are many proposed reasons for why teams above this range are less effective. The loafing effect first observed by Ringelmann, for example, seems to still play a role in knowledge work tasks. (Summarized simply: the more people working on a project, the easier it is to get away with putting in less effort.) But another key factor is the rising complexity of communication. It's easy for six elephant hunters to coordinate their attack by just speaking up when they have something relevant to say. But if you increase this size to sixty, the effort would devolve into an incomprehensible scrum of competing voices and misunderstood ideas, which is why military units of this size almost always feature strict chains of command.

Pulling together these threads, we can weave a compelling narrative that helps explain the hyperactive hive mind's spread. Throughout most of human history we worked together in small groups, communicating in an ad hoc fashion without any particular structure or rules. The rise of the large office in the early twentieth century completely disrupted these natural modes of collaboration, requiring us instead to send memos to be carbon-copied in typing pools, or have secretaries arrange one-on-one phone calls. When email arrived, we found a way to bring back a more primal mode of communication to our otherwise alienating office environments—we could just talk, on the fly, sending messages as the thoughts arrived, and expect responses promptly: the elephant hunt reenacted over network wires. The result was the hyperactive hive mind workflow—which made sense at an instinctual level, even while at a practical level it began to drive us toward misery as we misjudged its ability to scale up to large groups.

Put another way, although the now common tableau of the frantic business executives furiously typing on their phones might seem like the personification of our modern moment, it's perhaps downright Paleolithic in its origins.

Peter Drucker and the Tragedy of the Attention Commons

As a child in Austria during the first decades of the twentieth century, Peter Drucker was exposed to some of the foremost economic thinkers of the age, including notables like Joseph Schumpeter of "creative destruction" fame, who attended evening salons held by Drucker's parents, Adolph and Caroline.[29] The intellectual energy of these salons laid the foundation for Drucker's eventual emergence as one of the most important business thinkers of the modern period; he is widely acknowledged as the "founder of modern management."[30] His career produced thirty-nine books and countless articles before his death in 2005 at the age of ninety-five.

Drucker's sprint toward significance first picked up speed in 1942, when, as a thirty-three-year-old professor at Bennington College, he published his second book, *The Future of Industrial Man*. It asked how an "industrial society"—one unfolding within "the entirely new physical reality Western man has built up as his habitat since James Watt invented the steam engine"[31]—might best be structured to respect human freedom and dignity. Arriving in the midst of an industrial world war, the book found a wide readership. It impressed the management team at General Motors, who invited Drucker to spend two years studying how the world's largest corporation operated.[32] The 1946 title that resulted from this engagement, *Concept of the Corporation*, was one of the first books to look seriously at how big organizations actually operated. It laid the foundation for management as something that could be studied, and it made Drucker's career.

For our purposes, Drucker is more than just a famous business theorist. His influence also helps answer a pressing question that likely snagged your attention as you read this chapter: Even if we accept that the hyperactive hive mind arose largely of its own accord, why did we let it stick around once its flaws became obvious?

During his time at GM in the 1940s, Peter Drucker got to know its larger-than-life CEO, Alfred P. Sloan Jr. As Drucker later recalled, Sloan once said the following about being a successful manager: "He must be absolutely tolerant and pay no attention to how a man does his work."[33] This idea re-emerged in Drucker's thinking in the 1950s and 1960s, a period in which he coined the term *knowledge work* as he began to grapple with an emerging economy where the output of brains was beginning to prove more valuable than the output of factories.

"The knowledge worker cannot be supervised closely or in detail," Drucker wrote in his 1967 book, *The Effective Executive*. "He must direct himself."[34] This was a radical idea. In the nation's factories, centralized control of workers was the standard. Influenced by the so-called "scientific management" principles popularized by Frederick Winslow Taylor, who would famously prowl the factory floor with a stopwatch, rooting out inefficient movements, industrial management saw workers as automatons executing optimized processes carefully designed by a small cadre of wise managers.

Drucker argued this approach was doomed to fail in the new world of knowledge work, where productive output was created not by expensive equipment stamping out parts, but instead by cerebral workers applying specialized cognitive skills. Indeed, knowledge workers often knew more about their specialties than those who managed them. The best way to deploy these highly skilled individuals, Drucker concluded, was to give them clear objectives and then leave them alone to accomplish their brainy work however they saw fit. While it might have been efficient to tell an assembly line worker exactly how to install a steering wheel, it was futile to try to tell a marketing copywriter exactly how to brainstorm a new product slogan.

Drucker preached this idea of knowledge worker autonomy throughout his long career. As late as 1999, he still emphasized its importance:

> [Knowledge work] demands that we impose the responsibility for their productivity on the individual knowledge workers themselves. Knowledge workers *have* to manage themselves. They have to have *autonomy*.[35]

It's hard to overestimate the influence of this idea. With the exception of some routinized bureaucratic processes, like filing expense reports, the intricacies of how the myriad demanding tasks that define modern office work are accomplished remain largely beyond the scope of management. They're pushed instead into the hazy realm of personal productivity. Want to know how to get things done? Buy a book on how to better organize your tasks (Drucker himself wrote one of the first such books, *The Effective Executive*), or use a new planner, or, as is more commonly suggested in our culture of "crushing it," simply work harder. Knowledge workers don't expect their organization to take an interest in how much work falls on their plate, or how they get it done.

In our shift from industrial to knowledge work, in other words, we gave up automaton status for a burdensome autonomy. It's in this context that the hyperactive hive mind, once in place, became devilishly difficult to eradicate, as it's hard to fix a broken workflow when it's no one's job to make sure the workflow functions. In 1833, the British economist William Forster Lloyd proposed a hypothetical scenario, now a classical example in game theory, that can help us better understand this dynamic. The scenario, which eventually became known as the *tragedy of the commons*,[36] considers a town that maintains common grazing land for cattle and sheep, as was typical in Great Britain in the nineteenth century. Lloyd pointed out an interesting tension: it's in the individual interest of each herder to graze his animals as much as possible on the commons, and yet when all herders act in their best interest, they'll inevitably overgraze the commons, rendering it useless to everyone. Similar scenarios of individual interest leading to collective hardship turn out to be common in many different settings—from unstable ecologies, to resource mining, to the behaviors surrounding shared refrigerators. Using the mathematical tools introduced in the mid-twentieth century by John Nash (of *A Beautiful Mind* fame), you can even precisely analyze this situation, which turns out to be a nice example of what game theorists would call an "inefficient Nash equilibrium."

This economic trivia informs our discussions here because when the hyperactive hive mind emerged due to the drivers summarized earlier in this chapter, communication in the modern office became yet another example of Lloyd's thought experiment in action. Once your organization has fallen into the hive mind, it's in each individual's immediate interest to stick with this workflow, even if it leads to a bad long-term outcome for the organization as a whole. It makes your life strictly easier in the moment if you can expect quick responses to messages that you shoot off to colleagues. Similarly, if you unilaterally decrease the time you spend checking your inbox in a group that depends on the hive mind, you'll slow down other people's efforts, generating annoyance and dissatisfaction that might put your job in jeopardy. At the risk of stretching this analogy beyond comfort, in knowledge work, we're overgrazing our common collection of time and attention because none of us wants to be the one who lets their cognitive sheep go hungry.

The negative consequences of the hyperactive hive mind, in other words, are unlikely to be resolved by small shifts in individual habits. Even good-natured attempts to nudge the behavior of an entire organization, such as promulgating better norms around email responsiveness or attempting one-off experiments like email-free Fridays, are doomed to fail. As 150 years of economic theory has taught us, to solve the tragedy of the commons, you cannot expect substantially better behavior from the herders; you need instead to replace the free-for-all grazing system with something more efficient. The same holds for the hyperactive hive mind: we cannot tame it with minor hacks—we need to replace it with a better workflow. And to do so, we must soften Peter Drucker's stigma against engineering office work. Drucker was right to point out that we cannot fully systematize the specialized efforts of knowledge workers, but we shouldn't apply this to the workflows that surround these efforts. A manager can't tell a copywriter how to come up with a brilliant ad, but she can have something to say about how these commissions are assigned, or about what other obligations are allowed onto the copywriter's plate, or about how client requests are handled.

This goal of putting into place smarter workflows that sidestep the worst impacts of the hyperactive hive mind is of course a substantial endeavor—one that will require trial and error and many annoyances. But with the right guiding principles it's absolutely possible, and the competitive advantage it will generate is potentially massive. The second part of this book, at which we have now arrived, is dedicated to explaining these principles.

Part 2

Principles for a World Without Email

Chapter 4

The Attention Capital Principle

On Model Ts and Knowledge Work

We begin our efforts to unseat the hyperactive hive mind workflow in a perhaps unexpected place: Henry Ford's first car factories. During the early years of the twentieth century, Ford's newly minted Ford Motor Company produced its vehicles in much the same way as its competitors. "We simply started to put a car together at a spot on the floor," Ford once explained. "Workmen brought to it the parts as they were needed in exactly the same way that one builds a house."[1] These partially assembled cars were raised on wooden sawhorses to prevent unnecessary stooping as teams of workmen swarmed around them, shaping and filing the various parts and pieces into tight fits. The factories deploying this "craft method," as it became known, were directly scaling up the same natural approach Karl Benz had used to assemble the first practical automobile in the late 1800s.[2]

After working his way from the Model A, which seated only two and cost extra if you wanted a roof, through Models B, C, F, K, and N, Ford finally arrived in 1908 at what would become his masterpiece of pragmatic conveyance: the Model T. With this new design, Ford set out to innovate not just the features of the vehicle but also the entire process by which it was constructed. The first major step in this innovation was the introduction of interchangeable parts. Drawing from techniques that had emerged originally from New England armories around the time of the Civil War, Ford reinvested profits from the early versions of this popular vehicle to engineer specialized tools that could produce car parts with enough precision to eliminate the lengthy process of filing and grinding otherwise needed to get these parts to fit together.[3] As the company boasted: "You might travel around the world in a Model T and exchange crankshafts with any other Model T you met en route, and both engines would work as perfectly after the exchange as before."[4]

By eliminating grinding, interchangeable parts made faster assembly feasible, but Ford still had to figure out how to get the roughly one hundred precisely engineered pieces that made up a Model T to come together into a working automobile in the shortest amount of time possible. To accomplish this goal, he tried out many different ideas. In its standard form, the craft method originally had teams of fifteen working on a single car. Ford experimented with having one man dedicated to building each car, with other workers bringing him the pieces. The need for this single worker to context switch between all the different assembly steps, however, still caused delays, so Ford then introduced a system where each worker was dedicated to a specific single task—say, bolting a bumper to the car—and would walk the factory floor, from car to car, executing exactly that step on each vehicle. This was somewhat better, but it was devilishly difficult to orchestrate these rotating specialists.

It was in 1913, around five years after the introduction of the Model T, that Ford made the next logical leap in this process tinkering: What if instead of moving workers between stationary cars, the cars moved past stationary workers? He began tentatively, with a mini assembly line designed to speed up the production of the coiled-wire magnetos that supplied the sparks for the Model T's ignition system. It used to take a single worker around twenty minutes to manufacture a magneto from scratch at his workbench. After Ford introduced a basic, waist-high conveyor belt and broke down the construction into five steps, implemented by five workers standing shoulder to shoulder, a magneto could now come together in five minutes.

The proverbial light bulb lit up. After the magneto came a new assembly line for the vehicle's axle, reducing construction time from two and a half hours to twenty-six minutes. Then came a moving line for the vehicle's three-speed transmission, helping drop the engine assembly time from ten hours to four. Confidence buoyed, Ford made the final step toward his new and improved production system by building the heavy-duty, chain-driven conveyors needed to move an entire car chassis on a continuous-motion assembly line.[5]

In today's world, we've become used to complex manufacturing processes, but it's hard to overestimate the magnitude of this innovation when it was first deployed at a large scale by Ford. It used to take more than twelve and a half labor hours to produce a Model T. After the assembly line, this time dropped to ninety-three minutes. Ford went on to sell 16.5 million units of the iconic vehicle. At its height, his mammoth Highland Park factory would roll a new Model T through its doors once every forty seconds.

The clanking chains and sparking welders of an early twentieth-century automobile factory might seem far removed from our current moment of knowledge workers tapping out emails on sleek computer monitors. But as I hinted earlier, Ford's innovation, and its subsequent impact on the world of industrial manufacturing, will provide an immensely useful analogy for understanding what it will take to escape the miseries of the hyperactive hive mind workflow.

———

In the fall of 2019, *The Wall Street Journal* reported on a German entrepreneur named Lasse Rheingans, who had adopted a novel practice at his sixteen-person technology start-up: a five-hour workday. Rheingans wasn't just reducing the time his employees spent in the office, but the total time they spent working each day. They arrive at around eight each morning and leave at around one in the afternoon. During the day, social media is banned, meetings highly restricted, and email checks constrained. When they're done with work, they're actually done until the next morning—no late-night sessions at the keyboard, no surreptitious smartphone messaging during their kids' sporting events—as professional efforts are restricted to time spent in the physical office. Rheingans's bet was that once you eliminated both distractions and endless conversations *about* work, five hours per day would be sufficient for people to get done the main things that mattered for the company.

Soon after this profile on Rheingans was published, *The New York Times* invited me to write an op-ed about his experiment, which appeared in the paper a couple of weeks later.[6] "The *Wall Street Journal* described Mr. Rheingans's approach as 'radical,'" I wrote. "[But] I've come to believe that what's really radical is the fact that many more organizations aren't trying similar experiments." To justify my claim, I pointed to the story of Henry Ford and the assembly line. A fundamental lesson of the story is that when it comes to manufacturing products in a capital-driven market economy, the amount of resources you have is not enough by itself to predict your profitability. During the lead-up to the Model T, for example, Ford didn't have more capital than his competitors. If anything, at certain key points, he probably had less. (At the time when Ford's first Model A was sold, for $750 to a Chicago dentist, he was down to only $223 in cash reserves.[7]) And yet, by the end of 1914, Ford was producing cars at a cost that made it ten times more profitable than rival automobile companies. What mattered just as much as how much capital he had was how he *deployed* it.

In the aftermath of the Ford revolution, this principle became foundational for industrial management. It's now widely accepted that continued industrial growth requires continual experimentation and reinvention of the processes that produce the stuff we sell. As Peter Drucker argues in a classic 1999 article, this obsession with industrial improvement was enormously successful. As Drucker reminds the reader, since 1900 the productivity of the manual laborer increased by *a factor of fifty*! "The productivity of the manual worker has created what we now call 'developed' economies," he writes. "On this achievement rest *all* of the economic and social gains of the 20th century."[8]

But when we turn our attention back to knowledge work, we find this same spirit of experimentation and reinvention lacking. This is what I meant when I wrote in the *Times* that the rarity of experiments like Lasse Rheingans's five-hour workday was itself "radical." Rheingans is thinking about his organization with a Henry Ford mindset, by which I mean he's looking for bold new ways to deploy his capital to produce more value. Soon after my *Times* op-ed was published, Rheingans reached out to me and we began a conversation about life at his company. He explained that his five-hour workday experiment had been running for two years so far and that he had no intention of changing this setup anytime soon.

Accomplishing this transformation, however, proved challenging.

I asked Rheingans how he persuaded his employees to not check email constantly. "The answer is not as easy as you might expect," he told me. Suggesting they check email less was not enough for many on his team. He ended up hiring external coaches to reinforce "that checking email or social media all the time won't help them." The coaches also encouraged employees to embrace stress-reducing mindfulness exercises like meditation and to improve their physical health through practices like yoga. Rheingans's goal was for everyone to slow down; to approach their work more deliberately and with less frantic action; to realize that they were "running all the time without getting anywhere." With these changes in place, five hours suddenly proved to be more than enough to accomplish the work that used to require a much longer day.

Rheingans is one of the few business leaders willing to drastically change the fundamental building blocks of work in our age of networked brains. At the moment, most organizations remain stuck in the productivity quicksand of the hyperactive hive mind workflow, content to focus on tweaks meant to compensate for its worst excesses. It's this mindset that leads to "solutions" like improving expectations around email response times or writing better subject lines. It leads us to embrace text autocomplete in Gmail, so we can write messages faster, or the search feature in Slack, so we can more quickly find what we're looking for amid the scrum of back-and-forth chatter. These are the knowledge work equivalents of speeding up the craft method of car manufacturing by giving the workers faster shoes. It's a small victory won in the wrong war.

Lasse Rheingans and I aren't the only ones to notice the stakes on the table in this discussion. In the same 1999 article cited earlier, Peter Drucker notes that in terms of productivity thinking, knowledge work was where industrial manufacturing was in 1900—that is, right before the radical experiments that increased productivity by fifty times. We're poised, in other words, to make similarly massive increases in the economic effectiveness of the knowledge sector, *if* we're willing to get serious about questioning how we work. Drucker calls this push to make knowledge work more productive the "central challenge" of our times, writing: "It is on [knowledge work] productivity, above all, that the future prosperity—and indeed the future survival—of the developed economies will increasingly depend."[9]

We can capture both the necessity and the potential of this mindset shift in the following principle, which provides the foundation for all the practical ideas that populate part 2 of this book.

> **The Attention Capital Principle**
>
> The productivity of the knowledge sector can be significantly increased if we identify workflows that better optimize the human brain's ability to sustainably add value to information.

In the industrial sector, the primary capital resources were materials and equipment.[10] Some ways of deploying this capital returned far more value than others (think: the assembly line versus the craft method). In the knowledge sector, by contrast, the primary capital resources are the human brains you employ to add value to information—what I call *attention capital*. But the same dynamics hold: different strategies for deploying this capital will generate different returns. Based on the evidence I reviewed in part 1, it's clear that the brain-addling constant network switching required by the hyperactive hive mind is far from optimal, providing, in some sense, the cognitive equivalent of the old craft method for building cars. To obtain the dramatic productivity increases that Peter Drucker prophesied for the twenty-first century will require a commitment to finding approaches to knowledge work that can generate much better returns.

The chapters that follow will explore specific ideas about what these better deployments of attention capital might include. You'll learn about the value of switching your focus from optimizing people to optimizing processes, and about the importance of separating specialized work from administrative efforts. You'll also hear my argument for greatly reducing the raw quantity of work that the average knowledge worker is quixotically expected to complete, and you'll encounter many case studies along the way of individuals, like Lasse Rheingans, and organizations that are willing to experiment with better alternatives. Before moving on to these specifics, however, the remainder of this chapter will focus on a collection of *general* best practices for putting the attention capital principle into action.

Case Study: Devesh Ditches the Hive Mind

Let's start our exploration of the attention capital principle with a concrete case study: an entrepreneur named Devesh, who applied these ideas to rethink work in his small marketing firm. Devesh's company employs a group of largely remote employees spread out across the United States and Europe. This geographic diversity, which covers a wide range of time zones, required a dependence on asynchronous communication tools like email. Like so many other firms in similar situations, Devesh's company soon found itself tangled up in the hyperactive hive mind workflow, with its activities unfolding as a never-ending jumble of back-and-forth email messages. As Devesh explains, this resulted in frustrating days spent tending an inbox "filled with notes and design files, one-off messages, and single emails that talked about multiple different projects."

Like many business owners feeling overwhelmed by the hive mind workflow, Devesh first attempted to fix the problem by making the communication more efficient. Among other steps, he switched the company to Gmail, which does a better job of automatically grouping messages into threads and provides a sleek smartphone app that allows employees to keep up with their conversations while away from their desks. These bids for efficiency, however, didn't fix the underlying sense that there was something fundamentally wrong with the sheer volume of the frantic communication that drove their efforts. As Devesh explained to me, he and his employees felt "bombarded" by messages, which "dictated" how they spent their time. It became increasingly clear that this couldn't possibly be the best way to execute cognitive work. To use our new terminology, Devesh feared he was getting a weak return from this deployment of his company's attention capital.

Taking a page out of Henry Ford's playbook, Devesh began experimenting with radical new approaches to organizing his firm's work. His core insight was that when his employees relied on the hive mind, their days were structured by incoming messages, which dictated what they worked on and kept them jumping back and forth between many different projects simultaneously, limiting the quality of attention they devoted to any one objective. Devesh decided to reverse this dynamic. He wanted his employees to decide what to work on and then, once they made that decision, limit their attention to this choice until they were ready to move on to something else. To realize this new goal, Devesh abandoned the hive mind model in which all work passed through each person's general-purpose inbox. He rebuilt his company's workflow around an online project management tool called Trello.

When you set up a project in Trello, you create a dedicated web page called a "board" that's shared with relevant collaborators. You then add named columns to the board, and under each column you arrange "cards" in a "stack," creating a solitaire-style collection of cards lined up vertically. Each card has a short description on the front, and when you click on it, you gain access to much more detailed information on the back, including file attachments, task lists, notes, and discussion.

At my request, Devesh sent me a screenshot of a Trello board used for one of their ongoing marketing projects. It contained the following four named stacks:

☐ **Research & Notes.** The cards in this stack each contain background information relevant to the marketing campaign. One of the cards, for example, has notes from a recent client call, while another contains some thoughts on ways to grow the client's email list.

☐ **Backlog.** The cards in this stack each describe a project step that needs to be completed at some point but is not actively being worked on by anyone at the moment. One of these cards, for example, details a step in which new client testimonials need to be added to the client's website.

☐ **Designing** and **Implementing.** The cards in these final two stacks describe project steps that are currently being executed. The *designing* stack contains, naturally, design-related steps, and the *implementing* stack focuses on the other steps relevant to carrying out the marketing campaign. Different people work on these two elements, so it makes sense to keep them separate. Crucially, each of these cards, when clicked on, reveals not only a description of the step, but both its current status and a vibrant comments section where people can ask and answer questions and delegate responsibility for accomplishing key tasks related to the card.

Some of these cards even have checklists of sub-tasks, while others have deadlines that show up in bright colors under the card's title. Many have relevant files directly attached.

As Devesh explained to me, his company's efforts now revolve around Trello. If you're assigned to a project, all of your work, including discussion, delegation, and relevant files, is coordinated on its corresponding board—not in email messages, not in Slack chats. When you decide to work on a project, you navigate to its board and work with the cards. As project steps are completed, cards can be moved from *backlog* to the active columns. As new ideas come up or clients send extra requests, they can be added to the *research & notes* column. When questions arise or work needs to be delegated, these notes are appended to the discussion on the back of the relevant card, where everyone involved in the project can see them.

Before these changes, each employee's workday was driven by their inbox. They would open it up when they started work in the morning, then answer messages until quitting time. In the new Trello-based workflow, each employee's effort is now driven by project boards, which they rotate through during the day. Though email is still used for non-urgent administrative issues and private one-on-one conversations, its importance is greatly diminished. Inboxes are something you might now check once or twice daily, similar to a physical mailbox.

This new workflow encourages single-tasking. When one of Devesh's employees decides to work on a given project, the only information or discussion they see on its board relates to the project. This allows them to remain focused on one thing until *they're* ready to move on. When using a general-purpose inbox, by contrast, they were constantly switching back and forth between many different projects, sometimes even within the same message—a cognitive state that's both unproductive and misery-inducing.

Another advantage of this workflow is that it clearly structures all the relevant information about a given project. When Devesh's firm used to rely on the hyperactive hive mind, this information was spread out haphazardly in email messages buried in many different employees' inboxes. To have it instead neatly arranged in named columns, with the relevant files and discussion attached to clearly marked cards, is a much more efficient way to keep track of this work and effectively plan what needs to be done next.

When I saw Devesh's Trello boards, my reaction was likely similar to that of rival automakers who first encountered a fully functioning assembly line at Henry Ford's Highland Park factory: a gut realization that this was simply a better way to organize work. Devesh agrees. His employees seem much happier now that they're freed from email as the main driver of their efforts, and there have been no major complaints or drops in productivity. More telling, Devesh has no interest in changing back to the old way of working. To emphasize how much things have changed in his professional life, he sent me a screenshot of his business email inbox. In the entire preceding month, he had participated in only eight email threads, sending and receiving a grand total of forty-four messages. This averages out to slightly more than two messages per workday. "It's a godsend," he summarized.

This type of radical workflow makeover is easy to describe but often tricky to successfully implement. There are many obstacles, from figuring out where to focus your experimental energies, to shifting how you think about issues like inconvenience or extra overhead, to getting everyone on your team on the same page. The rest of the chapter will explore some best practices for overcoming these obstacles when you attempt to apply the attention capital principle in your own organization or professional life.

Build Structures Around Autonomy

In chapter 3, we tackled a key question: *If the hyperactive hive mind is so ineffective, why is it so popular?* Ironically, a major part of the answer I provided concerned the very same person who identified knowledge worker productivity as the central challenge of the twenty-first century: Peter Drucker. As detailed earlier, during the 1950s and 1960s, Drucker helped the business world understand the emergence of knowledge work as a major economic sector. One of his central messages was the importance of autonomy. "The knowledge worker cannot be supervised closely or in detail," he wrote in 1967. "He must direct himself."[11]

What Drucker realized was that knowledge work was too skilled and creative to be broken down into a series of repetitive tasks that could be prescribed to workers by managers, as was the case with manual labor. There was simply no easy way to take something as abstract as coming up with a new business strategy, or innovating a new scientific industrial process, and reduce it down to a clear series of optimized steps to be followed unthinkingly.

This emphasis on autonomy proved influential, and it goes a long way toward explaining the stubborn persistence of the hive mind. As I argued, when you delegate productivity decisions to the individual, it's not surprising that you end up stuck with a simple, flexible, lowest common denominator–style workflow like the hyperactive hive mind.

It's here that we arrive at an impasse. On the one hand, autonomy is unavoidable in knowledge work due to the complexity of these efforts. On the other hand, autonomy entrenches hive mind–style workflows.

To succeed with applying the attention capital principle, we must somehow escape this trap. To do so, we'll have to pick up where Drucker left off and clarify exactly where autonomy really matters.

Knowledge work is better understood as the combination of two components: *work execution* and *workflow*. The first component, work execution, describes the act of actually executing the underlying value-producing activities of knowledge work—the programmer coding, the publicist writing the press release. It's how you generate value from attention capital.

The second component, workflow, is one we defined in the introduction of this book. It describes how these fundamental activities are identified, assigned, coordinated, and reviewed. The hyperactive hive mind is a workflow, as is Devesh's project board system. If work execution is what generates value, then workflows are what structure these efforts.

Once we understand that these components describe two different things, we find a way to escape the autonomy trap. When Drucker emphasized autonomy, he was thinking about work execution, as these activities are often too complicated to be decomposed into rote procedures. Workflows, on the other hand, should not be left to individuals to figure out on their own, as the most effective systems are unlikely to arise naturally. They need instead to be explicitly identified as part of an organization's operating procedures.

If I manage a development team, I shouldn't tell my computer programmers how to write specific routines. I should, however, think a lot about how many routines they're asked to write, how these tasks are tracked, how we manage the code base, and even who else in the organization is allowed to bother them, and so on. (For more on radically original workflows for software developers, see the case study on *extreme programming* in chapter 7.)

We see this division in action in Devesh's marketing firm. By moving project management to Trello boards, Devesh didn't constrain how his team actually executed the core activities of designing and deploying marketing campaigns. What he did change, however, was the workflows that supported these activities—including how information about these projects was tracked, and how relevant information and questions were communicated. He innovated workflows but left the details of work execution up to his skilled employees. You'll see this same division in most of the case studies and examples you'll encounter in the chapters ahead.

To be fair, we cannot blame Drucker for not making this distinction in his original research on knowledge work. In the 1950s and 1960s, when he first began tackling this topic, the notion of *any* employee autonomy was so radical that there wasn't much room left for nuance. It was hard enough to simply convince people that the authoritarian approach that had produced such miraculous growth in the industrial sector might not apply to this new type of brain-centric activity.

Drucker succeeded in his efforts to preach the gospel of autonomy to a skeptical audience, and those of us who participate in the knowledge sector today are beneficiaries of these clear-sighted arguments. We cannot, however, stop here. To deliver the great promise of the attention capital principle, we must stand on Drucker's shoulders and push these theories toward their next evolution in complexity. Differentiating workflows and work execution is crucial if we're going to continue to improve knowledge sector productivity. To get the full value of attention capital, we must start taking seriously the way we structure work. This doesn't stifle the autonomy of knowledge workers, but instead sets them up to make even more out of their skill and creativity.

Minimize Context Switches and Overload

Henry Ford began experimenting with better ways to make cars in the early 1900s. A century later, Devesh began experimenting with better ways to serve marketing clients. In these efforts, we must admit, Ford had an advantage. When it comes to manufacturing cars, it's immediately obvious what makes one process superior to another: speed. This design principle—faster is better than slower—drove Ford's efforts and allowed him to directly connect improvements in low-level manufacturing processes to the bottom line. In knowledge work, this equation becomes murkier. When trying to engineer your workflows to generate a better return from your attention capital, what are you looking for? What is the cognitive work equivalent of production speed?

In answering this question, we can build on the insights of part 1 of this book, which documented the problems with the hyperactive hive mind workflow. In these previous chapters, I argued that there's a large cognitive cost to switching your attention from one target to another. Any workflow that requires you to constantly tend conversations unfolding in an inbox or chat channel is going to diminish the quality of your brain's output. I also argued that communication overload—the feeling that you can never keep up with all the different incoming requests for your time and attention—conflicts with our ancient social wiring, leading to unhappiness in the short term and burnout in the long term.

Drawing on these observations, I suggest the following design principle for developing approaches to work that provide better returns from your personal or organizational attention capital: seek workflows that

(1) minimize mid-task context switches and (2) minimize the sense of communication overload. These two properties are the knowledge work equivalent of Henry Ford's obsession with speed.

To unpack this claim, let's start with the first property. A mid-task context switch is when you have to stop an otherwise self-contained task and switch your attention to something unrelated before returning to the original object of your attention. The classic example of such switches is the need to continually return to an email inbox or instant messenger channel to keep up with drawn-out conversations about unrelated issues. Such switches, however, can also be analog. In open office settings, for example, you might be frequently interrupted by people stopping by your seat with questions, and if your workflow demands constant meetings, then this, too, will fracture your schedule into slivers too small to support start-to-finish work on tasks.

Regardless of the source of these interruptions, when it comes to producing value with your brain, the more you're able to complete one thing at a time, sticking with a task until done before moving on to the next, the more efficiently and effectively you'll work. As elaborated in part 1, this holds for many different types of knowledge work, be it deep thinking, managing, or even support roles. The optimal way to deploy our human brains is sequentially.

The second property cited above attempts to reduce the cognitive toll of feeling like everyone needs you at all times. All things being equal, workflows that minimize this never-ending stream of urgent communication are superior to those that instead amplify it. When you're at home at night, or relaxing over the weekend, or on vacation, you shouldn't feel like each moment away from work is a moment in which you're accumulating deeper communication debt. In the age of the hyperactive hive mind, we've become used to this despondent state as a necessary consequence of our high-tech world, but this is nonsense. Better workflows can tame this sense of overload and, by doing so, make you not only happier but also more effective and less likely to burn out over time.

When we return to Devesh's story, we see these design principles in action. His new project board–based workflow eliminates mid-task context switches. Communication about a project now happens only when you decide to load that project's board and review the relevant cards. There's no general-purpose inbox where you encounter messages about one project while trying to work on another. Devesh called this "flipping the script": *you* decide when to communicate about a project; you don't let *the project* decide for you.

Devesh's new workflow also minimizes communication overload. When interactions are moved onto task-specific cards associated with a project, the sense of requests *piling up* is diminished. When you decide to visit a particular project board, you contribute to the conversation. When you're not there, there's no inbox specific to you that's growing with impatient requests and notices.

Minimizing context switches and overload is not the whole story when it comes to engineering better workflows. This should guide your experiments in the short term, but in the long term, you must still monitor the key bottom line metric: the quantity and quality of valuable output you're producing. For a knowledge work organization, this means tracking the impact of new workflows on revenue, while for an individual knowledge worker, this might describe the rate at which you're hitting milestones or completing projects.

Seeing these numbers improve over time will provide the confidence needed to stick with new ways of working. Equally important, if your changes lead to these measures degrading, you have clear evidence you went too far, accidentally impeding activities crucial to your success. The key is to find ways to minimize context shifts and overload *while still getting done what needs to get done.*

Don't Fear Inconvenience

When I told Devesh's story to other knowledge workers, they predictably raised concerns. When they imagined shifting their own organizations away from the hyperactive hive mind and toward something more structured, like Devesh's project board–based workflow, they easily conjured potential issues. Losing the ability to grab people's attention for anything at any time might lead to deadlines getting missed, or urgent tasks not getting completed, or long delays before you get the answers you need to make progress on key project steps. Leaving behind the simplicity of the hyperactive hive mind, in other words, might create a steady stream of inconveniences for everyone involved.

This objection is important because it's relevant to most attempts to apply the attention capital principle. As argued, one of the key explanations for the hyperactive hive mind's persistence in the knowledge sector is that it's really convenient *in the moment* for the individuals who use it. There are no systems to learn or rules to remember; you simply grab people electronically as you need them. Almost any alternative to this workflow is going to be less convenient, in the sense that it will require more effort to follow, and lead to short-term problems, like missed tasks or occasional long response delays. This reality helps explain why so many work reform movements, born out of inbox exhaustion, end up reduced down to only small tweaks—like promoting better "etiquette" surrounding messaging—as these toothless suggestions prevent anyone from having to confront the hardships that follow real changes to the hyperactive hive mind status quo.

Imagine you want to make a major change to your own or your organization's workflow. How can you avoid the inconveniences associated with this experimentation? *You can't.* You must instead adjust your mindset so that you no longer fear these annoyances. To support this advice, let's turn back to the industrial sector, where an embrace of inconvenience is commonly accepted. Consider, for a moment, what it must have been like at Henry Ford's Highland Park factory during the radical experimentation that occurred between 1908 and 1914. At the beginning of this period, the way Ford was building cars made perfect sense. Deploying the same craft method that had dominated for decades, he had workers stand around stationary vehicles, bolting and filing parts, carrying supplies back and forth to the machine shop, and generally building the vehicles the way people had always naturally built complicated things: in place, one piece at a time.

Ford's early assembly line, by contrast, must have been a nightmare for his employees. Nothing about it was natural. For one thing, it required more complicated machinery that was prone to breaking down. Carrying a bumper from a pile to a stationary car was a simple and reliable process. Trying to pull an entire car chassis on a variable-speed winch system toward a worker who would then bolt on a bumper as it passed was a much more complicated way to accomplish this same step.

Then there were the custom tools. Part of what makes continuous production possible is specialized rigs that can execute precision tasks quickly. Ford, for example, invented a drilling machine that could simultaneously bore forty-five holes into an engine block.[12] The thing about custom tools, however, is that it's hard to get them running consistently. It's a fair guess that during these early years there was a lot of frustrated downtime at Highland Park spent tweaking and repairing these cumbersome rigs.

Another annoying reality of an assembly line is that a snag at any stage of a process—an installation step taking too long or a part not making it to where it's needed in time—can halt production altogether. Such shutdowns must have been common as the kinks were being worked out for the early lines. Imagine the frustration of shifting from the steady reliability of the craft method to a process that forced you to stop working completely again and again. To make matters even worse, the assembly line also required the addition of more managers and engineers to supervise. It was not only more annoying but also much more expensive to operate!

To summarize, Henry Ford took a reliable and intuitive process for building cars and replaced it with something that was more expensive to run, required a lot more management and overhead, was not at all natural, and frequently broke down, sometimes leading to major production delays. Nothing about this would have been easy or obvious. If you were a Ford manager, laborer, or investor during this period, you probably would have much preferred a safer and less disruptive focus on making the tried-and-true method slightly more efficient—the industrial equivalent of promoting better email etiquette.

We recognize now, of course, that these misgivings were misguided, as the assembly line ended up making Ford Motor Company one of the largest and most profitable corporations in the world. In the context of industrial production, we readily accept these stories, because when we think about a factory, it makes sense that the goal is not convenience, or simplicity, or preventing bad things from occasionally happening—it's instead manufacturing products as cost-effectively as possible.

Indeed, if you read twentieth-century management literature, the idea of achieving more effectiveness through your ability to tolerate added complexity is celebrated. In his 1959 book, *Landmarks of Tomorrow*, Peter Drucker lauds the "steady slugging away on improvement, adaptation, and application," led by applied researchers and engineers, that enabled companies to manufacture new and improved products faster than ever before.[13] Similarly, in James McCay's classic business advice tome *The Management of Time*, also written in 1959, McCay connects leadership in the modern world to the ability to constantly experiment with how work is accomplished, while stoically handling the resulting complexity:

> The man of the hour is the one who can handle the complex problems created by the increasing speed of invention. . . . He is the man of exceptional originality. He is the man who has disciplined himself to keep acquiring new knowledge and skills. He has created new production concepts, marketing concepts, approaches to financing.[14]

In modern knowledge work, we've largely lost interest in moving boldly ahead, embracing the resulting hardships as the cost of doing business better than before. We still talk about "innovation," but this term now applies almost exclusively to the products and services we offer, not the means by which we produce them. When it comes to the latter topic, business thinkers tend to focus on secondary factors, like better leadership or clearer objectives to help stimulate productivity. Little attention is dedicated to the actual mechanics of how work is assigned, executed, and reviewed.

This focus on secondary factors is not due to timidity on the part of knowledge work leaders. It's instead largely a result of the autonomy trap discussed earlier. A natural consequence of leaving the details of *how* knowledge workers work up to the individual is an entrenchment in workflows that prioritize convenience in the moment above all else. Once we free ourselves from this trap, however, and start systematically rethinking how we work, we'll inevitably create short-term inconvenience on our way to long-term improvement. As my industrial history hopefully underscores, this inconvenience shouldn't be feared. In business, good is not the same as easy, and fulfilling is not the same as convenient. Deep down, knowledge workers want to feel as if they're producing important output that takes full advantage of their hard-won skills, even if this means they can't always get a quick response to their messages.

An Aside: Weren't Assembly Lines Awful for Workers?

When I was in the early stages of my thinking about this book, I attended a family wedding. During the rehearsal dinner, I began chatting with a relative. He wanted to know what I was working on, so I told him about this book and tested out my ideas about the assembly line's relevance to rethinking knowledge work. I still remember his reaction word for word: "That sounds awful."

The issue in using the assembly line as a positive example is that the experience of actually working on one of these lines was anything but positive. As the historian Joshua Freeman argues in his 2019 book, *Behemoth*, when we think about the productivity gains of the assembly line, we focus too much on efficient material handling. Many of these gains came instead from the "sheer intensification of work."[15] If you slacked off your attention for even a moment, you could stall the entire line—forcing workers into an unnatural combination of boredom and constant attentiveness. Frederick Winslow Taylor had earlier tried to boost efficiency by measuring workers' performance with a stopwatch and offering incentives to those who were fast. Henry Ford bypassed Taylor's approach by simply making it impossible to be anything but fast. "For assembly-line workers, work was relentless and repetitious," writes Freeman. "Assembly-line work proved physiologically and psychologically draining in ways other types of labor were not. More than ever before, workers were extensions of machinery, at the mercy of its demands and pace."[16]

In 1936, Charlie Chaplin satirized this grim reality with his land-mark film *Modern Times*, which features his Little Tramp character trying to keep up with an assembly line that runs faster and faster. Wielding two large wrenches, Chaplin turns bolts on each item that passes. As the foreman increases the line's speed, Chaplin's actions be-come more frantic, leading him to eventually leap onto the conveyor belt in a vain last attempt to keep up with the items whizzing past. He's whisked away through a chute and ends up ground among the plant's oversized gears. Chaplin made the film soon after visiting one of Henry Ford's factories.[17]

This general understanding that assembly line work is dehuman-izing was what prompted my relative's negative reaction. He was imag-ining a future of knowledge work in which we end up in a digital-era reboot of *Modern Times*, with the frantic wrenching now replaced with frantic typing, and the sequence still ending with us mashed by the pro-verbial machinery of productivity. This is a natural concern to raise about the attention capital principle, but when we consider specific case studies of this principle in action, the feared drudgery doesn't materi-alize. Consider Devesh's marketing company. Nothing about the idea of switching work from a jumbled inbox to structured project boards indicates a shift toward more monotonous or soulless work. If anything, this change initiated the opposite effect. In a reversal of what happened when Ford introduced the assembly line, Devesh's employees found their professional lives less grueling and more sustainable *after* Devesh inno-vated their workflow.

As you'll encounter in the case studies that follow throughout part 2, the benefits of Devesh's workflow transformation are the rule, not the exception. This makes sense once we take a closer look at my use of the assembly line analogy. My goal in pointing to Henry Ford is not to highlight the effectiveness of the *specific manner* in which his workers built automobiles, as there are few useful connections between, say, assembling a magneto and designing a marketing strategy. It's instead to point out the power of experimenting with different ways of deploying capital—a process that differs greatly between the industrial and knowledge sectors. As Peter Drucker established, in knowledge work you must maintain skilled workers' autonomy in how they actually apply their craft. The attention capital principle asks you to experiment instead with the workflows that structure how this work is assigned and reviewed. The goal of these changes is to make it both easier and more sustainable for the knowledge worker to actually accomplish important things, not to coerce them into doing more things, faster—a strategy that's unlikely to succeed in the long term when dealing with cognitively demanding work.

Henry Ford took radical steps to rethink how to get more out of his factory equipment. Knowledge work leaders need to take radical steps to get more out of the human brains they deploy. But this analogy need go no further. In Ford's world, the workers were dispensable, while in the knowledge world, our brains are the source of all value. If anything, the hyperactive hive mind already has us trapped in a digital *Modern Times*, futilely trying to keep up with email messages that arrive faster and faster. The attention capital principle can help us move past this misery.

When Implementing Changes, Seek Partners, Not Forgiveness

In late 1984, Sam Carpenter, then thirty-five years old, bought a struggling telephone answering service.[18] It had seven employees and 140 clients. It cost him $21,000. Carpenter began boldly announcing to everyone he knew that "we would someday be the highest-quality telephone answering service in the United States." As Carpenter dryly summarizes in his 2008 book, *Work the System*: "Events did not unfold as anticipated."[19]

It turns out that the telephone answering service business is complicated. Clients call constantly, each representing an entirely new type of problem, from a medical emergency to an urgent business matter, each placing its own demands on the representative who takes the call. Like many small business owners, Carpenter found his life had become a "disorganized nightmare" in which he worked eighty-hour weeks, constantly putting out fires. He lost his house and car. He set up bunk beds at the office for his two teenage kids to sleep in. At one point, Carpenter was answering calls himself as the sole representative on duty during the midnight to 8:00 a.m. shift. He would then work from eight to five on the administrative minutiae generated by the business.[20]

None of this, of course, was sustainable. After fifteen years, Carpenter was near ruin, both physically and financially. It was then, as so often happens in these business memoirs, that he had an "earthmoving" insight. The acknowledgment that his business was in its final moments paradoxically gave Carpenter confidence to experiment with bold new approaches. It was this mindset that sparked that flash of insight: His company was like a mechanical device. It was composed of many assemblages that worked together in predictable ways. His problems, from the constant crises to the overwhelming amount of frantic administrative work drowning him, were not inevitable or the whims of circumstance, but instead the result of flaws in the underlying systems that made up his company's operation. If he could clearly identify each of these systems, write down how it worked, then optimize it as problems arose, he could get his organization humming without issues, and without requiring his constant, hands-on-the-controls interventions.

Carpenter created a master list of all the different activities that defined his company's operation, and began working with the relevant staff on an official system for each. One of the places he started was the company finances. He used to spend many hours each week paying bills and cashing checks, including regular trips to the bank—all of it a major source of stress. He replaced this chaos with a much more structured system for tracking expenses and revenue, and empowered his employees to make the bank trips on his behalf. What used to take hours each week was reduced to one short session during which he signed checks—a step he admits he could have also automated, but decided not to so he could maintain a more tangible understanding of his expenses. Another of these new systems streamlined customer service by providing clear guidelines that empowered employees to handle most service issues directly, without Carpenter's involvement. The basic operating procedure for how his call center staff answered calls also became strictly codified, providing much more consistent service (with fewer performance issues for Carpenter to address), and even the process for onboarding new employees was made largely automatic, greatly reducing the complexities created by staff turnover.

"The logic of it was crystal clear, exquisite," he writes. "I felt a quiet joy I had never felt before. To this day, I remember every moment of it."[21] Carpenter's optimism was well founded. As he worked to rebuild his company on a foundation of clear and optimized systems, profits grew for the first time. "My personal income is . . . let's just say, more than I need," Carpenter writes on his website. More important, his work obligations fell from eighty or more hours to less than two hours a week. By some statistical measures, the company even achieved Carpenter's original arrogant goal, ranking number one among the more than 1,500 answering services still active in the country.[22]

Sam Carpenter doesn't run a knowledge work organization. We shouldn't, therefore, pay too much attention to the details of the systems he put in place to improve the operations of his answering service. What makes him relevant to our discussion is a more general accomplishment: getting his employees to dramatically change the way they worked. The chapters that follow provide concrete ideas for how to put the attention capital principle into action by radically rethinking workflows. In most cases, the impact of these changes will extend beyond your own professional life to affect the daily experiences of other people— perhaps your employees, colleagues, or clients. This can create tricky dynamics, which is why before we move on to detailed suggestions for what to change, we should first address the question of *how* to make these general types of workflow modifications in a way that sticks. Carpenter's experience can help us with this goal.

———

There are two ways applying the attention capital principle can impact the people with whom you work. The first is when it alters workflows in such a way that people are forced to change how they *execute* their own work. This is what happened, for example, when Devesh moved his marketing company's workflow away from email and toward project boards. His employees needed to now log in to Trello and click on the cards to communicate about a given project instead of simply sending emails.

The second type of impact changes only other people's *expectations* about your own work. This applies when you focus on upgrading your personal workflow. If, for example, you now check your inbox only twice a day as part of a larger overhaul of how you work, your colleagues' expectations for how quickly you'll respond to their messages must shift.

We'll start by considering the first type of impact, as it's trickier to deal with. It's also the type of impact for which we can learn the most from Sam Carpenter. A key insight preached in Carpenter's book is the need to involve those who are affected by a new work procedure in the design of that procedure. His staff wrote 98 percent of the procedures currently in place and had a "heavy hand" in shaping the remaining 2 percent that Carpenter created himself. As a result, his employees are "fully vested" in these processes. Perhaps even more crucial, Carpenter made it easy to instigate further improvements. "If an employee has a good idea for improving a procedure, we will make an instant modification—with no bureaucratic hang-ups," he explains.[23] He takes this employee involvement so seriously that he now requires his service representatives to submit at least a dozen proposed improvements before they qualify to receive their annual performance bonus.

Carpenter's approach makes sense in the context of what's known as *locus of control theory*, a subfield of personality psychology that argues that motivation is closely connected to whether people feel like they have control over their ultimate success in an endeavor. When you have a say in what you're doing (placing the locus of control toward the internal end of the spectrum), you're much more motivated than when you feel like your actions are largely controlled by outside forces (placing the locus of control toward the external end).

This is what goes wrong if you defy Carpenter's model and instead attempt to deploy a brand-new workflow on your team by fiat. Regardless of the workflow's inherent benefits, you might be accidentally shifting your team's sense of control from the internal to the external, sapping motivation and making it unlikely that they'll stick with the changes. On the other hand, if your team members are involved in the construction of the new workflow and, equally important, feel like they're able to improve it as deficiencies arise, then the control remains internal and the workflow is much more likely to be embraced.

This concept doesn't apply as strongly to positions in which there are no expectations of autonomy. This is why, for example, the famously autocratic Henry Ford didn't feel the need to involve his workers in discussions of the assembly line's advantages and disadvantages. This also explains the success of military boot camps—the epitome of external control—in rapidly producing professional soldiers for volunteer armies: the new recruits enter the process trusting the time-tested system to get them where they need to be. As we've known since the forward-thinking theories of Peter Drucker, however, knowledge work will always be defined by large amounts of autonomous action. Locus of control theory therefore unavoidably applies: it simply won't work to radically change workflows without the input of those who must use them.

There are three steps necessary to keep these experiments collaborative. The first is education. It's important that your team understand the difference between workflows and work execution, and why the hyperactive hive mind is just one workflow among many—and probably not a very good one. For many knowledge workers, email is synonymous with work, so it's crucial to break up this misunderstanding before you discuss breaking up their comfortable reliance on the hive mind for getting things done.

The second step is to obtain buy-in on new workflow processes from those who will actually have to execute them. To accomplish this goal, these ideas should emerge from discussion. There should be general agreement that trying the new workflow is a worthwhile experiment, and following Carpenter's lead, its details should be captured with crystal clear specificity so there's no doubt about what exactly is being implemented.

The third step is to further follow Carpenter's lead by putting in place easy methods for improving the new workflow processes when issues arise. There's perhaps no better way to keep the locus of control internal than to empower your team to change what's not working. In practice, you might be surprised by how few changes are actually suggested. It's the *ability* to make changes that matters, as it provides a psychological emergency steam valve, neutralizing the fear that you might end up trapped in some unexpected hard edge of the new workflow, unable to get your work done.

It's also common for those moving past the universal accessibility of the hyperactive hive mind to put in place an emergency backup system that can handle urgent issues that the new workflow might neglect. For such a system to truly be a backup, and not just a back door that returns you to the hive mind, it must induce enough friction that you won't use it unless the situation is sufficiently urgent. The classic example is to use phone calls as the catchall fallback: your colleagues can call your cell phone if something pops up that's too urgent for the official workflow to reliably handle in time. These backup systems provide the peace of mind that nothing *too* bad can happen in the time it might take to recognize and fix flaws with new processes.

———

Let's now turn our attention to the other type of impact to other people caused by applying the attention capital principle: changes to others' expectations about your own behavior. As explained, this applies when you transform your personal workflow, moving your daily rhythms away from the unpredictable back-and-forth of the hyperactive hive mind. These shifts are likely to create changes that are visible to your colleagues and clients, with the most notable being that you're no longer always answering emails or instant messages promptly. Other people will, in other words, need to shift their expectations about working with you.

A common method for handling these personal workflow over-hauls is to clearly explain the structure of your new approach to your colleagues, perhaps accompanied by an unassailably logical explanation for why you're making these changes. A famous example of this idea in action is the following email autoresponder that Tim Ferriss cited in his 2007 mega-bestseller, *The 4-Hour Workweek:*[24]

Greetings, Friends [or Esteemed Colleagues],

Due to high workload, I am currently checking and responding to e-mail twice daily at 12:00 P.M. ET [or your time zone] and 4:00 P.M. ET.

If you require urgent assistance (please ensure it is urgent) that cannot wait until either 12:00 P.M. or 4:00 P.M., please contact me via phone at 555-555-5555.

Thank you for understanding this move to more efficiency and effectiveness. It helps me accomplish more to serve you better.

Sincerely,

[Your name]

Due to the success of Ferriss's book, there was a period of a couple of years in which tens of thousands of knowledge workers around the world began receiving some variation of the above autoresponder from their life-hacking colleagues. From a rational perspective, this strategy makes complete sense: it resets expectations so that your correspondents aren't wondering when they'll hear from you, and it provides a rock-solid explanation for the shift; it's terse, it's clear, it's hard to argue with. This is why so many people were so excited when they first encountered it. The problem, however, is that it also turned out to be really annoying for those who received these automatic replies.

It's hard to put your finger on what exactly rubbed people the wrong way—perhaps the cold formality, which has a way of accidentally bleeding over into the realm of condescension, or the implication that the author of the autoresponder is trying to neutralize the receiver's bad work habits. Whatever the specific reasons, Ferriss's fans came to realize that this particular hack wasn't working as well as they had hoped. Anecdotally, it seems that these autoresponders are now much rarer than they were at their peak, in the immediate aftermath of Ferriss's book coming out. They were a good idea in the abstract but degraded under the friction of real-world application.

The lesson lurking in this case study is that care must be taken in how you publicize changes to your personal work habits. Over the years of observing many different attempts by individuals to push back against or change their dependence on the hyperactive hive mind, and having attempted more than a few such changes myself, I've come to believe that these experiments are best executed quietly. Don't share the details of your new approach to work, unless someone specifically asks you out of genuine interest. Be wary of even providing new expectations, such as "I generally don't see email until after 10:00 a.m." or "I check my inbox only a few times a day." These provide hard edges that skeptical colleagues, clients, or bosses can begin to easily chip away. ("What if I need something urgently from you earlier? No . . . I don't like this at all—I think you need to stay better on top of your messages.") Similarly, if you get in the habit of asking for forgiveness—as is often suggested—people around you will get in the habit of thinking your work strategies must be broken, because why else would they keep causing you to apologize?

A better strategy for shifting others' expectations about your work is to consistently deliver what you promise instead of consistently explaining how you're working. Become known as someone who never drops the ball, not someone who thinks a lot about their own productivity. If a request comes your way, be it in an email or hallway chat, make sure it's handled. Don't let things fall through the cracks, and if you commit to doing something by a certain time, hit the deadline, or explain why you need to shift it. If people trust you to handle the work they send your way, then they're generally fine with not hearing back from you right away. On the other hand, if you're flaky, others will demand faster responses, as they'll feel they have to stay on you to ensure things get done. The professor and business writer Adam Grant uses the phrase "idiosyncrasy credits" to describe this reality.[25] The better you are at what you do, he explains, the more freedom you earn to be idiosyncratic in how you deliver—no explanation required.

Another issue that comes from transforming your personal workflow concerns system interfaces. If you put in place the types of advanced workflow systems discussed in the upcoming chapters, you'll have to figure out how you want other people, who are used to just grabbing your attention with a quick message, to interact with these more structured alternatives.

For guidance in this matter, we can learn from the world of IT support. As discussed earlier in the book, a couple of decades ago, IT support staff began internally organizing the technology issues they were tasked with fixing using so-called ticketing systems. These systems assign each problem a single *ticket*. All conversations and notes about the problem are attached to its ticket, where they can be easily reviewed.

IT professionals quickly realized the futility in requiring those they served to interface directly with the ticketing system; for example, by having them log in to a special support site to create and track these tickets. This might be the most efficient way to handle these issues in the abstract, but the concrete reality of many organizations is that most people wouldn't put up with the extra overhead. The solution to this issue was to create a *seamless interface*. In most IT setups, you now submit a problem in the most natural possible manner: by sending an email to a general-purpose address like support@companyname.com. Most ticketing systems can be configured to receive these emails directly, then transform them into tickets and place them in a virtual inbox to be processed. As the IT staff works on a ticket, the system can then send automatic updates, as email messages, back to the originator of the issue. The person interacting with IT doesn't have to know anything about ticketing systems. They simply send an email and receive email updates back in response. Internally, however, something much more structured is unfolding.

This lesson applies to the systems you put in place to organize your personal workflows. Don't require the people you work with to learn about your new systems or change the way they interact with you. Instead, when possible, deploy a seamless interface. We can use my own recent experience as a professor to help elaborate this approach. During the year in which I'm writing the bulk of this manuscript, I'm taking a turn as the director of graduate studies for the computer science department at Georgetown. One of the responsibilities of this role is to head the graduate committee, which oversees our graduate program, including approving changes and answering requests about policy.

As you might imagine, this leads to a large number of incoming issues that I'm in charge of resolving. Taking a page out of Devesh's playbook, I internally deploy a Trello board to help make sense of these requests. My board has the following columns:

- ☐ *waiting to deal with*
- ☐ *waiting to deal with (time sensitive)*
- ☐ *to discuss at next graduate committee meeting*
- ☐ *to discuss at next meeting with department chair*
- ☐ *waiting to hear back from someone*
- ☐ *working on this week*

When someone sends me an email or stops by my office with an issue concerning the graduate program, I immediately transform it into a card and place it in the applicable column on the Trello board.

At the beginning of each week, I review this board and move cards around as appropriate: deciding, for example, what I want to work on this week, or what needs to be discussed in upcoming meetings. I can also follow up on issues I'm waiting to hear back from someone about. My general rule is that when I move a card to a new column, I send an email update to the person who brought me that issue. For example, if I move something from a *waiting* column to the *discuss at next graduate committee meeting* column, I'll send a note to the appropriate person telling them that we'll be discussing their issue soon. If I take a card off the board because I completed the corresponding task, I'll let the relevant people know the ultimate resolution. And so on.

The key property of this system is that the professors and graduate students in my department know nothing about it. I suppose I could try to insist that they all log in to my Trello board to enter new issues or check on the status of old issues. In theory, this might save me a few extra messages, but in reality, no one would actually do this—and I can't blame them! It takes me about thirty minutes, once a week, to process my board and send update messages. I receive massive benefits from structuring all these issues so clearly, and because I spent a little extra time to make my interface seamless, my colleagues can enjoy these benefits as well.

———

At first encounter, my advice for applying the attention capital principle to groups seems at odds with my advice for applying the principle to individuals. The former emphasizes the need for clear communication about the workflows replacing the hyperactive hive mind, while the latter suggests you keep these changes largely private. A closer look, however, reveals that both approaches are based on the same principle: people don't like changes they can't control.

When modifying the workflow of an entire team or organization, everyone can be involved in this change and feel empowered to optimize it. As discussed earlier, this provides a sense that the locus of control is internal, motivating people to stick with the changes. When you alter your personal workflow, by contrast, those you work with didn't really have a say in what you decided to do. If they're then presented with a new system that will impact their own work, but for which they had no input, the locus of control moves toward the external, creating irritation and a tendency to try to push back and reassert some control. They don't applaud your clever new autoresponder; they instead find ways to tear down the restrictions it has imposed on them.

The psychology at play here is perhaps a bit subtle, but also crucial to master if you hope to succeed in maximizing your attention capital. Work is not just about getting things done; it's a collection of messy human personalities trying to figure out how to successfully collaborate. The three chapters that follow look closely at specific strategies for replacing the hyperactive hive mind with much more effective workflows. The value of these detailed approaches, however, will be greatly diminished if you don't first master the subtle art of putting them into action in a way that sticks.

Chapter 5

The Process Principle

The Power of Process

Early in my work on this book, I found myself browsing a little-used shelf, buried deep in the stacks of Georgetown's Lauinger Library, filled with titles dissecting the nuances of industrial engineering. I came across a collection of articles from a now defunct, early twentieth-century business magazine called *System*, a publication dedicated to case studies about the then new "scientific" approach to management. These articles were almost universally breathless with excitement about how much more money could be made by industrial organizations once they began to think more systematically about how their work was actually conducted. The articles were also, it soon became clear, largely quite boring to the modern reader. Scientific management in this era seemed to have a lot to do with filling out forms in triplicate. *System* magazine loves forms. In its pages, you'll find pictures of forms, and you'll learn about their colors, how they're perforated, even the material of the folders that hold them (manila is preferred).[1]

Hidden among these minutiae, however, I found a case study from a 1916 issue that caught my attention. The subject was so old-fashioned as to border on caricature: increasing the efficiency of the brass works operating within the Pullman train car company's massive factory complex on Lake Calumet, fourteen miles south of Chicago. But there was something about the story, written under the direction of Pullman president John Runnells, that came across as surprisingly contemporary. Many of Pullman's thirty-three departments depended on the brass works for key components, keeping the roughly 350 men working the foundries and machine tools in the brass works building perpetually busy. The problem with their system for dealing with all this work, as the article explains, was that there wasn't really any system at all, but instead just a jumbled mess of "slipshod methods."[2]

The brass department had only seven managers to help make sense of the constant influx of work requests. These managers were, of course, overwhelmed. As a result, everyone had to get informally involved in managing the workflow. "In many places throughout the plant, one man or another was devoting a part of his time to assist the active seven," it notes. "All the planning was being done somewhere. And every man contributing by that much demoralized his own particular work by the interruption." As the article elaborates, it became common for workers from other parts of the factory to show up at the brass department and wait around most of the day, bothering employees they knew, until they got the part they needed.

In the first decades of the twentieth century, in other words, the Pullman brass works had devolved into something that looks a lot like the hyperactive hive mind workflow. However, unlike the many knowledge work organizations of today that are suffering from a similarly informal workflow, the leaders of Pullman, swept up in the excitement of scientific management, were willing to experiment with radical solutions.

To make the brass department more efficient, Pullman's executive team did something counterintuitive: they made its operation more complicated. If you needed some brass work done, you now had to submit an official form that contained all the relevant information. To prevent employees from circumventing this process and reverting to the more convenient status quo of informally bothering workers, they literally locked the door and screened the windows. You now had no choice but to use the newly enforced "regular channel."

Once a request was submitted through a slot dedicated to this purpose, it was subjected to a rigorous procedure. A clerk would be tasked with figuring out a reasonable plan for accomplishing the work, including what raw source materials would be needed and how many worker hours were required to build the finished product. The details of the plan were then distributed to the proper subdepartments to ensure its timely execution. The specifics of the process get intricate at this point, but also fascinating. Using armies of clerks, the Pullman brass works seems to have replicated many of the tasks that today we can implement instantaneously with a click of a button on a computer application, implementing a sort of steampunk IT system, made up of step-by-step instructions and endless forms routed from desk to desk, like packets in a modern network. They even built custom hardware, my favorite example being an analog spreadsheet system that involved hanging brass tags on a large wooden board divided into a grid, which somehow allowed the work planners to quickly "cross-index" the current assignment of workers to machines.

To implement this more structured workflow, Runnells had to spend more money. There used to be seven administrative staff to help organize the efforts of the 350 brass workers. Now there were forty-seven. "Here is a vast increase in overhead," the article admits. Each of these new managers earned around $1,000 a year, significantly increasing the department's salary costs. "But does it pay?" it asks. "It certainly has done so." The new process dropped the production cost of each train car by $100, which not only covered the expense of the extra overhead but turned a "substantial profit."

The article makes it clear why the additional overhead increased profit. The old process—which was really no process at all—required the 350 workers who actually produced the department's valuable output to constantly switch back and forth between informally managing their workflow and actually executing the work itself. This "demoralizing" double duty made them much slower at their actual skilled efforts, reducing the return the department was getting from its frontline workers.

When the workflow was restructured to largely eliminate this double duty, the same workers could produce much more finished brass in the same amount of time. "The old lack of method is and never will be conducive to a betterment of standards," the article concludes. "But systemization promptly showed a surprising rise in quality; workmen concentrated and the product showed the result."

What industrial productivity hackers like John Runnells began to discover in the first decades of the twentieth century is that efficiency extends beyond the actions involved in physically manufacturing something. Equally important is how you coordinate this work. The problem with the Pullman brass works, in other words, was not that the workers were bad at casting and polishing brass components, but instead how these efforts were assigned and organized.

Like many fundamental ideas, it took a while for this new mindset to take hold in the industrial sector. When Frederick Winslow Taylor, the father of the scientific management revolution, was first rising to prominence in the late 1890s, most of the energy in this movement focused on the act of production itself. This is the era that gave rise to the image of the draconian Taylorist consultant, stopwatch in hand, trying to eliminate wasted motion on the factory floor. Taylor himself made his reputation working with Bethlehem Steel between 1898 and 1900, where, among other improvements, he famously changed the style of shovel that workers used to move slag, increasing the speed with which they could transfer the material between piles. Pullman had integrated many of these ideas when they built their factory during this period. John Runnells mentions that the brass works had been laid out carefully with wide aisles, and tools organized on racks, to increase the efficiency with which the work was conducted. But as they learned, focusing only on physical productivity wasn't enough to get the department humming.

By the time the Pullman case study was published in 1916, a year after Taylor's death, magazines like *System* had increasingly broadened their attention to include the information and decisions that surrounded manual labor. The magazine was less about better shovels and more about better forms to help figure out how much shoveling needed to be done. To be more concrete, we'll use the term *production process* to talk about this combination of the actual manufacturing work with all the information and decisions that organize this work. The production process thinking demonstrated in that 1916 article went on to dominate industrial management, where it remains a core idea. In his 1983 cult business classic, *High Output Management*, for example, former Intel

CEO Andy Grove dedicates the first two chapters to explaining the power of production process thinking. He notes that without this structure, you're left with only one option for increasing productivity: figuring out how to get people to "work faster." Once you see the whole process, however, a much more powerful option emerges: "We can change the nature of the work performed." Optimize processes, he urged, not people.[3]

Which brings us back to the subject of this book: knowledge work. In this sector, we stubbornly reject this insight from industrial management. We largely ignore processes, investing our energy instead in figuring out how to make people faster. We obsess over hiring and promoting stars. We seek leadership consultants to help us motivate people to work longer and harder. We embrace innovations like the smartphone that allow more hours of the day to be punctuated with work. We put dry cleaners on our corporate campuses and wi-fi on our corporate buses, all in the service of finding faster ways to shovel more proverbial slag.

Not surprisingly, this hasn't worked out well at all.

The core claim of this chapter is that production process thinking applies equally well to knowledge work as it does to industrial manufacturing. Just because you produce things with your brain instead of your hands doesn't change the fundamental reality that these efforts must still be coordinated. The importance of organizing decisions about who is working on what, and finding systematic ways to check in on this work as it evolves, applies as much to generating computer code or client proposals as it does to casting brass.

In knowledge work, any type of valuable result that you or your organization regularly produces can be understood as the output of a production process. If you're a marketing firm that runs publicity campaigns for your clients, your firm has a publicity campaign production process. If you work on an HR team that resolves salary issues, your team has a salary issue resolution process. If you're a professor teaching a class that requires you to assign and grade problem sets, you have a problem set process.

In the pages ahead, I'll argue that if knowledge workers admit that these processes exist, and then clarify and optimize their operation, then they'll discover the same result as the Pullman brass works: the expense of the extra overhead will be far outweighed by the boosts in productivity. When the costs and benefits are compared, it's common to end up with a "substantial profit." The problem, of course, is that few knowledge workers are used to thinking this way: they focus on people, not processes. As a result, the knowledge sector prefers to leave these processes unspecified, relying instead on the hyperactive hive mind workflow to informally organize their work.

For sure, a major explanation for this process aversion is the insistence on knowledge worker autonomy that we explored earlier. Production processes, by definition, require rules about how work is coordinated. Rules reduce autonomy—creating friction with the belief that knowledge workers "must manage themselves," as Peter Drucker commanded. This dislike of processes, however, goes beyond a general bias toward autonomy. There's a belief, implicitly held by many knowledge workers, that the lack of processes in this sector is not just an unavoidable side effect of self-management, but actually a *smart* way to work. A lack of processes, it's commonly understood, represents nimbleness and flexibility—a foundation for the type of outside-the-box thinking we're constantly told is critical.

This vision is fundamentally Rousseauian, a reference to the eighteenth-century Enlightenment philosopher Jean-Jacques Rousseau, who believed that human nature, before the introduction of political influence, was fundamentally virtuous. It claims that when left alone to work in whatever way seems natural, knowledge workers will adapt seamlessly to the complex conditions they confront, producing original solutions and game-changing innovations. In this worldview, codified work processes are artificial: they corrupt the Edenic creative, leading to bureaucracy and stagnation—a *Dilbert* comic brought to life.

Having spent years studying the nuances of knowledge worker productivity, I believe this understanding is profoundly flawed. To stick with the analogy to Enlightenment philosophy, the reality of knowledge work is much more Hobbesian, a reference to Thomas Hobbes's belief, originally detailed in *Leviathan*, that without the constraints of the state, human life is "nasty, brutish, and short." When you reduce work to a state of nature by allowing processes to unfold informally, the resulting behavior is anything but utopian. Much as is observed in actual natural settings, in the informal process workplace, dominance hierarchies emerge. If you're brash and disagreeable, or are a favorite of the boss, you can, like the strongest lion in the pride, avoid work you don't like by staring down those who try to pass it off to you, ignoring their messages, or claiming overload. On the other hand, if you're more reasonable and agreeable, you'll end up overloaded with more work than makes sense for one person to handle. These setups are both demoralizing and a staggeringly inefficient deployment of attention capital. But without a countervailing force, these hierarchies are often unavoidable.

Also as in natural settings, in workplaces without well-defined processes, energy minimization becomes prioritized. This is fundamental human nature: if there's no structure surrounding how hard efforts are coordinated, we default to our instinct to not expend any more energy than is necessary. Most of us are guilty of acting on this instinct when given a chance. An email arrives that informally represents a new responsibility for you to manage; because there's no formal process in place to assign the work or track its progress, you seek instead the easiest way to get the responsibility off your plate—even if just temporarily—so you send a quick reply asking for an ambiguous clarification. Thus unfolds a game of obligation hot potato, as messages bounce around, each temporarily shifting responsibility from one inbox to another, until a deadline or irate boss finally stops the music, leading to a last-minute scramble to churn out a barely acceptable result. This, too, is obviously a terribly inefficient way to get work done.

A well-designed production process, in other words, isn't an obstacle to efficient knowledge work, but is instead often a precondition. Which brings us to the principle that this chapter elaborates.

The Process Principle

Introducing smart production processes to knowledge work can dramatically increase performance and make the work much less draining.

To move past the shortcomings of the hyperactive hive mind workflow, we must abandon our Rousseauian optimism that knowledge workers left to a state of nature will thrive. To get the most out of our attention capital, we need processes, and this is true for both organizations and individual knowledge workers. To reiterate the obvious, I'm not talking about processes that somehow attempt to reduce the skilled and dynamic elements of knowledge work to step-by-step recipes. As we established in the last chapter, our reform efforts in this book focus on the *workflows* that coordinate knowledge work, not the skilled *execution* of the work itself. This holds true for our discussion of production processes, which help make sense of who is working on what but don't specify the details of how this work unfolds; replacing, in other words, endless back-and-forth hive mind messaging with guidelines that let knowledge workers spend more of their time actually working instead of talking about their work—the cognitive equivalent of John Runnells's revamped brass foundry.

The remainder of this chapter explores ideas for building smart production processes in both your knowledge work organization and your individual professional life. We'll begin, as is now our habit, with a concrete case study that we can reference in the discussions that follow. In this case, we'll take a close look at a twelve-person media company that's pushed its embrace of the process principle to a profitable extreme.

Case Study: Optimizing the Optimizers

Optimize Enterprises is a media company that focuses on self-improvement content. Its core product is a subscription service that provides weekly in-depth book summaries, as well as daily lessons, delivered as short videos. You can access the service through a website or a smartphone app. Optimize also recently began a coach training program, which proved a surprise hit. More than one thousand coaches signed up for the first round of training, a cycle that lasts three hundred days. The company employs twelve full-time team members, who work in tandem with eight to twelve part-time contractors. There's no physical headquarters for Optimize, meaning this team operates entirely remotely. As the president and founder, Brian Johnson, told me when I interviewed him for this book, the company is on track for $2.5 million in annual revenue.

The reason Johnson's company interested me is not its size or product offerings, but instead the details of how it operates. As Johnson explained early in our conversation: "We don't email at all. Zero. There will never be an email between a team member and another team member." Though he doesn't use this exact terminology, Johnson and his team were able to sidestep the hyperactive hive mind by adopting a production process mindset. Motivated by his intuitive dislike of interruption and harried busyness, Johnson had his team methodically break down their work into processes that could be clearly stated and (appropriately enough) optimized to maximize the time spent doing useful work and minimize the time spent moving back and forth between work and inboxes. "Our team is absolutely committed to single-tasking," Johnson told me. "You do one thing at a time."

One of Optimize's more intricate processes, for example, involves the production of the daily lesson videos that get delivered to multiple platforms each morning. The work required for this production is substantial. Johnson is responsible for actually coming up with and writing the lessons. He's also the person who delivers the lessons on camera for the video. But beyond this, other tasks lurk: the text versions of the lessons must be edited, the videos must be filmed, the film clips must be edited, and everything must be launched to multiple platforms at just the right time. Around a half dozen people are involved in executing these varied steps.

In many organizations, the sheer volume of interconnected action required to keep this content production machinery working would seem to necessitate endless back-and-forth urgent emails or hyperactive Slack chattering. But not at Optimize: over the years, they've built a production process for these efforts that eliminates almost all informal interaction, allowing those involved to focus nearly 100 percent of their energy on actually performing the skilled work needed to keep the pipeline of high-quality content filled and flowing.

The process starts with a shared spreadsheet. When Johnson comes up with an idea for a lesson, he adds a title and subtitle to the spreadsheet. Each row has a *status* column, which Johnson sets to "idea," marking the lesson as still in the earliest stages of development. Once Johnson gets around to writing the lesson, he'll upload it to a shared directory in the company's Dropbox account, then add a link to this draft to the spreadsheet row for the lesson. At this point, he'll change its status to "ready for editing." Johnson's editor doesn't interact directly with Johnson, but instead monitors the spreadsheet. When he sees a lesson is ready to be edited, he downloads it, puts it into the right format, edits it, and then moves it into a postproduction Dropbox folder that holds text that's ready to go live.

At this point, the editor changes the status of the lesson to "ready for filming." Johnson has a studio in his house where he films lessons. He has a standing schedule with his film crew that specifies which days each month they come to knock out a chunk of lesson videos. When the crew arrives, there's no ambiguity about what they'll be filming: all lessons currently in the "ready for filming" status. After a film day, the crew will upload the raw files to a shared Dropbox directory dedicated to the editing process. The statuses of these lessons are now changed on the spreadsheet to indicate they are ready to be edited. At this point, Optimize's film editor will download the clips from the dedicated directory, run them through the standard processing to get them ready for release, and then upload them to a shared postproduction folder. The lessons' statuses are changed to indicate they are ready for release, and a release date is chosen and added to each corresponding row.

The final step is the actual release of the written and video versions of the lessons on their scheduled release dates. Two content management service (CMS) specialists execute this last step. They monitor the spreadsheet to see which lessons are scheduled for which days. They download the content from the postproduction directories and sched-

ule it for release using the CMS platform. When the time comes, the
lesson that started as just an idea in Johnson's mind goes live across the
Optimize networks.

Here's what amazed me about this production process: it coordi-
nates a fair-sized group of specialists, spread out around the world, to
accomplish the complicated feat of releasing highly produced multimedia content on a demanding daily schedule—all without requiring
even a single unscheduled email or instant message. Not one of the
skilled knowledge workers involved in this process ever needs to load
up an inbox or glance at a messenger channel. Almost 100 percent of
their time is dedicated to actually doing the work they're trained to perform, and when they're done working, they're done working—there's
nothing to check, nothing urgent requiring a reply.

To be fair, media production is a structured endeavor. Many knowledge workers deal instead with a more amorphous and constantly shifting set of demands. To understand how these latter efforts can be tamed
with processes, I asked Johnson to walk me through a typical day of one
of the higher-level managers in his company—someone who has to over-
see various onetime projects, as well as produce original strategy on
a regular basis. As Johnson explained, the manager in question has a
schedule that begins every day with three hours of uninterrupted deep
work before he receives "even a single input." This is time set aside for
the manager to think intensely about his projects—making informed
decisions on how to go forward, where to focus next, what to improve,
and what to ignore.

Only after this morning block ends does the manager turn his attention to actively managing the projects he runs. To make this project
management more systematic, Optimize deploys an online collaboration tool called Flow. In its simplest form, Flow allows you to track tasks
associated with projects. Each task is represented as a card that can be

assigned to particular people and given a deadline. Files and information related to the task can be attached to the card, and discussion tools allow those working on the task to hold conversations directly on the virtual card in a forum-style format. Finally, these cards can be moved around and arranged into different columns, where each column is labeled to represent a different category of task or status.

Similar to how Devesh's marketing firm used Trello in the case study reviewed in the last chapter, these virtual cards arranged on virtual boards are the hub around which work on projects unfolds. Instead of having all communication for all work flow through a general-purpose inbox or channel, you now choose to work on a specific project by navigating to its page and checking in on the tasks to which you're assigned. This is exactly what our Optimize manager does after his deep work block concludes: he checks in on the projects one by one, joining the card-centric conversations when needed and more generally seeing where things currently stand.

After checking in on these projects in Flow, the manager typically has one-on-one FaceTime meetings with the various team members he supervises. These conversations are used to discuss new initiatives or resolve issues with ongoing tasks. Most projects also have a regular meeting scheduled each week to help synchronize everyone's efforts and efficiently solve group issues. The manager participates in these meetings, updating the corresponding project pages as needed to reflect any decisions made about the work. Like all Optimize employees, his day ends between 4:00 and 5:00 p.m. Johnson is insistent on enforcing a "digital sunset" for his company: he wants his employees to end their workday at a reasonable hour to spend time with family and recharge. Because there are no email inboxes to check, our manager, as with all Optimize employees, will actually be free from work until the next morning.

Here are a few other odds and ends I learned about Optimize's processes. Though they forbid internal email, they do use email to communicate with external partners. Their interaction with these inboxes, however, is highly structured. Johnson says those responsible for these external-facing email addresses have "discrete blocks" in which they check for messages, typically once a day. To handle customer service, Optimize deploys a tool called Intercom that streamlines the process of responding to the most common requests and prevents pileups of ambiguous emails from customers. Optimize also hosts a company-wide meeting every Monday (using teleconferencing software) to synchronize efforts.

Perhaps most interesting of all—and a real surprise when I first heard it—Optimize does use Slack. As Johnson explained, however, its engagement with this tool looks significantly different from the cliché of constant hive mind chatter. Because almost all the interactions required for Optimize's core work efforts are already captured by well-defined processes, there's not much left to discuss on these chat channels. This tool is mainly used for two purposes. The first is to "celebrate wins": if someone accomplishes something important, either professionally or personally, they might share it on the company Slack channel. Johnson describes this as a chance to virtually "high-five" one another. Because the company is virtual, he explained, it's important to have some outlet for social interaction. Their other use for Slack is to schedule the meetings in which most actual work interaction occurs.

Optimize employees truly do use Slack asynchronously—checking it only once or twice a day in between other tasks. It would be pointless to check Slack more often, as there is not enough actually shared on the channel to make it worthwhile. In a typical day, an Optimize employee might end up using Slack for perhaps a handful of minutes—maybe to deliver a virtual high five or provide a time to a manager trying to set up a meeting.

Finally, to support this process-centric approach to work, Johnson insists that the whole company take processes seriously. He sees getting these processes right as the core to their success. Every employee of Optimize is expected to spend at least the first ninety minutes of every day in a deep work block, free from inputs (some people, like the manager profiled above, spend much more). One of the key uses of this morning block is to think about processes and how to improve them. As Johnson explained to me, it takes time to figure out how best to structure the crazy inputs and interaction that surround most work processes. He's diligent in making sure that everyone keeps prioritizing this. "You need time away from inputs to figure out how best to systematize those inputs," he explained. This is perhaps Optimize's most important process of all: the process that helps improve the existing processes.

Who's Doing What and How?
Properties of Effective Processes

Let's say you've accepted the challenge of designing better knowledge work production processes. What makes a process effective in this context? Consider the production process used by Brian Johnson's Optimize Enterprises for producing daily multimedia content. Once Johnson enters a new lesson title and subtitle into his team's shared spreadsheet, the steps for getting from this initial stage to released content are all organized in a sequence of predetermined phases. At each phase, it's clear what work needs to be accomplished, where the relevant files can be found, who is supposed to accomplish the work, and what happens once they're done.

Optimize's processes for handling the more varied onetime projects can't rely on exact sequences of predetermined phases, as each of these projects is different. But the overall workflow remains highly structured. Information about who is working on what, as well as how it's going, is captured using the Flow project management tool. Decisions about what tasks to add and who to assign to them are made in regularly scheduled meetings. If you're working on one of these projects, the rhythm of your work is unambiguous. You check in on the task cards assigned to you in Flow, then put your head down to work on these tasks, updating the cards when done. Occasionally, you attend meetings when more involved discussion or decisions are required. The results of these meetings are immediately reflected back in Flow. This project-focused process similarly minimizes the time spent communicating about work and maximizes the time spent actually taking productive action.

These examples of effective production processes share the following properties:

1. It's easy to review who is working on what and how it's going.

2. Work can unfold without significant amounts of unscheduled communication.

3. There's a known procedure for updating work assignments as the process progresses.

For our daily lesson example, the first property is satisfied by the *status* field in the shared spreadsheet, which tells the team exactly where each lesson currently resides in the production pipeline. The second and third properties are satisfied by the predetermined sequence of phases, which specifies exactly what you should be doing when it's your turn to work on a lesson, where to find the needed files when you begin, where to put these files when you're done working on them, and what comes next once the phase is complete.

For the project process, the first property is satisfied by Flow, which provides a nice visual interface that displays all the active tasks for a project. Small headshot icons on each task represent the people who are assigned to it. When working on one of these projects, there's no ambiguity about what you're supposed to be doing in the moment. The second property is satisfied by a combination of Flow's collaboration tools, built right into the task cards, and the rhythm of regular short status meetings. Communication about the project is confined to these narrow channels. Finally, to satisfy the third property, decisions about who should be working on new tasks are typically made during meetings and are then reflected in Flow.

A good production process, in other words, should minimize both ambiguity about what's going on and the amount of unscheduled communication required to accomplish this work. Notice, nothing about these properties restricts the knowledge worker's autonomy in figuring out *how* they get their work done; the focus remains on coordinating this work. Also notice that these properties are unlikely to lead to stifling bureaucracy, as the processes they produce are optimized to *reduce* the overhead—in terms of both context shifts and time—surrounding the actual act of producing valuable things. Workers at the highly systematized Optimize Enterprises likely feel much more empowered and much less overwhelmed than those shackled to the status quo of the hyperactive hive mind workflow.

The main issue with production processes in the knowledge work context is that they often must be custom-built to fit each circumstance. What works for Optimize, for example, might not work for a mobile-app development company, and what works for the app company likely won't work for a one-person accounting shop. With this reality in mind, the remainder of this chapter explores several different best practices that you can deploy when trying to design the production processes that will work best for your specific situation.

Cards in Columns: The Task Board Revolution

An executive whom I'll call Alex runs a fifteen-person team that operates like an independent start-up within a major national healthcare provider. His team focuses on data analysis. If, for example, you're a researcher working for this provider, and you win a grant that requires you to perform some complicated number crunching, Alex's team can build you the tools you need. They also implement internal projects that help the provider run more efficiently, even spinning off some of these solutions as standalone software products. Given these various roles, Alex, as you might expect, has to juggle many different demands on his team's time.

A big part of how he pulls off this feat is immediately visible when you walk into his office. Dominating one of the walls is a three-by-eight-foot chalkboard. It's divided into five columns: *plan, ready, blocked, work,* and *done.* The *work* column is further divided into two sub-columns: *in development* and *testing.* Taped under each column are stacks of hand-labeled notecards. If you stick around Alex's office longer, a pattern will emerge. Most mornings, the project leaders on Alex's team gather around "the big board," as they've taken to calling it, and discuss the cards. As they talk, the cards are moved: some are shifted from one column to another, while others are arranged into a different order in their current column. What you won't see is these project leads splitting their attention between the discussion at hand and their email inboxes. Alex's team isn't big on email (or instant messenger for that matter): they see this technology primarily as a tool for interacting with external partners. The information that really matters for their getting things done is all right in front of them, scrawled on cards taped to a chalkboard.

As Alex explained to me when I asked him how he avoids the hyperactive hive mind workflow, the chalkboard in his office is not the only tool used by his team. Each notecard taped to the big board corresponds to a project. When a project makes it to the *work* column, the group of employees assigned to the project will create their own board dedicated to the tasks required to accomplish the project. Unlike the big board, these smaller boards are typically implemented in software. Alex's team prefers two tools that are popular in the software development community, called Asana and Jira, for creating these digital boards. Once a project is underway, those working on it will hold their own regular meetings to update the project's board—discussing the cards and rearranging them among the columns.

When I spoke with Alex, for example, there was a card on the big board labeled with a project that involved the process used by one of the provider's hospitals for storing the results of the genetic tests they conduct on babies. At the time, the data was housed on an FTP server. Alex's team was tasked with figuring out how to move this information into a more flexible database. He explained to me how this project would advance:

> We know about this project. It's represented as a card in the *plan* column. It's ordered behind three other things that have to get done first. Once it comes up to the top of this column, we will discuss it and come up with detailed tasks to add into Asana or Jira. On the big board, we'll then move its card to *in development*.

Alex typically holds these discussion meetings every morning. If his development teams are fully engaged in projects—"rock and rolling"—

he'll temporarily scale back these big picture meetings to once per week until there's more planning to be done.

———

This is the third time we've encountered a similar pattern: information about knowledge work arranged into columns of cards on a board. Alex's team uses both physical chalkboards and virtual boards implemented by Asana. Optimize Enterprises relies on Flow. Devesh, from the last chapter, uses Trello.

The general idea of posting tasks on boards to organize work is not new. Hospital ERs, for example, have long relied on *tracking boards*: whiteboards, divided into a grid, that list every patient being treated, including their room, the doctor or nurse assigned, and their triage level. For the harried staff, the tracking board provides, at a glance, a good overview of the current state of the emergency room. It also simplifies the tasks of figuring out where to put new patients and where doctors should dedicate their time. As mentioned, even the early twentieth-century Pullman train company relied on boards. They used brass tags hung on a wooden board to summarize the assignment of brass workers to machinery.

Recently, a more refined approach to deploying tasks on boards as a productivity tool has emerged. In this approach, boards are divided into named columns, and work tasks are arranged as vertical stacks of cards under the column that best describes their status. Sometimes, as with the *plan* column on Alex's big board, the vertical ordering of cards indicates priority. This is the general setup deployed by Alex, Devesh, and Brian Johnson.

The source of this approach to organizing work can be found in the software development community, which over the past couple of decades has increasingly embraced so-called *agile* methodologies for producing software. The basic ideas behind agile were first summarized in a 2001 manifesto penned by a group of seventeen programmers and project managers. The manifesto opens optimistically: "We are uncovering better ways of developing software." It then lays out twelve principles, each explained in plain language. "Our highest priority is to satisfy the customer through early and continuous delivery of valuable software," reads one principle. "Simplicity—the art of maximizing the amount of work not done—is essential," reads another.[4]

To understand agile, you must understand what it replaces. Software development used to rely on lumbering, complicated project plans that would quixotically attempt to figure out in advance all the work required to produce a major piece of software. The idea was that, given one of these plans, often lovingly rendered in striated, multicolored Gantt charts, you could know exactly how many programmers to assign at each stage and provide your customers with accurate release schedules. This approach made sense in theory, but for anything but the simplest projects, these plans almost never proved accurate. Producing software is not like producing cars: it's hard to accurately estimate how long different steps will take or what problems might arise. It also turned out that customers didn't always know everything they needed in advance, so the features being developed would change on the fly, further undermining the schedule.

The agile mindset argues that software development should be broken down into smaller chunks that can be released into the wild as quickly as possible. As users provide feedback, the information can be quickly integrated into future updates—creating a fluid feedback cycle that evolves useful software instead of trying to build it perfectly all at once before releasing. As more and more software became web-based, simplifying the process of releasing updates and soliciting feedback, various agile methodologies became extremely popular in the world of developers.

The word *various* is important here. Agile by itself is not an organizational system; it instead defines a general approach that is realized by multiple different specific systems. Two of the more popular systems at the moment are Scrum and Kanban, which, if you have any involvement with software, are terms you've at the very least heard mentioned. Generally speaking, Scrum breaks work down into *sprints*, where a team dedicates itself completely to delivering a particular update before moving on to the next. Kanban, by contrast, emphasizes a more continuous flow of tasks through a fixed set of phases, with a general goal of minimizing the current *works in progress* at any one phase, preventing bottlenecks.

Which brings us back to boards. When you look past the low-level details of their implementation, you'll notice that what Scrum and Kanban share is the use of a *task board* in which cards corresponding to tasks are stacked vertically in columns corresponding to phases of the software development process. In Scrum, for example, there's often a column called *backlog* for features that have been identified as potentially important but have not yet been tackled. There's also a column for features currently being worked on by a team of programmers engaged in a sprint, a column for features that have been completed and are now being tested, and a column for features that are complete, tested, and ready for release.

It's no coincidence that both these systems ended up using the same means of organizing tasks. A key idea driving agile project management is that humans are naturally pretty good at planning. You don't need complicated project management strategies to figure out what to work on next; it's usually sufficient to just have a group of informed engineers get together and discuss what makes sense. The key caveat in this belief, however, is that we're able to effectively apply our planning instinct *only if we have a good grasp of all the relevant information—what* tasks are already being worked on, what needs to be done, where there are bottlenecks, and so on. Cards stacked on boards turn out to be an amazingly effective method for quickly communicating this information.

This property of task boards makes them applicable to more than just software development, which is why we see them show up frequently in examples of forward-thinking knowledge work organizations trying to become more systematic about their processes. It's also why I recommend them as something to consider when developing processes for your own organization. To aid in this task, I've collected several best practices for getting the most out of task boards in the context of knowledge work.

Task Board Practice #1:
Cards Should Be Clear and Informative

At the core of the task board method is stacking cards in columns. These cards typically correspond to specific work tasks. It's important that these tasks are clearly described: there shouldn't be ambiguity about what efforts each card represents.

Also critical to successfully deploying this approach is having a clear method to assign cards to individuals. Digital systems such as Flow provide assignment as a native feature, allowing you to see small thumbnail headshots of the people associated with a task card. But even in systems that don't offer assignment functionality, it's easy to add this information to the card's title. In some cases, the assignments are implied by the columns; perhaps, for example, on a small development team, there's a certain person who's always responsible for the tasks in the *testing* column. What's important is that when a card gets moved to a column indicating that it should be actively worked on, there's no uncertainty about who is responsible for this work.

Finally, there should be an easy method to associate relevant information with each card. When using digital board tools such as Flow or Trello, you can attach files and long text descriptions to the virtual cards. This is immensely useful, as it organizes all the information relevant to the task in one place. This was something that struck me when I was studying the Trello boards used by Devesh. One of the cards I encountered on his boards, for example, corresponded to the task of writing up an analytics report for a client. Attached to the card were the relevant files containing the data for the report and some notes on how to format it. For the person working on this task, there's now no need to sift through cluttered inboxes or chat archives to find these materials. When it comes time to work on the report, everything that's needed is all in one place.

If you're using a physical board, then you obviously can't directly attach digital files or long descriptions to cards. But you can achieve more or less the same effect by using a service like Dropbox to set up a shared directory for the board, with a subdirectory for each column. You can store information relevant to the cards in a given column in the corresponding subdirectory—simplifying the task of finding this information when the time comes.

Task Board Practice #2:
When in Doubt, Start with Kanban's Default Columns

Once you leave the comfort of the entrenched guidelines surrounding the use of task boards in software development, it's not necessarily obvious how to set them up for your specific knowledge work context.

When in doubt, start with the default setup from the Kanban methodology, which includes just three columns: *to do, doing,* and *done.* You can then elaborate this foundation as needed.

On Devesh's boards, for example, he had a column for design tasks and a column for implementing client campaigns. This modification to the Kanban defaults proved useful in the context of his marketing firm because design and implementation work pull from two different pools of employees. The Flow boards used at Optimize Enterprises, by contrast, tended to deploy the simpler setup of a single column dedicated to all tasks being executed for the project at the moment.

Another useful expansion of the Kanban defaults is to include a column for storing background notes and research generally relevant to a project. This hack technically breaks the convention that every card corresponds to a task, but when using digital boards it can be a useful way of keeping information close to where it might be needed. At Devesh's marketing company, for example, a column of this type was used to capture notes from client phone calls.

Task Board Practice #3: Hold Regular Review Meetings

As argued earlier, a key property for any knowledge work production process is an effective system for deciding who is working on what. In the context of task boards, these decisions are reflected by the cards on the board and to whom they're assigned. But how should these decisions be made? A foundational idea in agile methodology is that short meetings held on a regular schedule are by far the best way to review and update task boards. Agile rejects the idea that you should let these decisions unfold informally in asynchronous conversations on email or instant messenger. When using task boards for your own knowledge work production processes, you should abide by this same rule.

A standard format for these meetings is to have each person briefly summarize what they're working on, what they need from other people to make progress for the rest of the day, and what happened with the tasks they had committed to working on the day before. It's during these *review meetings* that new tasks can be identified and new people assigned to them. The meetings also help remove bottlenecks caused by one person waiting to hear from another person, and they provide an important sense of accountability: if you slack off on the task you committed to during today's meeting, you'll have to reveal this lack of results publicly during tomorrow's review.

These regular review meetings work well in part because they're collaborative: everyone feels like they were part of deciding what tasks they're tackling. They also work well because they're unambiguous: everyone is present for the conversation that decides current work assignments. Finally, as argued in part 1 of this book, real-time communication is typically a much more effective means of coordinating individuals than drawn-out back-and-forth messaging. One ten-minute gathering can eliminate dozens of ambiguous messages that would otherwise generate frequent interruptions throughout the day.

Of course, many modern knowledge work organizations include remote employees, making it impossible for everyone working with a given task board to show up in person for these review meetings. The standard solution is to use conferencing software such as Skype, Zoom, or FaceTime (if the groups are small). The key is real-time interaction.

Task Board Practice #4:
Use Card Conversations to Replace Hive Mind Chatter

One of the more powerful features of digital board systems is the discussion function built into each virtual card. In Trello and Flow, for example, in addition to attaching files and information to cards, you'll find tools for message board–style conversation stored directly on each card. People can ask questions, and others can later chime in with answers. In the knowledge work organizations I observed that used digital task boards, these *card conversations* proved a critical part of coordinating work on specific tasks. People would check in on these conversations several times each day, reducing the amount of discussion required at the regular review meetings and eliminating the need for general-purpose communication tools like email, which do a poor job of structuring information and quickly become cluttered.

A fair concern is whether these card conversations might allow hyperactive hive mind–style unstructured messaging to sneak back into your organization. Based on what I observed, however, the experience of card conversation was significantly different from the experience of hive mind chatter. Devesh, for example, described his shift from email to card conversations as "flipping the script" on communication. When you have a general email inbox through which all discussion flows, you're forced to continually check this inbox, which then confronts you with discussions about many different projects. When you rely on card conversations, on the other hand, the only way to encounter the discussion surrounding a given project is to navigate to that project's board. At this point, you're encountering conversation about *only* this project. This flips the script because now you decide what project you want to talk about, as opposed to allowing the projects to decide for you.

Card conversations also come with different communication expectations. It's generally assumed that you'll check in on your relevant task cards only a few times a day, so there's no sense of urgency or any expectation that you'll deliver rapid responses. The granularity of work therefore increases and people get used to tackling one thing at a time, for long periods, before moving on to the next. On the other hand, when these conversations occur on a general-purpose communication tool, the awareness that everyone is checking this tool more frequently leads to heightened expectations surrounding response time for all communication, leading inevitably back to a full-speed hyperactive hive mind workflow. (See the discussion in chapter 3 about the cycle of responsiveness.)

Card conversations are also much more structured than hive mind chatter, as conversations are attached to specific tasks and are accompanied by all the relevant files for that task. If I'm running a project, for example, and I want to check the status of a key task, I can simply flip the virtual card and quickly review all the relevant discussion—bringing me up to speed. This contrasts with the hive mind workflow, in which all this information exists scattered among various people's inboxes or buried in crowded chat channels.

There's a slower pace and peacefulness that seems to accompany this shift of discussion toward card conversations. To avoid the need to wrangle an always-filling inbox is a benefit that shouldn't be underestimated.

Personal Kanban: Organizing Your Professional Life with Individual Task Boards

Jim Benson thinks a lot about improving knowledge work. His consulting firm, Modus Cooperandi, specializes in building custom processes that improve collaboration at knowledge work organizations. Likely influenced by his former career as a software entrepreneur well versed in agile methodologies, Benson's processes often make use of task boards. The photos featured on the Modus Cooperandi website are filled with brightly colored Post-it notes arranged in complex columns.[5]

In personal productivity circles, however, Benson is better known for a slim volume that he self-published back in 2011. It's titled *Personal Kanban*, and it offers a seductive promise: the agile methodologies that help teams make sense of complex projects can be used to tame the complex mess of obligations in your individual professional life.

The core ideas behind *Personal Kanban* are simple enough that Benson can summarize them in a five-minute video that he features on the book's website.[6] In the video, Benson stands in front of a large white notepad mounted on an easel. He fills the center of the sheet with a jumble of colored Post-it notes, which represent "expectations" from family, friends, colleagues, bosses, and ourselves. "All of these things become this big kind of congealed mass in our minds that we have to pull apart every time we decide something we would like to do," he explains. This requires us to try to pick this "mass" apart and think through all these different obligations just to figure out what we should do next. "That's not fun," Benson concludes.

The Personal Kanban solution to this problem is to organize this mess of expectations with a personal task board. Benson suggests using three columns. The first is labeled *options*, and it's where you arrange all your obligations into neat stacks of Post-it notes: one note per task. "Now we've taken that horrible mass of work and turned it into a very cognitively pleasing rectangle." The second column is labeled *doing*. This is where you move the Post-its corresponding to the tasks that you're actually working on right now. The key to this column—and a big part of the secret sauce of Kanban systems in general—is that you should maintain a strict limit on how many tasks you're allowed to be doing at any given time. In Kanban-speak, this is called the *works in progress (WIP) limit*. In the video, Benson sets this limit to three. As he explains, if you instead try to make progress on dozens of different tasks all at the same time, you end up with a "messy life." He convincingly argues that it's better to do a small number of things at any one time: give them

your full concentration, and only when you finish one should you replace it with something new.

Which brings us to the *done* column. This is where you move the
tasks you complete. In theory, you could just discard a Post-it once you
completed its task, but as Benson implies, the psychological boost of
physically moving the Post-it from *doing* to *done* is a powerful moti-
vator.

In the years since Benson published *Personal Kanban*, the system
has gathered a cult following. A YouTube search reveals countless home-
made videos from fans explaining their own takes on Benson's approach
to personal productivity. If you assume that all these fans strictly ad-
here to Benson's original three-column design, then you must not know
much about the personal productivity community. As you watch these
fan videos, you'll encounter many intensely complex, custom-built
variations.

One such video replaces the *doing* column with a *ready* column
divided into three sub-columns: *cold, warm,* and *hot*—allowing a more
nuanced take on the status of pending tasks.[7] Another video, recorded
by a professor who teaches supply chain management, demonstrates a
personal board format so complicated that it seems to require graduate
training in supply chain management to even understand. He divides
his *options* column into color-coded rows that he calls "value streams,"
each dedicated to a different type of task and featuring Post-it notes of
a matching color. These rows are further divided into internal columns.
One column is a designated "holding tank" of tasks that he cannot get
to in the current semester, while the other column is for tasks that he
does hope to get done. Each row has a "staging area" position where the
next task of that stream to be accomplished can be moved. From this
larger number of staging areas, tasks can then be shifted into the small
number of *doing* slots, constrained by a WIP limit of three. His *done*

column maintains the same color-coded value stream rows as his *doing* column, allowing him, at a quick glance, to get a sense of how he has recently been allocating his time.[8]

The success of Personal Kanban among productivity aficionados underscores an important reality for anyone looking to escape the hyperactive hive mind: task boards are not just effective for coordinating work among teams, but can be incredibly effective in making sense of your individual obligations—even if you don't have graduate-level training in supply chain management.

As I mentioned briefly before, I've embraced this idea in my own professional life as a professor, where I use Trello boards to keep track of my obligations during my time as the director of graduate studies (DGS) for the computer science department at Georgetown. Following Jim Benson's basic structure, I have *doing* and *done* columns. Following the lead of the Personal Kanban community, I also deploy my own custom blend of columns for making sense of the tasks I plan to work on but am not actively tackling at the moment (more on this to follow). Every Monday, I review the board, updating the positions of cards and deciding what I'm working on that week. Throughout the days that follow, I reference the board to figure out what I should do with any time put aside for my DGS duties. As new tasks arrive—in the form of emails, or phone calls, or, as is also common, students dropping by my office to ask questions I don't know how to answer—I immediately put them on cards that I drop on my board to be dealt with later.

Without this task board system, I'd be dependent on the hyperactive hive mind workflow to accomplish my work as DGS, which would consign me to juggling an avalanche of simultaneous, slow-moving email conversations throughout the day. I'd be *that guy*, with his laptop open in every meeting, phone always in hand while rushing across campus, keeping the proverbial plates spinning one frantic reply at a time. Without this system, in other words, my job would be nearly unbearable. With it, the overhead of this position is greatly reduced—obligations get dropped on a board, where they're organized, and I then methodically accomplish them in times set aside for this purpose. Which is why, as you might expect, I've become a big advocate of deploying task boards not just to organize teams, but to organize your individual life as a knowledge worker as well.

To aid in this effort, here are several best practices for making individual task boards work well for you.

Individual Task Board Practice #1: Use More Than One Board

Many proponents of the Personal Kanban approach deploy a single board to make sense of all the tasks in their professional life. I recommend something slightly different: maintain a separate board for every major role in your professional life. At the moment, I play three largely distinct roles as a professor at my university: researcher, teacher, and DGS. I deploy a different task board for each of these roles, so when, for example, I'm thinking about teaching, I'm not also confronted with unrelated tasks about research or the graduate program. This reduces network switching and therefore increases the speed with which I'm able to resolve issues.

Similarly, I've also found it useful to sometimes set up a dedicated task board for large projects (say, any project that might take more than a couple of weeks of effort). Not long ago, for example, I was the general chair of a major academic conference. The demands of this role were so numerous that I found it easier to contain them on their own task board, isolated from other areas of my academic life. Once that project ended, I discarded the board.

There is, of course, a limit to how many boards you can manage before the upkeep becomes too arduous. This is why I think the rule of one board per role, and one board per major project, is probably about right. For most people this means two to four boards that run your life, which works well. If you have ten boards, on the other hand, the cost of switching between them will begin to swamp out the advantages of separating the tasks.

Individual Task Board Practice #2:
Schedule Regular Solo Review Meetings

When we discussed task boards for knowledge work teams, I argued that regular review meetings were the best way to update these boards. The same holds for your personal board. If you want to get the most out of this tool, you need set times each week to review and update your personal board. During these *solo review meetings*, go over all the cards on the board, moving them between columns and updating their statuses as needed. This shouldn't take long: five to ten minutes is usually sufficient if you're doing this regularly. And these sessions don't have to be too frequent: I find once a week to work well. But they shouldn't be skipped. As soon as you believe that a task board can no longer be trusted as a safe place to store your obligations, you'll revert to more frantic, hyperactive hive mind messaging. Put your solo review meetings on your calendar and protect them like any other meeting or appointment. Individual task boards can significantly improve the quality of your life as a knowledge worker, but only if you invest sufficient time in their upkeep.

Individual Task Board Practice #3: Add a "To Discuss" Column

In my work as DGS, there are several colleagues with whom I frequently need to discuss issues related to this role: my department chair, the graduate program manager, and the two other professors who make up the graduate committee I lead. For each of these three categories of colleagues, I added a column to my DGS task board labeled *to discuss at next meeting*. Whenever a task arises that requires input from one of these individuals, I sidestep my instinct to shoot them a quick email by instead moving the task to the appropriate *to discuss* column.

I meet with my program manager weekly on a set schedule. During each meeting, we go through all the tasks that built up in his column since the last meeting. For my department chair and graduate committee, I wait until their *to discuss* columns are sufficiently crowded before I arrange our next meeting to review these tasks in one big batch.

This hack might seem straightforward, but its impact on my work life has been profoundly positive. Imagine, for example, that a stack of five cards builds up under the *to discuss* column for my department chair during a given week. In a twenty-to-thirty-minute meeting, the two of us can come up with a reasonable plan for each of these cards. If I had to instead shoot off a quick email for each of the tasks, the result would be five different conversations occurring in my inbox that I'd have to tend throughout the week—leading to dozens of extra inbox checks each day and frustratingly fractured attention.

If you want to unlock the power of personal task boards to minimize hive mind–style back-and-forth messaging, this hack is probably the most important one you'll encounter in this chapter. A regular rhythm of efficient meetings can replace 90 percent of hive mind messaging, *if* you have a way to keep track of what needs to be discussed in these meetings. The task board makes this simple.

Individual Task Board Practice #4:
Add a "Waiting to Hear Back" Column

In collaborative knowledge work, it's often necessary for progress on a task to be halted while you wait for feedback, or for an answer to a question, or for a key piece of information from someone else. If you use an individual task board to organize your obligations, it's easy to keep track of these halted tasks by moving them to a column labeled *waiting to hear back*. When you move a task to this column, note on the card who you are waiting to hear back from and what the next step will be when you do hear back. This prevents you from losing track of efforts that have temporarily left your direct control, and allows you to make efficient progress when you learn what you need. Most important, these open obligations have a safe place to reside, freeing you from that lurking worry in the back of your mind that there are things being missed.

A Follows B: Automatic Processes

Let's return to Optimize Enterprises' process for producing its daily content. Unlike the examples we've just been considering, this process includes no task boards or review meetings. Indeed, there are almost no interactions or decisions being made at all. Once Brian Johnson puts a new lesson idea onto the shared spreadsheet, it moves from one status to the next like clockwork. At each phase, the relevant people know exactly what's expected of them.

This style of *automatic* production process plays an important role in many knowledge work settings. Not all processes, however, can be made automatic. For this strategy to apply, the process in question must produce some output in a highly repeatable fashion, where the same steps are implemented, in the same order, by the same people, each time. The types of processes optimized with task boards, by contrast, are more diverse and dynamic, requiring collaborative decision making to figure out what tasks to tackle next and who should be responsible for them.

Consider, for example, the task of putting together a quarterly budget for your team. This is probably something that can be reduced to a series of unambiguous steps that are executed the same way and in the same order each quarter, making the task a good candidate for automation. Updating your company website, on the other hand, is probably a project that's less well defined and will require more discussion and planning to get right, making it better suited for a task board approach. The process for adding new client testimonials to the website, however, probably could be automated, as it's highly repeatable. And so on.

Once you've identified a process that does seem like a good candidate for automation, the following guidelines will help you succeed with the transformation:

1. **Partitioning:** Split the process into a series of well-defined phases that follow one after the other. For each phase, clearly specify what work must be accomplished and who is responsible.

2. **Signaling:** Put in place a signaling or notification system that tracks the current phase of each output being generated by the process, allowing those involved to know when it's their turn to take over the work.

3. **Channeling:** Institute clear channels for delivering the relevant resources and information from one phase to the next (such as files in shared directories).

The daily lesson production process at Optimize clearly follows these guidelines. It's divided into well-defined phases, uses a shared spreadsheet to signal each lesson's current status, and makes use of shared directories to transfer files. Automatic processes, however, don't necessarily have to rely on software systems. Over the years I've been a professor, for example, I've optimized the automatic process I use to work with my teaching assistants to grade problem sets for my larger courses. When I write my problem sets, I concurrently write detailed sample solutions for each of the problems. I also add some rough thoughts on grading the problems, capturing what I think would deserve full credit, versus partial credit, versus no credit.[9] On the day that I post the problem set for my students, I send these documents to my TAs.

The students hand in their problem sets at the beginning of class, and I bring them back to my office and leave them in a mail sorter I had installed on the wall in the hallway beside my door. The TAs will later come to pick them up. I don't have to tell them to do this, as they already know the class schedule and therefore know the days that problem sets are returned. Once the TAs have the problem sets, they can start grading. As they assess the students' answers, they might update my grading notes to reflect common issues they come across or particular grading heuristics they decide to apply.[10]

When they're done, the TAs enter the students' grades into a shared grading spreadsheet that I set up at the beginning of the semester, and put the problem sets back in the mail sorter by my door. On the day I plan to hand back the assignments, I use the spreadsheet to generate statistics about the problem set scores (e.g., average and median scores), which I paste onto a document that also includes the sample solutions and the grading notes updated by my TAs. (I discovered through trial and error that detailed sample solutions and grading notes significantly decreased the number of students complaining about their scores.) I print out the sample solutions right before class, then distribute them along with the graded assignments.

This process always more or less follows the guidelines specified above. The phases are well defined, the current phase is clear to the people involved, and we have set channels in place for moving the relevant resources—problem sets, grading notes, solutions, grades— where they need to be. Unlike the Optimize example, however, a lot of this process is physical—involving actual pieces of paper being moved back and forth. This detail turns out not to matter much. As long as the phases and communication channels are clear, the process can be effective.

Like any good automatic process, my approach to problem set grading eliminates basically all unscheduled communication between me and my TAs about grading. After I'm done writing a problem set, my only interaction with the material is to bring the problem sets to my office mail sorter after the students hand them in, and then to carry them back to the classroom along with sample solutions once the TAs are done grading them. The only email involved in this entire process is when I send the sample solutions to my TAs (though even this step could be further automated by giving my TAs access to a shared directory where I keep these solutions). None of my cognitive energy is dissipated worrying about logistics or trying to arrange meetings. This might sound superficial—like someone trying to avoid work—but the reality is that the energy and attention saved from administrative wrangling can be invested into activities that actually improve the quality of the class, like polishing lectures or answering student questions. This advantage is true of most automatic processes: eliminating unnecessary coordination does not just reduce frustration, but also increases resources to invest in the activities that really matter.

Most organizations or teams have some processes that are good candidates for automation. This is not, however, a transformation to take lightly, as the overhead in working out all the details of these processes can be substantial. (It took me a couple of years of tinkering, for example, to arrive at the process I now use for problem set grading.) A good approach to figuring out whether this effort is warranted is to apply the *30x rule*. As explained by the management consultant Rory Vaden, in its original form, this rule states: "You should spend 30x the amount of time training someone to do a task than it would take you to do the task yourself one time."[11] We can loosely adapt this rule to automatic process construction: if your team or organization produces a given type of result thirty times a year or more, and it's possible to transform its production into an automatic process, the transformation is probably worth the effort.

Making Individual Work Automatic

Automatic processes aren't just applicable to streamlining work conducted by teams; they can also apply to regularly occurring efforts that you typically perform on your own. As with the team processes, the goal remains to minimize both the cognitive energy and the back-and-forth communication required to finish your tasks, only now, the steps of the process are entirely under your control.

For example, back when I used to write student advice books, I suggested that students create an individual automatic process for each type of regular assignment: problem sets, reading assignments, lab reports—anything they knew in advance they were going to have to do again and again throughout the semester. At the core of these processes was timing. I recommended that they designate set times on their calendar for when they'd accomplish each type of recurring work. Maybe Tuesday from four to six is when you write up your lab reports for BIO 101, and you tackle your statistics problem sets in the free blocks between classes you have on Mondays and Wednesdays from ten thirty to eleven thirty, and so on. I then recommended detailing how this work gets done during these set times, including where on campus you go to work, as well as any methods or materials you regularly use. The key was to reduce cognitive energy wasted on planning or decision making, allowing the student to focus simply on execution.

This advice often proved revelatory for the students. Whereas they used to wander through their week, always guilty that they were behind, driven by impending deadlines into all-nighters, they could now confidently execute their automated schedule, secure in their knowledge that what needed to get done would get done, week after week. The reduced overhead and cognitive toll made the same amount of work suddenly seem to require a lot less energy.

There's no reason why this approach cannot also apply to nonacademic knowledge work responsibilities. If there's a particular outcome or result that you're individually responsible for producing again and again, there's probably nothing to lose by trying to come up with a more structured process that specifies when and how you tackle this work. As in my student example, start with the question of timing: add set times on your calendar, which you can treat like meetings attended only by you, for the specific steps you know have to get done. Then put in place some rules about how you execute these steps, searching for optimizations or hacks that can make each step a little easier to dispatch.

Crucial to this optimization is to minimize the back-and-forth communication associated with your processes. Consider, for example, a consultant who is responsible for producing a weekly report for a client that describes the hours her team spent on the project. Assume she needs to gather these hours from her colleagues on the team. Further assume that she needs to give her boss a chance to look at the report before sending it out.

Once our consultant puts aside a set time to work on this report each week, she can begin to optimize the communication required to complete it. She might, for example, create a shared spreadsheet where her colleagues can enter their hours. Two days before the report is due, she can send a reminder to her colleagues about entering their hours. In fact, she doesn't even have to send this message manually, but can instead schedule it to be sent automatically (many email clients, including Gmail, offer this feature).

Similarly, because the consultant now knows *when* she'll work on the report each week, she can have a standing agreement with her boss about when the report will be ready for review. For example: "I'll always have the report ready for your review in our shared Google Docs directory by 11:00 a.m. on Tuesday; if you have any comments, add them to the document during the day; I'll check for any notes at 4:00 p.m. before I send off the final version to the client at the end of the day."

A weekly task that might have once generated multiple back-and-forth urgent emails now adds no extra messages to our consultant's inbox. It also takes up much less cognitive energy. Our consultant sees the standing solo meetings on her calendar and executes the same steps every time: no urgency, no frantic messaging, no late-night worries about forgetting key steps.

This is the promise of introducing automatic processes into your individual professional responsibilities. Whether you're deploying complex automation or just following handcrafted procedures, these processes will reduce your dependence on the hyperactive hive mind workflow and reward you with extra cognitive energy and mental peace. Make automatic what you can reasonably make automatic, and only then worry about what to do with what remains.

Chapter 6

The Protocol Principle

The Invention of Information

Claude Shannon is one of the most important figures in twentieth-century science, yet few outside the specialized fields he helped innovate know his name. Perhaps his largest intellectual leap was his 1937 MIT master's thesis, which he submitted at the age of twenty-one and, among other contributions, laid the foundation for all of digital electronics.[1] But it's toward another of his most famous works that I'll turn our attention now, as it will prove useful in our quest to move beyond the hyperactive hive mind workflow. I'm talking about Shannon's invention of information.

To be more precise, Shannon wasn't the first person to talk carefully about information or to try to quantify it. But his 1948 paper, "A Mathematical Theory of Communication," established a framework called *information theory* that fixed the flaws of earlier attempts to study this topic formally and provided the tools that ended up making the modern digital communication revolution possible. Underlying this framework is a simple but profound idea: by adding complexity to the rules we use to structure our communication, the actual amount of information required by the interactions can be reduced. In this chapter, I'll adapt this principle to workplace communication, arguing that by spending more time in advance setting up the rules by which we coordinate in the office (what I'll call *protocols*), we can reduce the effort required to accomplish this coordination in the moment—allowing work to unfold much more efficiently. Before we elaborate this claim further, however, we must make a brief diversion to better understand Shannon's transformative insight.[2]

––––––––––

Shannon developed his groundbreaking work on communication while he was a scientist at Bell Labs in the 1940s. Building on the earlier efforts of fellow Bell Labs scientist Ralph Hartley, Shannon began by stripping away any notion of the "meaning" conveyed by information. In his framework the challenge is more abstract. A sender wants to transmit a message from a set of possible messages to a receiver by sending symbols from a fixed alphabet over a channel. The goal is for the receiver to identify which message from the original set the sender had in mind. (Shannon also added the possibility of noise on the channel that can corrupt some of the symbols, but we'll put that aside for now.) To keep things as clear as possible, Shannon further simplified the symbol alphabet to just two possibilities: a zero or a one. Putting this all together, in this framework, communication is reduced to the following game: a sender chooses a message from a well-known set of possible messages and transmits a sequence of zeros and ones over a channel monitored by the receiver, who then attempts to identify the message.

Before Shannon, Ralph Hartley had already identified something roughly like this setup as the right way to think about transmitting information. But Shannon added a twist: in many cases, a sender might be more likely to choose some messages than others, and this might help the sender communicate using fewer symbols on average. Imagine, for example, that a sender is transmitting letters from the English alphabet as part of a longer message. If the first two letters sent are "t" and "h," then this severely restricts which letter is likely to be sent next. The probability, for example, that the sender will next transmit "x" or "q" or "z" is zero. But the probability that the sender is about to transmit "e" is quite high. (Like his better-known British counterpart in the pantheon of computing pioneers, Alan Turing, Shannon had done some work on code-breaking during World War II, and therefore would have been familiar with the idea that certain letters are more common than others.)

Shannon argued that in this case, when the sender and receiver are trying to work out in advance the rules for how they will map transmitted symbols to letters, the *protocol*[3] they come up with should take into account these varying likelihoods, as this might allow them, on average, to get away with using far fewer symbols to communicate.

To make this idea more concrete, consider the following scenario. You're in charge of monitoring a meter that measures some important piece of equipment. The meter has a dial with 256 different values that span from –127 to 128. The chief engineer wants an update on the meter reading every ten minutes. Because she works in a different building, you rig up a telegraph wire so that you can communicate this information using a binary code of dots and dashes, preventing you from having to go find her in person to deliver each report.

For this scheme to work, you and the engineer must first agree on a protocol for how you'll encode the meter readings. The simplest thing to do would be to map each of the 256 meter readings to a unique sequence of dots and dashes. Perhaps, for example, a reading of –127 is transmitted as dot-dot-dot-dot-dot-dot-dot-dot, while a reading of 16 is transmitted as dash-dot-dash-dot-dot-dash-dash-dot, and so on. Some simple math ($2^8 = 256$) tells us that there are exactly 256 different sequences of eight dots and dashes, so you'll be able to assign a unique pattern to every possible meter reading.

This protocol would require you to send eight telegraph symbols for each meter reading. But let's say your goal is to minimize the number of symbols you have to send, as the telegraph key is annoying to use and hurts your hand. At this point, according to Shannon, you should take into account the likelihood of the different readings. In this scenario, let's assume you know that the meter is almost always going to read zero, as this is the normal operating state of the machinery being monitored. If it reads something different, this means there's a problem, and problems are relatively rare. To be more concrete, let's say that you expect the meter to read zero 99 percent of the time.

You and the engineer might now agree on the following more nuanced protocol. If you send a single dot, this means the reading is zero. If you send a dash, this means the reading is not zero and that you'll follow this dash with an eight-symbol pattern that maps to the specific nonzero reading you're measuring. Notice, with this new protocol, in the worst case you are sending *more* symbols than the simple protocol, as for a nonzero reading the new protocol requires nine symbols to be sent (the dash followed by an eight-symbol pattern), while the simple protocol always requires only eight symbols. But in the best case, the new protocol requires only one symbol, compared to eight for the simple alternative. How do you compare the costs of these two scenarios? Shannon suggests you use the specific probabilities to calculate an average cost. We calculate the average number of symbols per message in our new protocol like so: $.99 \times 1 + .01 \times 9 = 1.08$. In other words, if you average the number of symbols you send per measurement over a long period of time, it will work out that you're sending only slightly more than one symbol per message, making this new protocol massively more efficient over time than the original protocol.[4]

This was the central idea of Shannon's information theory framework: clever protocols that take into account the structure of the information being communicated can perform *much* better than naïve approaches. (This wasn't the only contribution of information theory. Shannon's paper also showed how to calculate the best possible performance for a given information source and revolutionized the way engineers thought about reducing interference from noise, making both high-speed electronic communication and dense digital storage possible.[5]) Without these insights, something as routine as downloading a movie from iTunes might take multiple days instead of a handful of minutes, and the images making up your Instagram feed might require an hour to appear instead of just the seconds we've come to expect.

These same ideas apply beyond digital communication. Soon after Shannon's seminal 1948 paper began to spread, engineers and scientists in a variety of fields recognized the general usefulness of his framework. Information theory began popping up in many contexts far separated from the world of digital files and computer networking, from linguistics, to human vision, to the understanding of life itself (biologists realized that DNA can be understood as an efficient, Shannon-style information protocol). We will now add one more area where Shannon's framework provides insight: coordination in the office.

In a standard work scenario, various parties need to communicate with one another about various issues—agreeing on a time for a meeting, determining the next step for a joint project, answering a client question, providing feedback on an idea. These coordination activities are structured by rules. Often these rules are implicit, in that they capture norms that aren't written down anywhere, and sometimes they're more formal. Consider, for example, a small consulting firm that regularly receives requests from potential clients that need to be evaluated to determine which are worth pursuing as new business. If the firm embraces the hyperactive hive mind workflow, then their implicit rule for deciding how to respond to these requests is likely to just initiate an email conversation among the relevant team members and hope to eventually arrive at a conclusion. A more formal rule, by contrast, might be to hold a meeting every Friday morning to go through that week's requests as a group and decide right then which ones to pursue and who will take the lead. Whether implicit or formal, many office activities are structured by some manner of rules. In honor of Shannon, let's call these collections of rules *coordination protocols*.

Shannon's information theory framework teaches us that for a given task, the protocol you choose matters, as some are costlier than others. In classical information theory, the *cost* of a given protocol is the average number of bits you need to transmit to complete the task—as with our simple meter reading example from above, a protocol that uses fewer bits on average is better than one that uses more. When evaluating coordination protocols in the workplace, however, we'll need some more nuanced notions of *cost*.

We might measure cost, for example, in terms of *cognitive cycles*, which describes the degree to which a protocol fragments your attention. To be even more precise, we can follow the lead of the RescueTime researchers discussed in part 1 and divide the workday into five-minute buckets. To measure the cognitive cycle cost of a particular coordination protocol, we count the number of these buckets in which at least some effort was expended toward the coordination task. To stick with our consulting firm scenario, the hyperactive hive mind protocol for evaluating new client requests probably generates several dozen back-and-forth emails, with each message corrupting a different five-minute bucket, creating a large overall cognitive cycle cost. The meeting protocol, by contrast, requires only one meeting per week. Assuming these meetings last something like thirty minutes, then the protocol corrupts only six or so of these buckets per week, making it much less costly by this measure.

Another relevant cost when considering workplace coordination protocols is *inconvenience*. If a protocol induces a long delay for someone to receive critical information, or requires extra effort on the part of the sender or receiver, or leads to a missed opportunity, then this generates inconvenience. For the sake of this thought experiment, let's imagine we have some sort of numerical scale for measuring inconvenience (actual numbers don't really matter here). Returning to our consulting firm example, the hive mind protocol probably scores better on this inconvenience scale compared with the weekly meeting protocol, as the need to wait for the next meeting before responding to a potential client might be perceived as an inconsiderately long delay. In some cases, this might even lead to lost business.

Shannon teaches us that we need to pay careful attention to these costs and be willing to tinker with our protocols to find ways to balance them optimally. In our scenario, the high cognitive cycle cost of the hive mind protocol for dealing with client requests seems prohibitive, even though it scores well on inconvenience. We might instead turn to the weekly meeting protocol, which scores well on cognitive cycle cost, and seek ways to reduce its inconvenience. Perhaps, for example, we introduce the following standard operating procedure: when a new client request arrives, whoever is in charge of monitoring that inbox immediately sends a reply to the potential client thanking them for their interest and promising a response within a week—reducing the probability that the client ends up annoyed by the delay. It's still possible that a potential client could be turned off by this response, but given the timely initial reply and clear expectations, this worst-case scenario is made rare. This approach slightly increases the cognitive cycle cost, as now someone has to send a quick reply to each incoming message, but this cost remains muted compared with what's generated by the hive mind protocol, which initiates an extensive thread for each new potential client. On average, this hybrid protocol seems like it has a lower cost than either of the alternatives and is probably therefore the right choice for the consulting firm.

Our instinct in the knowledge work setting is to obsess about factors like worst-case scenarios—*how can we prevent bad things from ever happening?!*—or to prefer the convenience of simple (but costly) protocols to more finicky (but optimized) alternatives. The information theory revolution tells us that these instincts shouldn't be trusted. Take the time to build the protocol that has the best average cost, even if it's not the most natural option in the moment, as the long-term performance gains can be substantial.

We're now ready to pull together these various pieces to articulate the central principle we'll explore in this chapter. A key element of any workflow is the means by which people coordinate their work. This coordination requires communication, and whether or not you use this terminology, this in turn requires the people involved to agree in advance on a set of rules about how and when the communication occurs— what we call a coordination protocol.

Most organizations default to using a hyperactive hive mind–style protocol for most coordination activities, because it's simple to set up and persuade people to follow. Its flexibility also often allows organizations to avoid worst-case scenarios. Shannon teaches us, however, that if you're willing to put in the hard work up front to develop smarter protocols for these tasks, you can often drastically reduce their long-term cost. The hard work you invest in advance to deploy the optimized protocol will pay off many times over in the lower cost you experience as you subsequently use it. Formally:

> **The Protocol Principle**
>
> Designing rules that optimize when and how coordination occurs in the workplace is a pain in the short term but can result in significantly more productive operation in the long term.

The remainder of this chapter explores case studies of the protocol principle in action. You'll learn about the usefulness of corporate office hours and how restricting clients' access to you can make them happier. You'll also learn what happened when an academic research group began running structured daily status meetings like a software development team, and you'll hear an argument for why you should never again try to schedule a meeting over email. All these protocols are more complex than just rocking and rolling with your email inbox or Slack channel, and some make it more likely that the occasional bad thing will happen. But guided by Shannon's fundamental insight, they embrace the central idea that sometimes a little extra complexity can unlock a lot more performance.

Meeting Scheduling Protocols

In 2016, I spoke on a panel at a business event. One of my fellow panelists was a New York–based technology entrepreneur named Dennis Mortensen. As I learned when we later chatted, he was the CEO of a start-up that was in the process of leaving stealth mode and taking on beta testers. It was called x.ai, and its product deployed cutting-edge artificial intelligence technology to tackle a mundane task: scheduling meetings.

In its original iteration, x.ai implemented a digital agent named Amy. When you needed to schedule a meeting with someone over email, you would cc a special email address connected to Amy and then, in natural text, ask the agent to help set up the gathering. For example, you might write: "Amy, can you set up a meeting for me and Bob next Wednesday?" At this point—and this is where the magic happens—Amy would interact with Bob over email to find a time on Wednesday that worked for both his and your schedules, then add the event to your calendar. This might sound like a minor improvement to office life, but it attracted major investment. By 2016, when I met Mortensen, x.ai had already spent more than $26 million of investment capital on the Amy natural language interface. By 2018, they had received $40 million in total investments.[6]

There's a reason why automated meeting-scheduling companies like x.ai are receiving so much attention from investors: even the most die-hard hyperactive hive mind booster can't ignore the raw time-wasting inefficiency of the way most knowledge workers currently tackle this increasingly common task. The standard protocol for setting up meetings is what I call *energy-minimizing email ping-pong*. At some point during an email conversation it becomes clear that a meeting is needed. Because this task is annoying and non-urgent, all participants involved initiate a game whose unspoken rule is to see how quickly you can bounce the responsibility for the scheduling to someone else, even if just temporarily:

> "We should meet. Let me know when works for you."
>
> "Should we shoot for next week?"
>
> "Sounds good to me. Generally speaking, Tuesday and Thursday are probably best."
>
> "I'm sort of swamped those days. Friday?"
>
> "Sure, when?"
>
> "Morning?"
>
> "Maybe I could do 11:00 if not too late?"
>
> "I leave for an off-site meeting around then. How does the following week look?"
>
> *And so on . . .*

The cognitive cost of this protocol is large, as each one of these back-and-forth messages requires time spent in your inbox. To make matters worse, once a scheduling conversation is in progress, you have to check your inbox frequently while waiting for the next message to arrive, as it would be impolite to disappear for many hours in the middle of one of these quasi-synchronous back-and-forth interactions.

It would be bad enough if you had just one such meeting to schedule at any given time, but in reality, most knowledge workers find themselves juggling many different scheduling conversations simultaneously.

As reported in a 2017 *Harvard Business Review* article, dramatically titled "Stop the Meeting Madness," the average executive now spends twenty-three hours a week in meetings.[7] The sheer volume of the scheduling required to set up those meetings becomes a major driver of hyperactive inbox checking, and therefore induces a major cognitive cost. When you have to continually return to your inbox to nudge along one of many different meeting-scheduling conversations, your ability to perform valuable cognitive work significantly diminishes. This is why investors are willing to spend $40 million to see whether artificial intelligence might drastically reduce this cognitive cost—this price is small compared with the massive amount of productivity that would be unlocked if the knowledge sector could abandon energy-minimizing email ping-pong altogether.

When seeking better meeting-scheduling protocols, there are several solutions that are significantly less costly on average than ad hoc emailing. The first, and most extreme, is to hire an actual flesh-and-blood assistant who has access to your calendar and can schedule meetings on your behalf. There was a time when this option was prohibitively expensive for all but the highest-level executives, as it involved paying a full-time salary to a dedicated employee. This is no longer the case. Online freelance services have made it simple to hire assistants to work remotely for a limited number of hours on specific tasks. When I hired my first part-time virtual assistant, using a service called Upwork, I was surprised to discover that she could easily handle my meeting scheduling in no more than two to three billable hours a week. The real cost of meeting scheduling comes from the numerous interruptions required to check your inbox and keep the conversations moving, but all these costly interruptions don't actually add up to a large total amount of billable time when handed off to an assistant.[8]

Though hourly rates differ depending on the experience of the assistant, given the reality of how much time is actually involved in scheduling, it shouldn't be difficult to off-load the bulk of your meeting scheduling for around forty dollars a week on average. An extra $160 a month, of course, is a nontrivial amount of money. In my experience, the type of knowledge workers most likely to make this investment are entrepreneurs who are already used to investing money in themselves and their businesses to keep things growing. For those who work as employees for large organizations, on the other hand, the idea of trading your own money for increased productivity is more foreign, and in this context bringing in an outside assistant to interact with your colleagues might be viewed with suspicion, if not outright hostility. That's why in my professional life, I use my assistant to manage the overwhelming number of meeting and interview requests I receive in my writing business, not, for the most part, to deal with the demands of my other job as a university professor.

Successfully working with a part-time assistant to schedule meetings requires two things: access to your availability and a way to add new events to your calendar. There are many tools that can satisfy these requirements. I've been using an online scheduling service called Acuity. At the beginning of each semester in which I've hired an assistant, I'll manually enter into the system all the times I'm available for meetings in the months ahead. When my assistant needs to schedule a meeting, she uses Acuity to select a block within these available times. What makes this service useful is that it synchronizes with my Google Calendar. When my assistant books an appointment in Acuity, it shows up automatically on my calendar. Equally important, if I directly book something on my calendar, Acuity automatically removes that block of time from my availability.

The obvious question, of course, is why I don't just directly use Acuity to accelerate my meeting booking: if someone wants to meet with me, instead of passing them off to my assistant, I could just send them straight to Acuity to book a meeting time that works for both of us. The reason I don't default to this simpler and cheaper option is that I work with a diverse set of possible appointments, and they're not all created equal from a scheduling perspective. When booking a meeting that will be held in my Georgetown office, for example, I want to consider only times when I'm on campus. When booking a podcast interview, by contrast, I want to do the opposite, offering only times when I'm working from home and can make use of my in-home studio. Some meetings are urgent, and I want to find the nearest available time slot, while others are not, and I want to defer them to a less crowded period in the future. It wouldn't work for me to respond to each meeting request with a list of *all* times that I'm available; I can instead let my assistant navigate these different demands.

For most knowledge work jobs, however, these types of distinctions are less relevant. You have a standard workweek during which you block off some times for uninterrupted work, leaving the rest open for meetings and appointments. In this case, there really isn't a need for an actual human to help you with your scheduling. Tools such as Acuity, ScheduleOnce, Calendly, and, of course, x.ai (to name a few examples among many) make it easy for other people to set up meetings with you during times when you're available. When someone requests a meeting, you simply send them a link to your scheduling service and tell them to pick whatever time works best for them. Days of energy-minimizing email ping-pong have now been reduced to a single message and some clicking on a scheduling website.

If the meeting involves multiple people, then avoiding email ping-pong becomes even more urgent, as the number of messages required for scheduling often increases exponentially with the number of attendees. In these cases, it's worth using a group polling service like Doodle. For those who are unfamiliar, these services require you to set up an online poll by entering in multiple date and time options that work well for your calendar. You then send the poll to the other meeting participants, who each check off which of these times work for them, allowing you to easily identify a time that works for everyone.

I would go so far as to say that anyone whose job requires more than one or two scheduled events in a typical week absolutely should be using a scheduling service or, if the work demands it, a part-time assistant. There's really no reason why anyone should still have to waste cognitive cycles in dragged-out scheduling conversations. You might think that the gains here are small—*how hard is it to send some emails?*—but if you're like me, you'll likely be surprised by the feeling of a burden being lifted when you eliminate all these ongoing scheduling conversations, which have a way of nibbling at the borders of your concentration, driving you again and again back into the hive mind chatter.

Claude Shannon's framework underscores this reality. Meeting-scheduling protocols induce a small extra inconvenience cost, as you have to set up the system, and your correspondents now have to select times from a website instead of simply shooting back a short email reply in the moment. But the cognitive cycles saved are so substantial that there's no comparison: the average cost of these meeting-scheduling protocols is significantly lower than what's required by the status quo of energy-minimizing email ping-pong.

Office Hour Protocols

In early 2016, I published an article on the *Harvard Business Review*'s website that I gave a purposefully provocative title, "A Modest Proposal: Eliminate Email." Though I'd been writing about the unique miseries of this technology on my blog, this piece was one of my first mainstream essays on the ideas that would eventually coalesce into the book you're currently reading. At the halfway point of the article, after I'd reviewed the issues caused by the hyperactive hive mind workflow, I delivered my big conclusion: "There's great advantage for those organizations willing to end the reign of the unstructured workflow and replace it with something designed from scratch with the specific goal of maximizing value production and employee satisfaction."[9]

In my original draft, I was happy to leave the argument there. My editor didn't agree. He rightly pointed out that the idea of abandoning email was so novel that there had to be at least some suggestions about how an organization might function in its absence. I hadn't yet worked out the details of attention capital theory at this early point in my thinking, so I didn't have a ready answer to my editor's question of what replaces email. Grasping for an example, I found inspiration in an activity common in my own world of academia: office hours. As I elaborated:

> The concept is simple. Employees no longer have personalized email addresses. Instead, each individual posts a schedule of two or three stretches of time during the day when he or she will be available for communication. During these *office hours*, the individual guarantees to be reachable in person, by phone, and by instant messenger technologies like Slack. Outside of someone's stated office hours, however, you cannot command their

attention. If you need them, you have to keep track of what you
need until they're next available.

Much to my disappointment, this 2016 article didn't immediately
spark an anti-email revolution. One commenter pointed out, correctly,
that office hours would be a poor fit for organizations with employees
that spanned multiple time zones. Another wrote that they'd rather
have more email than more meetings. "To attempt to outlaw email now
is like trying to bolt the barn door after the horse has bolted," concluded another commenter. "It's just not gonna work." As my research
on email continued, I pushed the office hours concept to the periphery
of my thinking. As I later learned, however, I perhaps shouldn't have
been so hasty in dismissing this solution.

———

Let's jump ahead to 2018, when Jason Fried and David Heinemeier
Hansson, the iconoclastic cofounders of the software company Basecamp, published a book titled *It Doesn't Have to Be Crazy at Work*.[10] The
book describes a collection of ideas for cultivating an effective workplace culture they call "the calm company," and nestled among its suggestions is a familiar strategy: office hours. As Fried and Hansson note,
their company contains many subject matter experts: "people who can
answer questions about statistics, JavaScript event handling, database
tipping points." Accordingly, if one of their employees has a question
about one of these topics, they can simply "ping" the expert to get an
answer. Fried and Hansson have mixed feelings about this reality: "[It's]
wonderful. And terrible."[11]

The wonderful aspect is that these experts can help their coworkers
become unstuck or identify more effective solutions to their problems.
The terrible aspect, on the other hand, is that the experts get sucked

into the hyperactive hive mind—devoting more and more slivers of time throughout the day to fielding these ad hoc requests. Basecamp's solution, to my delight, was to introduce office hours. The experts now publish set hours each week during which they're available to answer questions. For some experts, these office hours might be sparse, such as one hour per week, while for others they might be frequent, such as one hour every day. The company trusts the experts to figure out the availability that best matches their demand. Questions for these experts are then confined to those set office hours.

"But what if you have a question on Monday and someone's office hours aren't until Thursday?" Fried and Hansson ask. They provide a blunt answer: "You wait, that's what you do." They note that these constraints might seem overly bureaucratic at first, but that they've ended up a "big hit" at their company. "It turns out that waiting is no big deal most of the time," they elaborate. "But the time and control regained by our experts is a huge deal."[12]

Further investigation reveals that Basecamp is not the only non-academic organization to deploy office hours in a limited manner. As I learned from Scott Kirsner, the Innovation Economy columnist for *The Boston Globe*, office hours have long been popular among venture capitalists. As he explains in a column titled "I'm Joining the Open Office Hours Movement," many Boston-area investment groups, including Flybridge, Spark Capital, and Polaris Partners, have taken to putting aside regular times each week in which anyone interested in technology startups can show up, "no strings attached," to ask for advice, pitch an idea, or just make a connection.[13] As I learned profiling a Silicon Valley-based venture capitalist named Mike Jackson for my 2012 book, *So Good They Can't Ignore You*, success in this industry depends on exposing yourself to lots of different ideas and people, but if this exposure is delivered through unsolicited email messages, you can accidentally drown trying to keep up. "It's so easy to just come in and spend your whole day on email," he warned.[14] Office hours proved a good way for investors to balance these competing forces.

Claude Shannon's framework helps explain why these examples work so well. For most types of coordination, moving to predetermined office hours will significantly reduce the cognitive cycle cost compared with simply bouncing messages back and forth in an ad hoc fashion. Having to wait until the next scheduled office hour to communicate, however, can induce an inconvenience cost. Office hour protocols seem to work best for activities that are not too negatively impacted by these delays. This is why Basecamp's experts and Boston's venture capitalists embraced office hours: they reduced the large cognitive cost of distracting messages while introducing delays that didn't yield any major impact on daily effectiveness. This is also why my 2016 suggestion of replacing *all* communication with office hours landed with a thud: there are many types of coordination currently handled over email for which long delays *would* be prohibitively costly. The conclusion is that any time you find yourself involved in a type of coordination activity that's both frequent and non-urgent, an office hour protocol might significantly reduce its cost.

Client Protocols

In the late 1990s, as a teenager caught up in the excitement of the first dot-com boom, I cofounded a technology company with my friend Michael Simmons. Because we lived near Princeton, New Jersey, and thought this was a prestigious-sounding address, we named the firm Princeton Web Solutions.[15] We focused on website design, starting off by hand-coding sites for small businesses in the area. At some point, however, Michael connected online with a group of freelance developers based in India. We soon realized two key points. First, this team was much better at web development than we were, and second, their rates were quite low by American standards at the time. We struck a deal in which we would find clients and manage the projects while the Indian team would do the actual graphic design and HTML coding. In my memory, our first contracts were around $1,000. With the new team on board, we began landing contracts in the $15,000 to $40,000 range. The problem with all this, of course, was that we were teenagers living in the 1990s, meaning that we were in school all day and didn't have cell phones. As a result, we were running large contracts for demanding clients who basically had no way to get in touch with us.

Our solution to this problem was to code up an elaborate client portal. Each client had their own username and password they could use to log in to the portal. Once inside, they were presented with detailed information about their project. Sample designs and pre-launch versions of their site were all available for review in the portal, as was a calendar that listed the major upcoming milestones. A "work diary" contained daily updates on what work had been completed that day. Most actual interaction about the projects was condensed to specific meetings that were connected to our detailed project process. Each of these meetings generated a corresponding memo outlining what we'd decided, which we asked the clients to sign, indicating that they approved. (We found that this minimized the chances that the client would later change their mind once development was underway.) Scans of these signed memos could be downloaded through the portal.

We never directly explained to our clients that we relied on our portal because we were in school all day—though I have to imagine they figured this out on their own—we just set things up so that this reality wouldn't be an issue. Designers today often complain about how much time they spend dealing with emails. We were doing more or less the same work back then, but did so with basically no emails at all.

Of course, we weren't unique in our commitment to becoming clever about client communications. Back in chapter 1, I told the story of Sean overhauling the workflow at his small technology start-up. In this story, it was overwhelming client communication, more than anything else, that drove him to a breaking point. For Sean, things really began to unravel when a particularly demanding client asked to be given access to their internal Slack setup—causing the pings of Slack notifications to become a constant background hum, with each message carrying yet another anxiety-producing demand from the client. Not surprisingly, when Sean finally decided to replace the hyperactive hive mind at the company with better practices, one of the main areas where he focused was how they interacted with their clients.

Sean's company began adding a section titled "Communication" to every statement of work. "We want the client to be aware of all of this at the front of the project," he told me. The new section specified the rules for communication between the client and the company, including, as Sean emphasized to me, what to do when urgent matters arose. In most cases, the standard setup was a prescheduled weekly conference call with the client, after which a written summary of the call was sent to the client. Sean's business partner, who was in charge of client relations, was anxious about this change. "He was worried the clients would not be happy about this because we are a user experience company, so the experience has to be top-notch," Sean explained. "But they are absolutely much happier. It's all about managing expectations."

––––––

Though we didn't use this terminology, both Sean and my high school company deployed improved communication protocols to handle interactions between our organizations and our clients. By doing so, we significantly decreased the average cost of this coordination. Having studied other examples of these client protocols, I've identified a few useful pointers for helping these efforts succeed.

First, when seeking to minimize costs, consider the client's cost in addition to your own. A key factor that helps a client protocol work is if it reduces the cognitive cycles or inconveniences that the *client* faces as well. Few clients actually like sending you endless messages. They often instead feel forced into this behavior because they don't know how else to get in touch or make sure work is being done. As I learned with Princeton Web Solutions, the structured nature of our portal didn't frustrate clients; it instead gave them peace of mind, as they didn't have to waste cognitive energy worrying about our contract. By contrast, if you come up with a communication scheme that makes your experience easier while simultaneously making the client's experience costlier— to provide an extreme example: forcing them to fax you detailed client request forms every time they need something—you'll have a much harder sell on your hands, and for good reason.

Another important point is the need for clarity. Sean's company included a detailed description of their client protocol in the statement of work all their clients signed. This was smart. If they had instead just casually suggested to their clients that a weekly call should work, the clients would have been much more likely to default to the hive mind as soon as the first minor inconvenience arose. When the language is contractual, however, the client is more likely to just suffer the minor inconvenience and learn over time how much they actually enjoy the lower average cost of a more constrained system.

Finally, despite your best efforts, there will always be some clients for which these types of protocols just won't work. I talked with a communication consultant who used to work at a twelve-person shop in

Washington, DC. She told me that for many of their clients, they used a variation of Sean's setup: a scheduled weekly call followed by a written summary of all the points discussed. For some of their clients, however, they offered crisis communication services. These clients needed a way of getting *immediate* attention when publicity crises occurred, so their protocol essentially simplified to "call right away if anything happens." The details of these protocols, in other words, can depend on the specific type of work.

There are also certain individuals for whom this approach won't apply, not because of the nature of their work but because of their personalities. To use the technical term, I'm talking about jerks who enjoy badgering people because it makes them feel important. Tim Ferriss wrote about this exact situation in his 2007 bestseller, *The 4-Hour Workweek*. In discussing how he upgraded the workflows of his supplement company, BrainQuicken, he talked about how he ended up "firing" one of his more stress-inducing and belligerent clients. This idea that you might fire toxic clients struck a nerve. "That passage just leapt off the page for me," explained Tobi Lütke, the CEO of the tech company Shopify, in a Ferriss profile appearing in *Inc.* magazine. "If you go into business school and suggest firing a customer, they'll kick you out of the building. But it's so true in my experience. It allows you to identify the customers you really want to work with."[16] Claude Shannon's framework helps validate the logic of this client-firing strategy. While it's true that you'll lose money in the short term, you'll also eliminate significant cognitive costs. Once you start treating the latter more seriously, it becomes easier to move on from clients whose costs to your psyche don't justify the improvements to your immediate bottom line.

Pulling together these pieces, it should be clear that if you deal with clients, an optimized client communication protocol will be crucial in your journey to move past the hyperactive hive mind workflow.

Nonpersonal Email Protocols

Some aspects of our daily lives become so familiar that we have a hard time imagining an alternative ever existing. One such example of this effect is the canonical format of email addresses: person@organization. There's an elegance to this structure. When you send an email, the underlying email protocol routes the message to the organization specified in the address. Once there, the organization's email server delivers the message to the specific recipient on the left side of the @ symbol. It's this element of the email address, the recipient field, that we take for granted. But if we step back and examine it from a fresh perspective, an intriguing question emerges: Why are the recipients in email addresses almost always *people*, and not, for example, departments, projects, or activities?

The historical answer to this question can be traced to one of the earliest proto-email systems. In the early 1960s, computers were still large and expensive mainframes that required dedicated rooms and maintenance staffs. To use these machines meant waiting your turn, at which point you would temporarily be given full control of the digital behemoth, hoping it would compute your program, likely inputted as punch cards, before your turn expired. Engineers at MIT, frustrated by this setup, figured there must be a better way to divvy up mainframe access. Their solution, launched in the MIT Computation Center in 1961, was called the Compatible Time-Sharing System (CTSS). And it introduced something revolutionary into the world of computing: the ability for multiple users to log in to the same mainframe at the same time using terminal machines hardwired to the mainframe. These users weren't literally controlling the computer simultaneously; instead, the time-sharing operating system running on the big machine would switch rapidly between the different users, doing a little computation for one user before switching over to do some computation for another, and so on. But from the perspective of the users, it truly felt to each as if they had the mainframe all to themselves.

The jump from CTSS to email was natural. One of the features time-sharing introduced was the idea that each user account had its own directory containing its own files, some private and some accessible to everyone else on the system. Clever early users of CTSS realized they could leave messages in one another's directories. By 1965, this behavior was standardized with the MAIL command, implemented by software engineers Tom Van Vleck and Noel Morris. It placed a file called "MAIL BOX" in each user's directory. When you sent a message to a specific user with the MAIL command, the note was appended to that user's MAIL BOX file. People could use the tool to read and delete messages in their own MAIL BOX files.

The very earliest email accounts were associated with individual people, in other words, because the user accounts for mainframe time-sharing systems were originally set up in this way. Once this connection was made, it stuck. Ray Tomlinson, the engineer perhaps most responsible for the person@organization address format that later became standard, had previously worked on more advanced versions of time-sharing messaging tools like MAIL.[17]

This arbitrary and seemingly innocent decision to associate email with individuals ended up playing a role in the rise of the hyperactive hive mind workflow. As argued in part 1 of this book, the hive mind scales up the natural way we have always coordinated in small groups: unstructured, ad hoc, back-and-forth chatter. Because email addresses are associated with people, it was easy to deploy this tool to support this type of conversation, starting us down the slippery slope that eventually led to uncontrolled messaging. In an alternative universe where email addresses were instead tied to projects or teams, the hive mind workflow might have felt much less natural, and therefore might have had a harder time gaining traction.

The point of detailing this history is to encourage you to consider breaking the convention of associating email addresses with individuals, especially when seeking out efficient communication protocols. By eliminating this connection between email and people, you will, with one grand gesture, destabilize everyone's expectations about how communication *should* unfold, making it much easier for you to rebuild these expectations from scratch with a protocol that makes more sense.

Consider, for example, the client communication protocols discussed in this chapter. When a client is used to contacting a specific individual in your organization when they have questions or issues, it might be hard to diminish their expectation of quick responses. They will personalize these interactions and begin treating delays as a personal affront (*why are you ignoring me?!*). Now imagine instead that each client is assigned a dedicated email address of the form client name@yourorganization.com. It's now much easier to break them from the idea that their messages are going to an individual person, who is seeing them right away and therefore better answer them quickly! By depersonalizing communication, you have many more options to optimize it.

I deployed protocols based on these ideas to help manage my author communication. When I used to offer only a single email address for readers to reach me, associated with my name, the messages became overwhelming: not in just their volume but also their complexity. When you think you're interacting with an individual, it's natural to assume that they'll be reasonable enough to read your long story and offer detailed advice, or set up a call to talk about your business opportunity, or connect you to relevant people in their network. I used to do this gladly, but as my audience grew it became more difficult.

To improve my author communication protocols, I introduced nonpersonal email addresses. One of these, for example, is interesting @calnewport.com, which my readers use to send interesting links or leads. Below the address is a simple note: "I really appreciate these pointers, but due to time constraints, I'm usually not able to respond." In my experience, if you put such a disclaimer next to a personalized address, like cal@calnewport.com, it will be widely disregarded, as our expectations for one-on-one interactions are so strong. But when the disclaimer appends a nonpersonal address, like interesting@calnew port.com, I receive few complaints—without preconceived expectations, you're able to set them from scratch.

There are many different ways to build low-cost protocols into your professional life or organization, but in many cases, freeing email addresses from individuals provides a powerful boost to these efforts.

Short-Message Protocols

In 2017, C. L. Max Nikias, an accomplished academic and then president of the University of Southern California, wrote a peculiar op-ed for *The Wall Street Journal*. He wasn't discussing the research accomplishments that had earned him memberships in the National Academy of Engineering and the American Academy of Arts and Sciences. He also wasn't writing about the $6 billion capital campaign he ran, or the new campus he opened, or the addition of one hundred endowed chairs that he had helped create during the previous seven years of his presidency at USC.[18] His topic was both more universal and more mundane: email.

As Nikias explains, in his role he received over three hundred emails a day—and this presented a problem. "The very point of being a leader is to move an organization in a meaningful direction," he writes, "yet email can have the opposite effect, blocking the leader from accomplishing anything proactive or of lasting substance." To avoid the fate of spending his time "glued to a screen and responding endlessly," Nikias came up with a simple solution: "I keep all of my emails brief— no more than [the length of] an average text message." What happens to the emails that demand an interaction more involved than what can fit into a text-length reply? Nikias calls the person or asks them to set up a meeting. "The crucial nuances of human communication don't translate well into cyberspace anyway," he explains.

Nikias is not the only person to experiment with shorter emails. In 2007, a web designer named Mike Davidson posted an essay on his personal blog titled "A Low-Fi Solution to E-mail Overload."[19] In this post, Davidson describes his frustration with the asymmetric nature of email communication. "Often times the sender will ask two or three open-ended one sentence questions which elicit multi-paragraph answers," he writes. "In these cases, the sender spends one minute and the receiver is asked, implicitly, to spend maybe an hour." He came up with the same general solution as C. L. Max Nikias: keep *all* of his emails short. He similarly identified the 160-character count of an SMS text message as a reasonable target, but, recognizing that counting characters would require some sort of special software plug-in, he instead used a simple approximation: he would keep all his emails to five sentences or fewer.

To "politely" explain this rule to his correspondents, Davidson launched a simple website, http://five.sentenc.es, that briefly explains the policy on a minimalist landing page. He then added the following signature to the bottom of all his emails:

Q: Why is this email five sentences or less?
A: http://five.sentenc.es

As Davidson concludes in this introductory post: "By ensuring that all e-mails I send out take the same amount of time to send (viz. 'not a lot'), I am evening the playing field between emails and attending to many more of them in the end."

The idea of strictly limiting email length is more than a gimmick. It instead represents a step that too few take in our current digital age: the placing of clear constraints around what email should and should *not* be used to accomplish. The hyperactive hive mind workflow wants email to be a neutral carrier that supports flexible, unstructured, ongoing conversations of all types. The short-email movement pushes back on this commitment. It specifies email as something useful for short questions, short answers, and short updates, but demands that anything more complicated be handled using a different type of communication better suited to the exchange. This might be a pain in the moment, but from the perspective of Claude Shannon's framework, it's a protocol that will deliver a lower average cost in the long run.

As Nikias explains in his *Wall Street Journal* op-ed, for example, when he was overseeing the largest campus expansion in his university's history, he regularly received emails from his construction managers with design updates or small change requests that needed quick approvals ("everything from brick samples to stained glass windows"). This is a great use of email: for the construction managers to interrupt Nikias with a phone call or meeting for every one of these approvals would have devoured his entire schedule. On the other hand, as Nikias elaborates, when a construction issue seemed to require "substantive" discussion, he immediately bounced it out of his inbox and would instead initiate a phone call.

When deployed properly, these short-message policies implement efficient protocols that use email for the type of communication for which it's best suited (quick and asynchronous), forcing people onto better mediums for everything else. Always keeping emails short is a simple rule, but the effects can be profound. Once you no longer think of email as a general-purpose tool for talking about anything at any time, its stranglehold on your attention will diminish.

Status Meeting Protocols

In 2002, Michael Hicks and Jeffrey Foster joined the computer science department at the University of Maryland as newly minted assistant professors, where they began working together to establish a research group. Faced with the need to mentor the students they were hiring, Hicks and Foster deployed a strategy that's nearly ubiquitous among computer science professors: they set up weekly meetings with each of their students to check in on progress and work together on research problems.

For a while, this approach worked fine. Like many junior professors, Hicks and Foster had only two or three students to supervise and a relatively light load of additional responsibilities outside of research and teaching. As they explain in a technical report on research productivity that they published in 2010, however, as their careers advanced, this standard mentoring strategy began to "reach its limits."[20] They went from supervising two or three students total to six or seven students each. As their mentoring load grew, so did their outside commitments to review papers and write grants, further restricting their free time.

Their weekly meetings with each student became "extremely inefficient," as they were always scheduled for the same amount of time, thirty minutes to an hour, which was almost never the right duration—sometimes they needed only ten minutes for a status update, while other times they needed a couple of hours to tackle a particularly hard problem.

Hicks's and Foster's increasingly busy schedules made it difficult to fit in additional student meetings beyond those already scheduled for each week. As a result, students began to fall through the cracks. If someone was struggling on a problem, it could take a week before any remedies could be discussed. Hicks and Foster also noticed that one-on-one meetings failed to produce a sense of community in their research group. "We had built up a set of great individual students, rather than a collaborative research group," they wrote. Considering all these issues, their conclusion was simple: "Clearly, something needed to change."

The instigation of that change was a research meeting that Hicks attended in 2006. He was chatting with his officemate from graduate school, who had since gone on to become a software developer. The old officemate began telling Hicks about how much he enjoyed Scrum, the agile methodology his employer used to organize software development work. Something about the idea resonated with Hicks. When he returned to Maryland, he suggested to Foster that these exotic organizational techniques from the world of software development might be just what they needed to get their research group operating more effectively.

I introduced Scrum, and agile methodologies more generally, back in chapter 5 as part of our discussion of task boards. Of this strategy's various elements, the one that most resonated with Hicks and Foster was the discipline of daily scrums. As you might recall, in standard Scrum, software development teams break up work into sprints: sessions lasting two to four weeks that are dedicated to developing a specific set of features. During the sprints, the team meets every morning for fifteen minutes, in a gathering called a scrum. During this meeting, each person in the group answers the following three questions: (1) What did you do since the last scrum meeting? (2) Do you have any obstacles? (3) What will you do before the next scrum? They then spend the rest of the day actually working on their objectives. In software, this coordination method turns out to be much more efficient than trading emails or instant messages throughout the day. To enforce the fifteen-minute limit, and thereby prevent the meetings from dragging on into time-wasting territory, scrums traditionally require everyone to stand up.

Hicks and Foster adapted the daily scrum concept to their research group. Instead of holding the meetings every day, they held them on Mondays, Wednesdays, and Fridays. They also changed the name to "status meetings." Otherwise, the details remained largely the same: these gatherings lasted for fifteen minutes, and everyone on the research team answered the traditional three questions. They even experimented with holding the meetings standing up and found that, "surprisingly," it really did help them stick to the constrained time limit. Hicks and Foster would participate as well, updating the students on their own daily activities. They called their modified system SCORE.

A key to Hicks and Foster's SCORE was clearly distinguishing these status meetings from more involved technical discussions. If during a status meeting it became clear a student needed a more detailed discussion to make progress, a separate "technical meeting" would be scheduled right there on the spot. Unlike the old weekly meeting system, these technical meetings were scheduled only when needed. Because their purpose was clear the moment they were scheduled, they also tended to be very efficient—everyone arrived knowing the goal of the discussion. As Hicks and Foster elaborate, because they had cleared the standing weekly meetings with every student off their calendars, there was more than enough schedule space to fit these on-demand meetings as the need arose.

Curious whether their students shared their appreciation of the SCORE approach, the professors conducted a formal survey of their research group. They asked them to rate seven different aspects of their research experience as graduate students, including "quality of interactions with adviser," "productivity level," and "enthusiasm for research." For those students who were around before SCORE was instituted, they were asked to also rate their experience with the old way of organizing the group. "The responses were uniformly positive," Hicks and Foster summarize. "SCORE improved students' experience in every way we considered."

The regular status meeting strategy that Hicks and Foster extracted from Scrum methodology is both a powerful and widely applicable communication protocol. For many different knowledge work settings, deploying these short meetings, three to five times a week, can significantly reduce ad hoc email or instant message interaction throughout the day, as everyone synchronizes during the regular gathering. This trades the small number of cognitive cycles needed for the status meetings for the large number of cycles needed to achieve the same coordination through sporadic back-and-forth messaging. As Hicks and Foster report, the regular rhythm of short meetings also creates a sense of "momentum" that helps people both feel better about their work and experience more productivity. It also increases group cohesion, as everyone knows what everyone else is working on.

This protocol brings with it some inconvenience costs. In particular, waiting until the next status meeting might be annoying if you need a quick answer to a question or help overcoming an obstacle. In the groups I've studied that use some variation of these regular meetings, however, these bad events seem to be much rarer than people fear. Fall-back protocols, of course, can always be put in place to mitigate such concerns (e.g., "If something urgent comes up before the next status meeting, knock on my door").

A bigger issue with this style of communication protocol is that its effectiveness will rapidly diminish if you allow the status meetings to become longer and less focused. As Hicks and Foster report about their own experience:

> In the Fall of 2007 the meetings were approaching 30 minutes as students talked more with their adviser, during the meeting, about particular technical issues. While the longer meetings produced more technical information, they did not generate more group interest or contribution. To the contrary, the longer meetings became boring and tedious, and so we redisciplined ourselves to keep the meetings short.

Many of the students they surveyed emphasized the importance of the length of the meetings. This is an idea that's well understood in the Scrum community. Short, structured check-ins can be empowering. As soon as you let these gatherings devolve into looser, more standard-style meetings, they become a tedious burden.

This distinction is important. In academia, for example, it's common for groups of professors to work collaboratively on projects, such as a co-authored research paper or a departmental committee. A standard technique to help "move the project forward" is to establish a regularly occurring meeting, usually held once a week for an hour. The motivation here is to use appointments on your calendar—a convention that most people respect—to spark productivity. If you're forced to meet every week about the project, the thinking goes, then this should encourage you to get work done on a regular basis. These meetings are *not at all* the same thing as Scrum-style status meetings. The former is essentially an abdication of responsibility—an admission that you're not organized enough to accomplish something independently, so you need meetings to force you into feeling like progress is happening— while the latter empowers you to get even more done on your own. Weekly meetings are too infrequent and vague. They take up too much time and often feature people trying to weasel out of commitments through doublespeak and conversational diversion. Status meetings, by contrast, are both frequent and structured in the questions they demand of participants: What did you do, what are you going to do, what's in your way? These two shouldn't be confused.

If you work in groups on common professional goals, and you find that this work is generating too many distracting messages or aimless meetings, a well-executed status meeting protocol might make a significant difference in your productivity. As Hicks and Foster discovered, it's surprising how much overwhelming, attention-fracturing, back-and-forth interaction can be compressed into a frequent schedule of very short check-ins.

Chapter 7

The Specialization Principle

A Productivity Puzzle

In his wide-ranging 1996 book, *Why Things Bite Back: Technology and the Revenge of Unintended Consequences*, the independent scholar and writer Edward Tenner tackles a "productivity puzzle" that's proven both significant and widely overlooked: Why did the arrival of personal computers in the workplace fail to make us as productive as we predicted? As Tenner writes, "the huge investment in computing in the 1980s and early 1990s" made office workers feel "autonomous, in control, more powerful, and absolutely more productive." It was compared to a second industrial revolution, something that would transform work in profoundly positive ways. "But toward the end of the 1980s, the sentiment grew that something was not right," and by the early 1990s, people "from within technocratic culture"—economists, business professors, consultants—began to notice that the computer's predicted gains were not fully materializing.[1]

This skepticism was sparked in part by discouraging data. Tenner cites a study by the economist Stephen Roach which found that between 1980 and 1989, investment in advanced technology in the service sector grew by over 116 percent per worker, while the workers' output increased less than 2.2 percent during the same period. He also cites a study by economists at the Brookings Institution and the Federal Reserve that calculated the "contribution of computers and peripherals as no more than 0.2 percent of real growth in business output between 1987 and 1993."[2]

Even without this data, many people were coming to similar conclusions about the failed promise of the PCs that had become ubiquitous seemingly overnight. These shortcomings were particularly noticeable in professions that existed both before and after the computer revolution. My grandfather, like me, was a college professor. I spend most of my day interacting with a powerful portable computer equipped with high-speed wireless access to the internet. My grandfather, by contrast, didn't buy his first computer until after he retired (I helped him set it up), and there was no evidence that he ever actually used it. He would transcribe his books on yellow legal pads to be later typed up by an assistant, and he didn't need the internet for research purposes, as he packed his office with a massive personal library covering the topics he studied. I can highlight many small-scale tasks in my life that my computer has simplified. But if we look at the big picture metric that matters most for scholars—research output and scholarly impact—I can't argue that I'm more productive than him, especially considering that he wrote many books and ended up with an endowed chair in religious studies at Rice University before ending his career in the role of provost at a large theological seminary.

Tenner offers several explanations for this puzzle, but one of his primary arguments is that instead of reducing labor, computers end up creating more work. Some of this extra work is direct. Computer systems are complicated and change every few years as existing technology becomes obsolete. They also break a lot. The result is a large time investment in learning new systems and trying to get them to work. Around the time I was writing this chapter, for example, my speaking agent stopped by my office for a visit. As we were talking about workplace inefficiency, he told me the story of the woes the agency was facing trying to get a customer relationship management system called Salesforce working properly for their particular needs. After endless hours of tinkering, they ended up having to hire an additional expert to do nothing but work with the system. My agent wasn't so sure they were really gaining a productivity bump compared with the old days of Rolodexes and business cards.

More insidious, however, are the indirect labor increases personal computing instigated. A major problem with personal computers, Tenner notes, is not that they make individual tasks harder, but that they make them *just easy enough*. To explain, he points to a remarkable 1992 paper, published in the journal *National Productivity Review* by a Georgia Tech economist named Peter G. Sassone.[3] Between 1985 and 1991, Sassone studied twenty departments at five major US corporations, paying particular attention to the impact of the arrival of new office technologies such as personal computers.

As Sassone documents, professionals paid to do highly specialized work were spending more and more time doing administrative work. "Intellectual non-specialization was the dominant characteristic at most of the organizations in this study," he writes. The immediate cause of this imbalance, he notes, is a top-heavy staffing structure that has a skewed ratio of skilled professionals to support staff. In seeking explanations, he points to "office automation," noting that many firms paid for costly computer systems by reducing support staff that used to perform the functions computers could now "simplify."

As Sassone argues, this trade-off can be lopsided. When you eliminate support staff, the skilled professionals become less intellectually specialized, as they have to spend more time on administrative work that computers made just easy enough for them to handle on their own. As a result, it now requires *more* of these professionals to produce the same amount of valuable output for the market, as they have fewer mental cycles free to conduct this specialized work. Because the professionals have much higher salaries than the support staff, replacing the latter with more of the former can be expensive. Sassone crunches the numbers and argues that the organizations he studied could immediately reduce their staffing costs by 15 percent by hiring more support staff, allowing their professionals to become more productive. To Sassone, this analysis provides a compelling answer to the stagnating productivity in the early personal computer age. "Indeed, in many instances firms have used technology to decrease, rather than to increase, intellectual specialization," he writes.

In the intervening decades, the non-specialization issues reported by Sassone have become even worse. Knowledge workers with highly trained skills, and the ability to produce high-value output with their brains, spend much of their time wrangling with computer systems, scheduling meetings, filling out forms, fighting with word processors, struggling with PowerPoint, and of course, above all, sending and receiving digital messages from everyone about everything at all times. We think we've advanced because we no longer need secretaries or typing pools, but we don't factor in how much less bottom-line-boosting work we actually accomplish. I became so frustrated with the loss of specialization in my own world of academia that in 2019 I wrote an article for *The Chronicle of Higher Education*'s magazine that detailed the many ways in which professors' potential intellectual output has been massively decreased due in large part to increased demands enabled by technological advances. My editor gave the piece a provocative title: "Is Email Making Professors Stupid?"[4] It became one of the magazine's most read articles of the year.

Tenner notes that economics textbooks used to introduce the idea of efficient labor markets by telling the story of the best lawyer in town who also happens to be the best typist. The obvious conclusion of the textbook story is that the lawyer would be foolish to not hire a typist. If the lawyer bills $500 an hour and a typist costs $50 an hour, then the lawyer will clearly end up better off outsourcing the typing so she can spend more time on legal work. The arrival of computers in the workplace, it seems, obscured this once obvious reality. We've all become the lawyer spending hours at the typewriter.

In this version of recent workplace history, the arrival of computer technology led to a diminishment of specialization in knowledge work. As the data cited above reinforces, this shift likely created major economic ramifications for this sector. It concerns us here, however, because it also has a significant impact on our journey to move past the hyperactive hive mind workflow. The sheer quantity and variety of tasks in a non-specialized work environment make the hive mind workflow *unavoidable*. When you're faced with an overwhelming incoming stream of unrelated tasks, you don't have enough margin in your schedule to create smarter alternative workflows—there's just too much bombarding you to individually tame everything with optimized processes. In other words, when playing defense against an onslaught of unpredictable obligations, ad hoc, unstructured messaging soon becomes the only reasonable option to prevent yourself from drowning.

This reality creates a nasty, productivity-sapping circularity. When you're overloaded, you're forced to fall back on the flexibility of the hive mind. This workflow, however, leads to even more fragmentation of your attention, making you even less efficient in getting things done. The result: overload increases! As this spiral continues, you'll eventually end up in an overwhelmed state of inefficient desperation, where the idea that you can somehow carefully engineer smarter workflows seems impossible.

If we want to tame the hyperactive hive mind, therefore, we must first tame the trend toward non-specialization. By reducing the number of different obligations you're required to tackle, you'll gain the breathing room needed to then optimize the workflows you deploy to handle what remains—creating a one-two punch of productivity gains that can completely transform your effectiveness or that of your organization. This chapter asks you to embrace the following principle as a crucial step toward moving past the hive mind:

The Specialization Principle

In the knowledge sector, working on fewer things, but doing each thing with more quality and accountability, can be the foundation for significantly more productivity.

The notion that less can somehow lead to more might be uncomfortable at first, especially in the context of a competitive workplace. Some might fear that if they reduce the obligations they accept, or push back on tasks that fall outside their specialty, they'll seem like less of a team player, or perhaps even lose their job. But as Greg McKeown argues in his 2014 bestseller, *Essentialism*, the opposite dynamic might be more likely. He tells the story of an executive he calls Sam, who, in an effort to be a "good citizen" in the Silicon Valley company where he worked, said yes to everything, leading to a severe case of chronic overload. Eventually, the company offered him an early retirement package. Sam considered accepting the package and opening his own consulting practice, but on the advice of a mentor, he decided he would try staying at the firm—except he would stop saying yes to everything and instead accept only work that he thought was essential. He figured he had nothing to lose: if this frustrated his employer, he still had the option of taking the retirement package and moving on.

As McKeown recalls, Sam stopped volunteering for last-minute presentations and ended his habit of being the first to jump in on email threads. He stopped attending conference calls that weren't relevant and learned that just because someone sent him a meeting invitation didn't mean he had to accept. He also started saying no more often. If he didn't think he had the time to do something well, or if it was not a top priority, he would just explain this frankly and decline. Sam worried this was all a little "self-indulgent," but his worries were misplaced. No one got mad at him; they instead admired his clarity. The quality of his work improved to the point where his managers awarded him the biggest bonus of his career.[5]

Sam's story highlights a truism we easily forget: there are few things more valuable than someone who consistently produces valuable output, and few approaches to work more satisfying than being given the room to focus on things that really matter. The strategies that follow in this chapter will help both individuals and organizations shift toward the type of specialization enjoyed by Sam: a state in which you work on less, but do this work much better; a state in which it's possible to move past the hyperactive hive mind to embrace slower and more effective ways of organizing work.

Case Study: Working at the Extremes

In the spring of 2019, I taped an interview for *The Rich Roll Podcast.* During the episode, we talked about some of the ideas explored in this book. I mentioned that the agile methodologies popular among software developers were an interesting example of a more thoughtful alternative to the hyperactive hive mind workflow. A few months later, soon after the episode was released, I received an old-fashioned printed letter in the mail, delivered to my office at Georgetown University. It was from a longtime Silicon Valley programmer and executive named Greg Woodward. He mentioned that he had just heard my interview with Roll and was particularly interested in our discussion of agile methodologies. As he explained, if I really wanted to understand the potential of optimized workflows, I needed to learn about the small software start-up where he was currently the CTO. They deployed a methodology that "takes all of the agile practices and dials them up to a 10." It was called, appropriately enough, *extreme programming*—and it blew my mind.

Woodward began writing code and managing development teams in Silicon Valley in the mid-1990s, after completing his PhD in mechanical engineering at Stanford. His dissertation applied an efficient style of algorithm to run physics simulations relevant to the NASA space shuttle program. He remembers his first decade working in software development, a period of lumbering waterfall schedules and novel-thick feature specifications, as "frustrating." In 2005, looking for a better way to write code, he managed to find a job at Pivotal Labs, a company that had developed a reputation among Silicon Valley insiders for its eccentric but outrageously productive approach to software development. They called it extreme programming, or XP for short. As Woodward explained to me, this methodology is relentlessly optimized. "XP has taken all of the software development best practices," he said, "honed them extensively, and then discarded anything that didn't work." Woodward became a believer. After working with Pivotal for several years, he brought the XP methodology with him to every company he's helped managed since.

Here are some (but not all) of the core ideas behind XP. Programmers who are working on a big project are divided into smaller development teams, typically consisting of no more than ten individuals. In an era where remote work is increasingly common, XP development teams work in the same physical room, where face-to-face communication is prioritized over digital alternatives. "We rarely check email throughout the day," Woodward told me, discussing the development team he currently manages. "Sometimes my developers will literally go days without checking emails." If you need something from someone else on your team, you wait until they look like they're at a natural stopping point and then walk over and ask them. Woodward describes these conversations as "one hundred times more efficient than email."

One complaint I've heard from many software developers is that they're often bothered electronically by people outside their team, such as members of the marketing department, or customers—leading to constant interruptions that pull them away from their primary work of making great software. I asked Woodward how XP handled these distractions. "The project manager serves as the liaison to the rest of the company and customers," he explained. "[These outsiders are] trained to funnel their feature requests, bug reports, and so on through the project manager. . . . The development team is shielded." The project manager places any tasks extracted from these interactions into a priority queue. The team works on tasks from the queue one at a time, deciding after each task is complete which they should tackle next.

One of the more extreme elements of XP is its commitment to what's known as pair programming. XP developers work in groups of two that share a computer. "Unenlightened managers would think that you would get fifty percent of the productivity with two developers working on the same thing at the same computer," Woodward explained. "In actuality, you get three to four times *more* productivity." As he elaborated, the crucial step in programming is not the actual act of mechanically typing commands into a computer, but instead crafting the underlying solution that is then translated into code. When you work with another person, you can push back on each other's ideas—finding flaws and coming up with new angles that might work better.

To illustrate this concept, Woodward gave me a recent example that had occurred a couple of weeks before our conversation. At the time, he explained, he had an idea for a software feature that would provide a "big performance boost." He was thinking about the idea on his commute into his San Francisco office. "By the time I got into work, I thought I had the strategy for implementing the feature pretty much all figured out." Woodward sat down with his pair programming partner for the day and began explaining his idea. They discussed it for forty-five minutes. During the conversation, his partner "poked a few holes" in the strategy and identified a few "edge cases" where it might not work as well as Woodward hoped. His partner then had a breakthrough thought about how they might eliminate one of the message types from the system, sidestepping some of the worst of these issues. By noon, they had the new and improved system up and running. As Woodward explained, "I feel sure that if I had just pursued the design I was thinking of in the car, the implementation would have taken me days; so right there is a three-to-four-times productivity boost." Reflecting on how much more effective programmers are working in pairs, he defaulted to superlatives: "It's amazingly powerful."

Another source of productivity in the XP method is its intensity. When you're working with a partner, you're locked into your work. There's no tactful way to disrupt your focus to check email or idly surf the web, as doing so would leave your partner just sitting there, annoyed, waiting for your attention to return.[6] Furthermore, given a work culture in which you're expected to give your full attention to the problem at hand, with a project manager shielding you from distractions, you end up spending most of your day actually accomplishing hard things. XP is as close to a pure deep work environment as I've ever seen deployed successfully.

Given this intensity, another core tenet of XP is "sustainable pace." Most practitioners of this methodology stick to traditional forty-hour workweeks, in defiance of the Silicon Valley norm of seventy to eighty hours. "With XP, we want you to come in, work super hard for eight hours, then go home and think about other things," Woodward explained. This is not an act of generosity, but instead a recognition of the limits of the human mind. "The average engineer at a non-XP company may only do two to three hours of actual work a day; the rest of the time is spent surfing the web and checking email." When you're actually *working*—not sending messages about work, not attending meetings about work—eight hours in a single day can be quite demanding. When an engineer joins an XP team, Woodward explained, it's common for them to feel "zapped." The intensity of actually focusing for eight hours can be overwhelming, and many XP rookies in their first week head straight to bed when they return home from work. Some engineers never adjust to this culture of focus or, more pressingly, to the extreme accountability that it fosters (there's no slacking off, or hiding a lack of ability, in an XP office). They soon flee for more traditional software companies, where they can hide shortcomings behind bluster, or default to highly visible busyness as an alternative to actually doing the hard but satisfying work of creating valuable output with their brains.

The core of the specialization principle is the idea that less can be more. If you design workflows that allow knowledge workers to spend most of their time focusing without distraction on the activities for which they're trained, you'll produce much more total value than if you instead require these same workers to diffuse their attention among many different activities. This latter course is often the more convenient option in the moment, but rarely the most productive in the long term. Extreme programming underscores the possibility of rejecting this status quo and going all in on specialization.

I imagine that XP development teams must be a pain to deal with in the context of the larger companies that employ them, but it's hard to care about such inconveniences when you see the awe-inspiring pace at which they produce amazing results. "An XP team of eight to ten can do the work of a non-agile team of forty to fifty," Woodward told me. "I've seen it over and over again." These are the productivity boosts at stake in any number of knowledge work fields currently suffering from a severe diminishment of specialization. The remainder of this chapter explores strategies for reaping the benefits of an XP-style specialization.

Do Less, Do Better

In a 2010 essay, Anne Lamott reflected on a particular piece of advice that distresses her writing students.[7] She tells them that creative pursuits can be deeply rewarding, but then she brings up the bad news: "You have to make time to do this." As she elaborates, this requires aspiring writers to understand the harm caused by their "manic forms of connectivity—cell phone, email, text, and Twitter." She then lists other seemingly critical activities that her students might have to reduce—gym trips, housecleaning, consuming news—if they really want to produce something important. This advice might sound straightforward, but Lamott notes that her students often find it challenging. They lead busy lives, and the thought of reducing that busyness seems like a step backward. "I know how addictive busyness [is]," she writes, but this "whirlwind" isn't compatible with producing accomplishments that provide lasting meaning and pride.

In rarefied pursuits like professional writing, the importance of doing fewer minor things so you can do the main things better makes a lot of sense. We like to imagine our novelists cloistered in sheds, toiling in undisrupted concentration, oblivious to the distractions of the world. But we also assume that this lifestyle doesn't generalize to the less romanticized setting of standard office work. The specialization principle argues it should. While it's true that most knowledge work positions lack both the autonomy and clarity of purpose found in writing, the same basic dynamic that drives authors toward a more minimalist set of obligations applies to any cognitive pursuit where you produce value by focusing your brain. In the world of computer programming, XP gained this minimalism through a strict set of rules, enforced by the management, that had been polished over decades of practice. Here we explore a pair of strategies for making progress toward this goal in knowledge work fields where such structures don't yet exist.

Work Reduction Strategy #1:
Outsource What You Don't Do Well

When I was early in the research process for this book, I received an email from an entrepreneur I'll call Scott, who four years earlier had started a successful home décor company. As Scott explained, soon after starting the company, he found himself suffering from chronic overload. "I did all the things most people do with start-ups," he told me. "I had a bunch of employees, reached out to lots of people for marketing and networking, and had a very active Instagram." He knew his value was in designing elegant and innovative furniture, but he was instead "spending [his] days in constant communication."

At some point, perhaps after one too many phone conferences with his Instagram consultants, Scott decided he was done with forced busyness. "I was no longer doing what I set off to do." In response, he sought ways to radically pare down his day-to-day responsibilities. His first move was to sign an exclusive wholesale agreement with a single national retail chain. Not only did this vastly simplify distribution, but it removed his company's need to deal with marketing, sales, and customer service. He then found a small number of manufacturing partners with large enough workforces to easily handle their typical orders.

Scott is "crystal clear and up-front" with these partners about what he wants, and then empowers them to make their own decisions to help keep the business moving. "I don't want to be a linchpin," he explains. To underscore the importance of this delegation, he told me the story of a meeting in which he was one of ten attendees. The objective: to confirm a new black glaze to use on one of their products. "It was infuriating," he said. "Trust *one* person to make that decision, stop cc'ing everyone on emails, and get to work!"

Scott reports that he now gets "only a few" emails a day. He dedicates his reclaimed mental bandwidth to the areas where he thinks he can bring the most value: "New design projects, big strategic decisions, and innovation solutions to age-old design problems." By outsourcing so much of his business to retail and manufacturing partners, Scott reduced the profit margin he sees. If he ran everything in-house, he could, given enough attention, squeeze out more efficiency and keep more of the revenue. He's also given up some control. He no longer individually curates the brand's image, as he did in his days of relentless Instagram engagement, and he has to work with the material limitations of his manufacturing partners. But Scott doesn't care. By focusing almost all his energy on his specialty—designing great products and making big picture strategic decisions—the long-term profitability of his company is vastly increased compared with the alternative scenario where all this thinking gets done in small slivers of time between endless meetings about glazing decisions.

Scott's story highlights an effective strategy for becoming more specialized in your work: attempt to outsource the time-consuming things that you don't do well. The key obstacle to overcome in applying this strategy is that you'll likely pay a price in the short term before you reap long-term benefits. Scott, for example, had to give up profit margin and some control over his business to create a company that would be massively more successful over time.

In many cases, the price you pay to outsource comes directly out of your pocket. In 2016, podcaster and entrepreneur Pat Flynn reached a tipping point with his email inbox. He remembered when he used to embrace the idea of *inbox zero*: the objective of reducing your email inbox back down to empty at the end of each day. At some point, as demands on his time from partners and listeners increased, he made *inbox 100* his new goal. Then one day he noticed his unread messages had ballooned to over nine thousand. He was trying to run a business but had instead become a professional email manager.

His solution was to hire a full-time executive assistant. As Flynn details in a podcast episode titled "9000 Unread Emails to Inbox Zero," it took him and his assistant several weeks to work out a system for her to successfully manage his inbox.[8] They produced a rule book that allowed her to handle almost every message on her own, bringing to Flynn's attention only what required his input. Most important, Flynn was freed from the sense that if he wasn't constantly checking his inbox, elements of his business might suffer. Hiring a high-end executive assistant is expensive. But Flynn had come to a similar conclusion as Scott: If he wasn't able to spend significant time on the specialized activities on which his business was built, then what was the point of running that business?

If you run your own business or freelance, once you adopt this mindset that unskilled activities slow down your growth, you'll begin to notice numerous opportunities to reduce non-vital efforts. Other examples I've encountered include hiring a bookkeeper to handle accounting and invoices, using a virtual assistant to book meetings and travel, having a web designer on retainer to keep your web operations humming, using social media consultants to handle your online branding, or bringing on experienced customer service representatives, empowered to make decisions without your input. The productivity writer Laura Vanderkam argues that we should in general be more aggressive in identifying work that can be delegated. "For instance, it doesn't make sense for licensed, experienced teachers to be grading most worksheets," she writes. "Automating this (via technology) or else hiring graders to report back the results would free up teachers to dream up better lessons and share best practices."[9] Once you start looking for opportunities to off-load nonessential tasks, you'll be surprised by how many you find.

All these outsourcing activities cost money, and some take you out of the loop on issues you might be used to monitoring, but they all have the potential to allow you to spend more time on the small number of things that actually move the needle in your professional context. This strategy is not for everyone. But if you have the luxury of autonomy over your work life, then realize that you don't have to tolerate overload. Outsource what you can so you can excel at what you can't.

Work Reduction Strategy #2: Trade Accountability for Autonomy

The strategy we just discussed is well suited for those who are their own bosses, but what about those suffering from chronic overload within large organizations? I learned an interesting solution for this common scenario from a reader I'll call Amanda, who has been working at a global engineering design firm since 2009. As Amanda explained when she contacted me, during the first six years of her job, she kept her head down and tried to earn the trust of her bosses by producing the best work possible. This wasn't easy given the culture of chronic overload in her office.

As Amanda elaborated, there are two categories of work possible at her firm. The first category she calls "reactive, easy, brain-dead work." As she explains: "This is where you show up, check your email, do what the emails tell you to all day, and then go home." The second category she calls "intentional, difficult, focused, creative work," which is when you "spend time thinking about what's the most important, long-term, impactful thing for you to do for your big projects." In the office where she works, the first type dominates. There's an expectation that you keep up with your inbox—"We use email a lot"—and once you're stuck monitoring the constant influx of random tasks and requests, you never quite make it over to that second category.

Somehow, amid this scrum of hive mind chatter and chronic overload, Amanda managed to carve out a valuable niche for herself within the company. The entire engineering industry was going through a shift from 2D to 3D information models, and Amanda was helping her company with this transition—fielding questions and assisting individual projects. During this period, she read my 2012 book, *So Good They Can't Ignore You*, which suggests among other things that once you have made yourself valuable to your organization, you should use this *career capital* as leverage to remake your position into something more satisfying. Inspired but nervous, Amanda proposed to her bosses that she shift into a more strategic role, where instead of fielding random questions and helping with individual projects, she would work on technology strategy for whole regions. In this role, she would be entirely remote, working on a small number of long-term projects at a time.

Amanda assumed her bosses would turn down her request, and she was prepared to leave the company to offer a similar service as a consultant. To her surprise, they agreed to give the new arrangement a trial. "Since I'm remote, I can no longer rely on 'showing up' functioning as a measure of my value to the company," Amanda explained. "It's all what I produce. So I turn off email, I put my phone on airplane mode, I give my colleagues emergency contacts, and then I focus." She left behind brain-dead work and committed herself fully to the alternative.

There's both opportunity and danger in Amanda's arrangement. The opportunity, of course, is that the combination of her reduced portfolio and results-oriented evaluations gives her the ability to remove herself from the hyperactive hive mind workflow. "Since I don't have any supervision over my daily routine," she said, "I have a lot of freedom to chart the shortest course to where I think I need to be to deliver maximum value." This makes it possible for her to vastly increase her value to her company, which, in a virtuous cycle, can gain her even more autonomy.

The danger, of course, is that now she *has* to produce. Her note about the comfort of "showing up" to demonstrate value is more than just a casual dismissal of normal work culture. For many people, this strategy provides a professional safety net. Busyness is controllable: if you decide to be visibly busy, you know with certainty that you can accomplish this goal. Producing high-value results under scrutiny, as Amanda is now committed to doing, is much more demanding! Just deciding to produce valuable things is not enough to ensure that you'll pull it off. Recall our XP case study, where Greg Woodward noted that a lot of developers dislike the extreme environment and end up leaving after a few weeks. The aspect that most distresses them? The transparency. You're either producing good code, or you're obviously not. Some are simply not comfortable with this blunt assessment of what they're actually accomplishing.

Amanda's general strategy of offering accountability to gain autonomy, therefore, is a powerful approach to escaping chronic overload, but it's also risky. If you're entrenched in a large organization where chronic overload reigns, and you've developed an expertise that obviously makes you valuable, then this strategy may be one of your best moves to gain the breathing room needed to remake your workflow into something more effective. You don't necessarily have to match Amanda's boldness when applying this strategy. Sometimes even just volunteering for a large initiative provides you enough cover to ignore messages and turn down meeting invites without annoying people, as you now have an unassailable excuse: "I would, but am swamped trying to handle [big thing]." But it's hard to avoid the underlying economics: to gain something valuable like autonomy means you have to offer something unambiguously valuable in return. You must, in other words, become accountable for what you produce if you want the freedom to improve how you do so.

There are many ways to combat the overload created by diminished specialization. The strategies explored here get straight to the value proposition of knowledge work. Not all efforts create the same value for your organization. If you spend more time on the high-value activities at the expense of spending less time on the low-value activities, you'll produce more value overall. In the short term, of course, there are other costs, such as up-front expenses, or inconveniences to your colleagues, or, as in Amanda's case, reduced job security. But as Anne Lamott emphasizes to her writing students: it's almost always worth it. The rewards of becoming significantly more effective at the things that really count will swamp the pain of overcoming the minor obstacles this specialization generates. Less *can* be more; the trick is building up the courage to embrace this in your own work life.

Sprint, Don't Wander

One of the key ideas from our extreme programming case study was the importance of working on one objective at a time, without interruption, until it's complete. This commitment to working in *sprints* is now widely held throughout the software development world, even in teams that don't adopt the full set of strict XP rules. The history of sprinting can be traced back to the creation of Scrum, one of the original agile methodologies for software development, back in the 1990s. During a Scrum sprint, a team works exclusively on a single specific deliverable, such as adding a new feature to a software product—no complex task lists, schedules filled with meetings, or intricate daily planning processes are needed.[10] This productivity hack has become an accepted best practice in this field. It's now widely agreed that it would be inappropriate to bombard a development team in the middle of a sprint with calendar invites for meetings, or to badger them via email to help out with unrelated projects. In most software companies, it's completely reasonable for developers to be unresponsive during a sprint, as the culture is one that accepts that this is the best application of their energy at the moment.

Software development, of course, is a highly specific endeavor. The question is whether this particular idea—working in sprints on a single objective—can apply beyond the world of programming as a general method for achieving more specialized work. Fortunately for our purposes, a partner at a tech-focused investment fund has spent the past decade exploring this exact question.

In 2009, Google started a venture capital fund to invest some of its earnings into up-and-coming tech start-ups. It was called Google Ventures. In 2015, the fund was spun off as a standalone entity, now called just GV, with Google's parent company, Alphabet, remaining its only limited partner (source of money). This close connection between GV and Google makes it inevitable that ideas from the search giant's software culture would make their way into the culture of the fund. One such idea to follow this path was the value of sprints.[11]

A GV partner named Jake Knapp knew a lot about sprints in software development. In his previous role at Google, he'd helped teams implement this strategy to increase their effectiveness. When Knapp transitioned to GV, he began experimenting with ways to apply this tool to other types of business challenges. He eventually came up with a revised version of the strategy that he called the "design sprint." The goal of the design sprint is to help companies efficiently answer critical questions by requiring executives to dedicate five consecutive days of (nearly) uninterrupted concentration to the problem at hand. In 2016, having deployed these sprints with over one hundred of their portfolio companies, Knapp and fellow GV partners John Zeratsky and Braden Kowitz introduced the design sprint methodology to a larger audience with their book *Sprint: How to Solve Big Problems and Test New Ideas in Just Five Days.*[12]

Design sprints are meant to help you figure out where your team or organization should focus its efforts. In a traditional workplace, these decisions typically unfold over months of meetings and debates, augmented with numerous email threads, ultimately leading to costly investments in new products or strategies that all too often fall short. A design sprint attempts to compress this work, from the initial debates all the way to receiving market feedback on the resulting decisions, into one highly efficient workweek. On the first day, you figure out the problem you're trying to solve. On the second day, you sketch out competing solutions. On the third day, you make the tough decision about which solution you want to explore, transforming it into a hypothesis that can be tested. On the fourth day, you throw together a rough prototype that allows you to test the hypothesis, and on the fifth and final day, you put real clients in front of the prototype and learn from their feedback. These sprints have been used to test new products, but they've also been used to try out advertising strategies and even to determine whether there's a reasonable market for a given idea.

The design sprint encourages specialization, as practitioners are asked to concentrate for five days in a row on a single important problem. Curious about the degree to which this single-minded focus is actually achieved, I got in touch with Jake Knapp and asked him a question I felt got to the core of this issue: "Are people still checking email during design sprints?" He explained that the hard rule during sprint sessions is "no laptops, no phones, no tablets, nothing." The only exception is the use of computers on the fourth day, if needed, to construct a prototype. When Knapp coaches a team through a sprint, he tells them to set out-of-office autoresponders so they won't be stressed out by their lack of connectivity. (He calls these autoresponders a "pressure release valve" for participants worried about stepping away from the constant thrum of the hyperactive hive mind.)

Participants *are* allowed to use devices before and after the sprint sessions, which last from 10:00 a.m. to 5:00 p.m. They may also check devices during breaks, but they must do so outside the room where the sessions occur. Knapp told me that he suspects a more extreme approach, in which communication outside the team is banned altogether throughout the week, could "yield even deeper focus and better results." But he thought it might be a "hard sell" to persuade a group of modern knowledge workers to sign up for five days of complete disconnection. After a beat, however, he noted that once they "experienced the benefits" of such disconnection, the idea might start seeming less extreme.

––––––

Jake Knapp's design sprint process works great for making high-stakes decisions about future directions for your business, but there are many other areas in knowledge work where sprints could prove effective. I talked with a communication consultant, for example, who told me that when her firm took on major event-planning contracts, the partner in charge of the project would schedule an in-office workshop, sometimes lasting multiple days, in which the team would sequester itself to work out the best possible game plan for the event. One could imagine similar sprints being deployed by academic research teams trying to make progress on a big open problem. Indeed, in *Deep Work*, I discuss how Wharton professor Adam Grant used exactly this strategy to become one of the youngest professors to earn tenure in Wharton's history.

Most knowledge workers are so entangled in obligations and commitments and legacy methods of getting things done that there's often no easy way to reduce this load in one bold move. Sprint processes offer an indirect alternative. If you put in place a culture of design sprint–style sessions, you don't eliminate the other work in the short term, but you do constrain its impact—allowing you to switch back and forth between a specialized existence and a hyperactive one (which is better than always being in the latter state).

Regular sprints also support longer-term changes to your workload by making it easier for individual knowledge workers to lobby for fewer obligations overall. In a standard hyperactive hive mind–style office, asking for less work might come across as laziness (*why do you get to do less?*). In a culture where sprints are common, however, you can point to the massive value these focused pushes are producing, and frame the minutiae that define chronic overload as impediments to this value. Once you can establish a clear dichotomy between convenient busyness and bottom-line-boosting sprints, it becomes harder to justify the former as more important.

For any sprint process to succeed requires buy-in from everyone involved. When you're in a sprint, you must trust that you really can step away from your inbox and chat channels, and do this without generating frustration or annoyance. If you're self-employed, you must clearly explain to your clients that your work is fundamentally bimodal, and during the sprint modes, you cannot be reached. If you work for a larger organization, enthusiasm for sprints must emanate from the top. But once this regular specialization is embraced, its benefits will soon become apparent. As Jake Knapp explained to me, one of the best things about helping teams run sprints is the enthusiasm it generates from the participants. Chronic overload makes us miserable. When we're given a chance to escape its frustrating clutches and instead do what we were trained to do, to apply our skills to produce the best possible results, work transforms from a chore into something we actually find satisfying.

Budget Attention

As mentioned earlier, in 2019 I published an article in *The Chronicle Review* titled "Is Email Making Professors Stupid?" The article discussed more than just email. I examined the many different ways in which the haphazardly constructed workflows common in academia sap professors of their ability to be productive. One of the topics I tackled was service. At most universities, professors dedicate some of their time to activities that help the school function, such as reviewing applications, or sitting on committees, or participating in self-governance. These obligations are essential to academic life. The problem, however, is that there are few controls on how these tasks are assigned. "A typical approach to service is to say 'yes' to a fire hose of incoming requests," I wrote, "until you become so overcommitted that you retreat in desperation to catch up."

In an essay written in response to my *Chronicle* article, a philosophy professor named Bruce Janz elaborated on the problem of overwhelming service obligations in higher education, writing:

It comes from the attitudes of many of those administrators, who think that their new streamlined procedure is the greatest thing ever and will only require just a little form or a little input by faculty, or a little something else. It is caused by . . . other committees [formed] to mentor or help or strategize or support or brainstorm or any number of other things, each of which requires just a little more from the same people. It comes from none of these administrative committees seeing any incentive to combine or rationalize anything, so the same work has to be done over and over.[13]

As Janz's analysis points out, a major source of service overload in academia is the asymmetry inherent in asking for someone's help. If you run an administrative unit within a university, or are tasked with forming a committee, then from your perspective, asking me or Bruce Janz to attend some meetings or participate in a survey or review some files seems completely reasonable. You're not demanding a huge time commitment, and our minor assistance is crucial for you to succeed with your major objective. For us to say no would seem uncivil, if not downright antisocial.

The problem, of course, is that these requests accumulate. If two dozen other units and committees all make these same reasonable requests, suddenly we're desperately overwhelmed by work that has little to do with our main objectives of research and teaching—a recipe not just for inefficiency, but outright frustration.

This dynamic extends beyond academia. Knowledge workers in general are pushed into chronic overload by similar asymmetries. It's so easy for the marketing department to shoot over a meeting invite to solicit your opinion on a new product campaign, or for your boss to send a quick email asking you to organize a lunch seminar series for your team. To say no to any one of these requests in isolation makes you seem curmudgeonly or lazy. But the sum total of many such "simple" requests leads you to become constantly overwhelmed by everything that has to get done.

In the extreme programming case study, the solution to this problem was to essentially forbid people in the company from directly asking the programmers to do things. Their focus is supposed to remain locked into implementing the feature at the top of their priority queue. If you need something from them, you can talk to their project manager, who will figure out what's actually reasonable to bother them about, all the while trying to protect their primary goal of producing code.

Sadly, this model doesn't necessarily extend to all knowledge work positions. If professors stopped doing all service, for example, the university would stop functioning. Similarly, while the programmers in an XP shop can afford to be isolated, many other knowledge workers really must be available to field questions and requests, as this is the essence of collaboration. What's needed is an idea that enables these work requests to exist, but prevents any one person from having to accept too many. In my article, I proposed one such idea.

"One solution is to directly confront the zero sum trade-off generated by service obligations," I wrote. "Professors have a fixed amount of time. . . . Instead of ignoring this reality, we should clearly articulate these trade-offs by specifying the exact amount of time a faculty member is expected to devote to service each year." As I then explained, in this plan, professors would not be allowed to exceed whatever time budget they had agreed on with their department chair for the semester.

My service budget proposal was meant more as a thought experiment than a concrete plan, but it highlights a crucial reality about overload: it's common, in part, because its magnitude is hidden. Professors are always vaguely and persistently busy. In this undifferentiated mass of activity, it's easy to push just *one more thing* onto someone else's plate. But now imagine, for the sake of argument, that a new rule was enacted that demanded that service time was carefully measured and not allowed to exceed a fixed budget without the explicit permission of your dean. Reaching a state of extreme service overload would become more difficult in this scenario. If you're the dean, for example, and you've invested a lot of money in bringing a top scholar to your university, when you're presented with a request to increase her weekly service budget to thirty hours so she can keep up with all her different service requests, you'd have a hard time signing that form! When facing stark numbers, it becomes difficult to justify overload—why bother hiring a hotshot if the bulk of their time is spent doing administrative work? When these numbers are obfuscated, it's much easier to just shrug about the reality that we're all busy.

In knowledge work more generally, approximating something like my hypothetical service budget could be a powerful strategy for pushing back against overload. There are three keys for a strategy of this type to work. First, it must start from the premise that your time and attention are limited. Second, it must quantify how much of your time and attention is currently dedicated to whatever category of work you're attempting to budget. And third, whoever is responsible for determining how much work of this type you have to do must confront your current commitments when asking you to do more, even if this person is you.[14]

One minor area in academia where strategies of this type are already prevalent is peer review requests. Academic publishing depends on peer review by professors in the relevant field. Accordingly, most professors receive a lot of requests to review articles. A common strategy to tame these demands is to fix a *quota* of how many reviews you do per semester. Once you hit your quota, you politely decline additional requests, explaining that you've hit your limit. This approach works well because it provides the reason why you cannot take on more work, meaning that the only way a requester can pressure you into taking on a review anyway is to implicitly argue that your reason isn't good.

If you ask me to review a paper, and I simply say, "I don't know—I'm really busy," it would be easy for you to keep pushing: "I know, but it's really important to me. Could you fit this in?" On the other hand, if I say, "I wish I could, but I already hit my quota of ten paper reviews per semester," for you to push back, you would have to argue: "You should be reviewing more than ten papers a semester." Which is not a strong argument, as ten is a lot of papers, and a quota of that level is quite reasonable.

Moving beyond academia, another budgeting strategy I've seen used with great success is the idea of deep-to-shallow work ratios, which I first proposed in my book *Deep Work*. The idea is to agree in advance with your supervisor how many hours each week should be spent on the core skilled activities for which you were hired, and how much on other types of shallower support or administrative work. The goal is to seek the balance that maximizes your value to your organization. You then measure and categorize your work hours and report back how close you came to achieving your optimal ratio.

After *Deep Work* was published, many readers reported success with this strategy. Crucial to its effectiveness is the way in which it forces your supervisor to get specific about workloads. Assuming you're good at something valuable, your supervisor is not going to insist on a work ratio made up almost entirely of shallow work, as this is self-evidently absurd when presented clearly. When you come back and report that according to your measurements this is what's currently happening with your time, it becomes much easier to authorize changes that will directly ease up the overload you're suffering, as the alternative would be for the supervisor to admit that your skewed ratio is in fact best for the organization (which it almost certainly is not).

Meeting budgets are also common. The idea is to block off on your calendar the times you're available for meetings. These blocks should add up to the total amount of time you think is reasonable to spend in meetings in a given week. When meetings are subsequently requested, you schedule them *only* in these slots, making meeting overload impossible. If you use a shared calendar or an online scheduling tool, you're saved from even having to say no; the person trying to set up the meeting will see that all your time slots are filled.

This strategy is especially popular among entrepreneurs who have great autonomy in their work. One company founder I know deploys a simple rule for his staff and clients: no meetings before noon. This allows him to get important work done without interruption every single day. Another founder I know is even more extreme: his schedule for meetings with people outside his company has available slots only on Thursday afternoons. It's not uncommon to have to wait weeks until his next available free time. He's completely unapologetic; he has a business to build.

The task boards discussed in the process principle chapter also provide a powerful tool for implementing workload budgets. Using a task board to organize work offers two benefits in this context: it makes it easy to determine how much work each person is currently doing, and it has a structured system for how these work assignments are updated, usually in the form of a status meeting attended by everyone. Imagine you're working on a team that uses task boards. If you're already tackling a heavy workload, this will be immediately clear on the board—making it much harder for your team leader to overload you, especially if other people have lighter loads. In the situation where overloading you is necessary, the magnitude of what you're being asked to do is unambiguous, meaning you'll receive the credit due for your efforts. In a hyperactive hive mind workplace, on the other hand, where these tasks are distributed in an ad hoc manner through emails, you could easily find yourself not only overloaded, but unrecognized for this sacrifice.

This latter point is critical, as it leads to inequities that are often overlooked. As I argued in the opening to chapter 5, when you run an office haphazardly, a Hobbesian dynamic arises in which those who are most brash and disagreeable get away with doing less work, while their more reasonable peers become overloaded. The late Nobel Prize–winning physicist Richard Feynman famously told an interviewer that his strategy for minimizing committee work was to do it really poorly so that people would eventually stop asking him for help. Few people would be comfortable with such brazen misanthropy. Do we really want to reward those who are?

An important study on this topic, published by a research team headed by Linda Babcock of Carnegie Mellon University, documented how this dynamic disproportionately affects women.[15] In both field and laboratory studies, the researchers found that women are more likely to volunteer for "non-promotable" service tasks than men. Women are also asked to do these tasks more frequently than men, and say yes more often when asked. "This can have serious consequences for women," the researchers note. "If they are disproportionately saddled with work that has little visibility or impact, it will take them much longer to advance in their careers."

Shielding our eyes to how work gets allocated can make things more convenient in the moment. If I'm trying to assign a project, I'd prefer not to confront the reality of how much work my team members are already doing—I just want it done! But the convenience of this obfuscation has real costs. It stymies moves toward productivity-boosting specialization and can disproportionately punish some groups over others. When you're forced to confront the quantitative realities of how much work is being done, casually pushing someone's load to an extreme level becomes itself more of an extreme act. Accountability, in other words, can go a long way toward achieving reasonability when it comes to how many obligations we expect knowledge workers to handle.

Supercharge Support

A key question to ask about any attempted shift toward specialization is what happens to the leftover work once everyone starts doing less? Many of these tasks will simply disappear as it becomes clear that they're not actually that important to producing valuable output. Programmers who deploy extreme programming, for example, spend much less time in meetings and answering emails than their peers, but their companies seem to do just fine without this extra activity. A shift toward a more focused workload, however, will inevitably orphan some administrative chores that cannot be eliminated. One solution to handling this remaining work is to reverse the trend toward diminishing intellectual specialization first observed by Edward Tenner and Peter Sassone, and instead *increase* support staff.

Most modern knowledge work organizations treat individuals as general-purpose computers that execute a turbulent mixture of value-producing and administrative tasks—often unequally distributed, and not at all optimized for any particular big picture objective. In a *specialized organization*, by contrast, the workforce is more bimodal, with one group focused almost exclusively on producing high-value output—like developers in an XP shop—and another group focused almost exclusively on handling all the other logistical work needed to keep the organization running. As Sassone's research points out, hiring more support staff in this manner won't necessarily decrease profitability. When you allow specialists to work with more focus, they produce more, and this extra value can more than compensate for the cost of maintaining dedicated support. Our rush to cut payrolls by having everyone handle their own administrative work through computer interfaces provided only the illusion of streamlining. These top-line numbers obscured the degree to which the cognitive gears that produce value in knowledge work began to grind and stick under these new demands.

Returning to a culture that allows more separation between specialized and administrative work is crucial to moving past the hyperactive hive mind and significantly improving productivity. This doesn't mean, however, that we must retreat to the lumbering *Mad Men*-style support setups that ruled before the office computer revolution—in which dedicated assistants sat at desks outside every office, executives dictated memos, and runners pushing mail carts and delivering coffees were ubiquitous. Technology has advanced significantly during the intervening decades to enable a much more sophisticated vision of support. As we return to a state of specialization, we should be able to supercharge the support roles that enable this shift in ways that make these roles much more efficient and satisfying for those involved.

Here are some ideas for how we might accomplish this goal.

Supercharging Idea #1: Structure Support

Veronica used to work as a customer service representative for a university, responsible for answering inquiries and processing orders. Her office handled all communication using email. "I would sort of go to work and 'finish' all my emails," Veronica told me when I interviewed her for this book. "Sometimes I would sit in my chair for eight hours straight or more, just so I could clear my inbox." Her work, in other words, was an exercise in overload—a constant influx of varied tasks that she struggled to tame. At the time, she explained, she thought this was just "normal work." Like many support staff members who mainly interact with the world through an inbox, she had a hard time understanding how else her type of job could be done.

Then she switched to a public sector position in the local court system. The general type of work was similar to her university role: she processed legal fees and updated case files. But the feel of the work was much different for one important reason: her new job didn't use any electronic communication in the office. As Veronica explained, there was a custom-built case management system where information about cases was entered and updated. The communication between support staff, however, was all delivered physically. The various tasks the staff executed were each associated with a specific workflow in which specific pieces of paper would be passed from one person to another. In some cases, for legal reasons, these handoffs required signatures or extra copies to be filed to maintain a paper trail. If you had an informal question, you walked over to the relevant person and asked them.

One could argue that the individual steps of these old-fashioned workflows could be made more efficient if implemented using digital networks. It seems like a waste of time to physically walk a form to someone's office when you could instead, for example, attach a PDF to an email. But having previously worked in an office where *everything* transpired in the supposedly more efficient world of email, Veronica wasn't so sure. She described the work in her new office as "transactional." If someone needed something, they brought it to you in person, and you would deal with it right then until done. It might be literally slower to walk a form down the hall than to email it, but from a productivity perspective, Veronica didn't feel less effective. When you're no longer required to fragment your attention by jumping back and forth between what's in front of you at the moment and any number of asynchronous conversations piling unpredictably in your inbox, each discrete task takes less total time.

Veronica also reported other, less tangible benefits of an office without email. "Because we all interact with each other in person throughout the day, there's more camaraderie," she said, unlike the isolation she felt at the old job, where her days were spent staring at a screen. There's also a great psychological benefit to avoiding inboxes full of obligations arriving faster than you can handle them. "The best result is that we do all of our work in the office," she told me. "There is no way to bring any kind of work home."

The lesson we should extract from Veronica's story is not that it's smart to revert to paper-based offices. It's instead that when it comes to support, workflows matter. Both of Veronica's jobs involved roughly the same type of support work, but the first defaulted to the hyperactive hive mind, while the second structured the efforts more carefully. The difference was stark: the first job made Veronica feel unhappy and ineffective, while the second reversed these faults.

In order to build a sustainable specialized organization, support roles need these types of structured processes. Hiring new support staff and then simply pointing them to an inbox and saying "Be useful" is a recipe for misery and high turnover. To succeed in reintroducing these roles requires more systematic workflows. The details of how these processes operate can differ significantly depending on the specific type of work. Generally speaking, however, processes should offer clarity about each step. A support staffer should not be faced with ambiguity about what to do next, as such uncertainty drains energy and can generate endless and frustrating ad hoc conversations.

In addition, it's important to remember that transactional work typically trumps concurrent efforts. If it's possible, set up a process that allows a support staffer to work on one thing at a time until done, and to deal with issues in person (not through back-and-forth messaging). In the moment, it might seem like the ability to just fire off messages would be a real time-saver, but when everyone is doing the same thing, everyone ends up buried in an inbox, struggling to make reasonable progress on anything.

Supercharging Idea #2:
Build Smart Interfaces Between Support and Specialists

To help keep my Georgetown University inbox reasonable, I set up a Gmail filter to automatically move administrative announcements out of my main inbox and label them for me to review later. My process for building this filter was simple: every time an administrative message made it to my main inbox, I would add the sender's address to my filter's rule. I was soon overwhelmed. I currently have twenty-seven different Georgetown email addresses included in my filter—each of which is a regular source of administrative announcements. At some point, I just gave up trying to update my filter: there were simply too many different entities vying for a share of my attention.

The issue at my university, which is common in most large knowledge work organizations, is that each of the support units operates more or less as a standalone entity, focused on trying to accomplish its own internal objectives as efficiently as possible. For the more than twenty-seven units that regularly send me emails, it makes perfect sense to send those messages. They have information they need to spread, and putting it in a bulk email is clearly an efficient way for them to accomplish their goal.

These same issues occur when interactions go in the opposite direction. Anyone who works for a large organization is familiar with the pain of struggling with a complex and ambiguous form that a support unit requires you to fill out to request some service. Once again, when we treat each such unit as a mini standalone entity trying to accomplish its individual objectives as effectively as possible, these complex forms make sense—if support staff can get everyone to enter information in a format maximally useful to them, they'll be able to process it more easily.

The problem, of course, is that these support units aren't standalone entities: they work within a larger organization, and their internal efficiency doesn't necessarily impact the bottom line. In most knowledge work settings, it's the specialists who directly produce the valuable output that sustains their organization. Given this reality, a better objective for support units would be the following: to effectively fulfill their administrative duties with *as small an impact as possible* on the specialists' main work obligations. If taken seriously, this metric might mean a given support unit needs to make its own work *less* efficient to better serve the organization.

The contact point where this idea becomes relevant is the various *interfaces* through which specialists interact with support staff. As underscored by my above mailing list example, if every unit is left to design these interfaces in a manner that makes its own operation easiest, soon everyone ends up deluged with more communication than they can reasonably handle. A better interface in this case might be a shared weekly newsletter that includes summaries of all relevant announcements with links to more details for those who are interested. This rule makes the operations of the support units slightly harder, as they can't simply blast out announcements whenever they want, but the information still gets spread, and this time it's done in a way that reduces interruption.

For a more extreme example, imagine an organization in which requests for a specialist's time and attention—such as the parking office asking them to fill out parking renewal forms, or the travel office demanding preregistration of all travel—go to some sort of *attention capital ombudsman* who can weed out unnecessary requests, consolidate others, and perhaps even negotiate with support units to make their requests easier to complete. This might sound absurd, but is it? Google, for example, already invests heavily in free food and subsidized dry cleaning to help its high-paid specialist developers produce more value. Against that backdrop, the cost of an ombudsman of this type might be minor relative to the additional value it would unlock.

Going the other direction, one might imagine also optimizing the interfaces specialists use to contact support units, with the goal of minimizing the impact on the specialists' time and attention. In the world of consumer interaction, there has been a push over the past decade toward what's known as *invisible UI*—interfaces that are so simple and flexible that the consumer doesn't even think of them as interfaces at all. Perhaps the most common current examples of invisible UIs are digital assistant appliances like Alexa and Google Home. Instead of requiring you to navigate through menus on a computer screen to find some information, or send a message, or play some music, you can ask out loud for what you want, and the appliance will figure out what you need. In the context of a large organization, imagine if instead of wrangling a complex web interface to request a vacation or submit a grant proposal, you could just type into a chat window what you're trying to do, and someone will stop by your office or call you to get the additional information they need.[16]

The examples above are meant only to prompt more concrete thinking. The details of how you actually optimize these interfaces depend on your specific type of work. A more abstract way to think about this optimization is to imagine that each support unit maintains a counter that, through some magic, is able to track the total number of minutes of attention the unit has commandeered from other employees so far that week. The goal could then be simply to minimize that number as much as possible while still executing core functions. No such counters exist, of course, but this neatly captures the shift in thinking this approach to support induces.

Finally, I should admit to feeling some trepidation about these concepts. An ethical pitfall in moving toward more specialization is the fear of creating a sharp divide between specialists who enjoy their work and an underclass of support professionals confined to overload. My suggestion here that support units should be willing to make their own work harder to make specialists' work easier, in addition to being self-serving, seems to nudge our discussion toward this pitfall. With this in mind, I want to propose two defenses.

First, reorienting support staff to optimize the production of specialists doesn't necessarily need to make the work life of the former more miserable. My first idea in this section dealt with ways to introduce more structure into support processes to sidestep hyperactive hive mind overload. That idea still applies: changing your objective from making your own unit as efficient as possible to helping your organization produce as much value as possible doesn't need to reduce the quality or sustainability of the work involved.

My second defense is that whether or not we like this suggestion, it's an economic reality. If a knowledge work organization is producing valuable cognitive output in a competitive marketplace, then it's self-evident that having support units prioritize this output will make an organization more successful than if it instead allowed every unit to focus myopically on its own internal objectives. To be clear, no unit should be disrespected or treated as less important, and nobody should ever have to tolerate a misery-inducing work environment. But beyond these fundamental principles, it's also true that companies aren't democracies, and employees are not all necessarily guaranteed the same types of liberties surrounding their efforts. Put more bluntly: no knowledge work organization ever conquered a market because of the internal efficiency of its HR department.

Supercharging Idea #3:
As a Last Resort, Simulate Your Own Support Staff

The two preceding ideas concern the role of support staff in large knowledge work organizations. Putting these ideas into action requires that you're in a position of power—perhaps CEO or head of a large division. If you're instead an employee without this control, but still suffering because you don't have enough support, you're not entirely out of luck. In this situation, as a last-resort measure, I suggest *simulating* your own support staff.

One way to accomplish this goal is to partition your time into two separate categories: specialist and support. For example, perhaps 12:00 to 1:00 p.m. and 3:00 to 5:00 p.m. are support hours. During all other hours, you act as if you work in a specialized organization: focus only on skilled work that directly produces value. Don't answer administrative emails or attend administrative meetings—just work on what you do best, as if you're an XP developer. During the support hours, by contrast, act as if you're a full-time support staffer whose objective is to make your specialist alter ego as effective as possible. Don't simply get lost in emails during these times, but actually follow the advice given above and put in place processes for minimizing the sense of overload you experience juggling these logistical matters. (The process principle chapter provides some specific strategies individuals can deploy toward this purpose.) You can even optimize the interfaces between these two sides of your work life by putting in place simple collection bins where your specialist self can store administrative work to be later tackled by your support self. Maybe you keep a text file for this purpose, or an actual plastic collection bin on your desk where you can drop forms, or reminders you jot down on paper (an idea originally proposed by David Allen).

If you want to get more advanced, consider using two separate email addresses. I do this to some degree in my role as a professor. I have an email address for the georgetown.edu domain that was assigned to me by the university. This is where I receive all official university correspondence, and I use it, as much as possible, for administrative issues. I also have an address hosted by a server in our department for the cs.georgetown.edu domain. I use this to interact with other professors, the students and postdocs I supervise, and my research collaborators. The former address belongs to my support self; the latter to my specialist self.

Another advanced tactic is to assign entire days to these roles. Perhaps Tuesday and Thursday are support days, and Monday, Wednesday, and Friday are specialist days. Not every job allows such a dramatic split in your behavior, but if yours does, there's great clarity in such a clean division. I've even met practitioners of this rule who use different locations—coming into the office for support days, for example, and working from home when in their specialist role.

This idea of pretending to be two different types of workers might seem heavy-handed, but there's a surprising amount of efficiency to be gained by isolating these distinct categories of effort. As discussed in part 1, rapidly switching back and forth between support and specialist work reduces your cognitive capacity, leading to less quality work produced at a slower rate. An hour dedicated exclusively to a hard project followed by an hour dedicated exclusively to administrative work will produce more total output than if you instead mix these efforts into two hours of fragmented attention.

Technology helped push us down the road toward diminished specialization and increased overload. Once personal computers made it feasible for specialists to handle more support work, tackling an overwhelming number of obligations became the new norm, helping to cement the hyperactive hive mind workflow as the best option for wrangling our hectic professional lives.

Reimagining work, therefore, first requires more specialization. Let the knowledge workers with value-producing skills focus on applying those skills, and put in place robust and smartly configured support staff to handle everything else. This move toward less (but better), built on a balance between specialization and support, is fundamental for the evolution of knowledge work from its current inefficient chaos toward something much more organized.

Conclusion

The Twenty-First-Century Moonshot

In 1998, the social critic Neil Postman gave an important speech titled "Five Things We Need to Know about Technological Change."[1] He opened by saying that although he didn't have solutions to all the problems surrounding modern technology, he could share some ideas based on his over thirty years of studying the topic. Each of his ideas is profound. He talked, for example, about the fundamental trade-off inherent in all technological change: "For every advantage a new technology offers, there is always a corresponding disadvantage." He also argued that these advantages and disadvantages are never "distributed evenly" among the population.

It's the fourth of his five ideas, however, that I want to dwell on, as it casts into sharp relief the intellectual framework I've attempted to build in this book:

Technological change is not additive; it is ecological. . . . A new medium does not add something; it changes everything. In the year 1500, after the printing press was invented, you did not have old Europe plus the printing press. You had a different Europe.

Postman's idea clarifies the confusing cognitive dissonance so many people feel about digital communication tools like email. Rationally, we know email is a better way to deliver messages than the technologies it superseded: it's universal, it's fast, it's essentially free. For anyone old enough to remember clearing jammed fax machines or struggling to open the red-thread ties of those worn memo folders, there's no debate that email elegantly solves real problems that once made office life really annoying. At the same time, however, we're fed up with our inboxes, which seem to be as much a source of stress and overwork as they are a productivity boon. These dual reactions—admiration and detestation—are confusing and leave many knowledge workers in a state of frustrated resignation.

Drawing from Postman, we can gain clarity. The issue is that we tend to think of email as *additive*; that the office of 2021 is like the office of 1991 plus faster messaging. But this is wrong. Email isn't additive; it's *ecological*. The office of 2021 is not the office of 1991 plus some extra capabilities; it's instead a different office altogether—one in which work unfolds as a never-ending, ad hoc, unstructured flow of messages, a workflow I named *the hyperactive hive mind*. We didn't used to work this way, but today, now thoroughly entangled in the hive mind's demands, we find ourselves crushed by shallow busyness and struggling to get important work done, all the while feeling increasingly miserable.

Part 1 of this book was my attempt to elaborate this dynamic. In addition to defining the hyperactive hive mind workflow and explaining the various ways in which it diminishes our work lives, I looked closer at the complicated forces that made it ubiquitous (which turn out to have a lot to do with management theorist Peter Drucker's early in- sistence on knowledge worker autonomy). As I argued: email made the hive mind workflow possible, but it didn't make it inevitable. We're not, in other words, stuck working this way. The title of this book, *A World Without Email*, turns out to be just an approachable shorthand for the more accurate portrayal of my vision: *A World Without the Hyperactive Hive Mind Workflow*.

With this reality established, in part 2 of this book I shifted my attention from the negative aspects of this workflow to the positive op- portunities that arise once we recognize that we can replace it. Perhaps the most important observation I made in the second half of the book came in its first chapter, where I noted that the productivity of the av- erage manual laborer increased by more than *fifty times* between 1900 and 2000. The reason this is important is that near the end of his life, Peter Drucker, the man who coined the term *knowledge work*, assessed the productivity of knowledge workers to be where manual labor was in 1900. In other words, we haven't even scratched the surface of how best to operate in this new economic sector. It follows that the potential productivity gains of breaking the stranglehold of the hyperactive hive mind workflow are staggering—on the order of hundreds of billions of dollars of increased GDP, if not more. As one prominent billionaire Silicon Valley CEO told me when we recently discussed our mutual obsession with this issue: "Knowledge worker productivity is the moon- shot of the twenty-first century."

To help structure this massively important endeavor, I introduced *attention capital theory*. Once you accept that the primary capital re- source in knowledge work is the human brains you employ (or, more accurately, these brains' capacity to focus on information and produce new information that's more valuable), then basic capitalist economics take over and make it obvious that success depends on the details of how you deploy this capital. When viewed through the lens of this theory, the hyperactive hive mind becomes just one of many ways to execute this deployment. This workflow has the advantage of being easy and flexible, but it also has the disadvantage of producing a low rate of return from your capital. This should sound familiar, as this story of starting with simple capital deployments before advancing to options that are more complex but also more profitable is one that, as I showed, was repeated many times during an earlier disruptive collision of technology and commerce: the industrial revolution.

The remainder of part 2 then explored different principles for designing smarter workflows—that is, ways to perform knowledge work that are more effective than simply hooking everyone up to an inbox and letting them rock and roll. The ideas in these latter chapters aren't meant to be a comprehensive playbook, as I'm an academic, not a business expert, but I hope that their specificity will be useful in sparking the development of new strategies custom-fit to the particular circumstances that define your organization or individual professional life.

Near the end of his speech, Neil Postman said: "In the past, we experienced technological change in the manner of sleep-walkers. . . . This is a form of stupidity, especially in an age of vast technological change." He was absolutely right. Digital-era knowledge work is, on any reasonable historical scale, a recent phenomenon. It's absurdly ahistorical and shortsighted to assume that the easy workflows we threw together in the immediate aftermath of these tech breakthroughs are somehow *the best* ways to organize this complicated new type of work. Of course we didn't get this exactly right on the first try—to have done so would have been exceptional. Once seen in this context, it should be clear that the efforts of this book have nothing to do with a reactionary rejection of technology. The Luddites in this current moment are those who nostalgically cling to the hyperactive hive mind, claiming that there's no need to keep striving to improve how we work in an increasingly high-tech world.

Once we understand the contours of our frustrations with knowledge work, we recognize that we have the potential to make these efforts not only massively more productive, but also massively more fulfilling and sustainable. This has to be one of the most exciting and impactful challenges that almost no one is talking about . . . yet. "We need to proceed with our eyes wide open," concluded Postman, "so that we may use technology rather than be used by it." If you're one of the many millions exhausted by your inbox, hopeful that there must be a better way to do good work in a culture currently obsessed by constant connectivity, then it's time to open your eyes.

Acknowledgments

I began working on this book almost immediately after finishing the manuscript for *Deep Work*. At the time, I knew I had only scratched the surface of the complex landscape of issues afflicting knowledge work in an age of digital networks, but I was struggling to cohere these lingering thoughts into a useful framework. In the fall of 2015, as *Deep Work* was being prepared for printing, and my thinking was moving on to what would come next, I found myself browsing paperback displays at a Barnes & Noble in Bethesda, Maryland (now, unfortunately, closed), when I came across a copy of Jaron Lanier's book *Who Owns the Future?* I was impressed by how he complemented his criticism on the economic impacts of the internet's architecture with a bold and clear proposal for an alternative. Standing there in the aisle, holding the book, a revelation hit me that all at once seemed to clarify the muddled mass of research and intuitions with which I'd been battling: What if work didn't require email?

The first person to whom I pitched this vision was my wife, Julie, who has been helping me assess and mold book concepts since I signed my first contract with Random House at the age of twenty-one. She's the key filter through which I run all early-stage book ideas, so her positivity set the whole process in motion. The second person to hear the pitch was my longtime literary agent and publishing mentor Laurie Abkemeier, who, improbably enough, has also been working with me since I was twenty-one. She, too, encouraged me to develop the concept, and so began a long, circuitous, intellectually exhilarating research process that ultimately led to my taking this book to the market, where my editor at Portfolio, Niki Papadopoulos, as well as the imprint publisher, Adrian Zackheim, were enthusiastic, and bought this book along with *Digital Minimalism* (which I ended up publishing first, in 2019). Niki went on to play an integral role in the shaping of this book, as well as the polishing of my tone and approach in tackling these topics more generally—efforts for which I'm endlessly grateful. I must also thank the publicity team at Portfolio, including Margot Stamas and Lillian Ball, with whom I worked closely on *Digital Minimalism* and am fortunate enough to work with again on this release, as well as Mary Kate Skehan, who coordinated the marketing, and Kimberly Meilun, who managed the publishing details.

The number of writing colleagues, friends, family members, and neighbors who have heard me talk about this book concept over the years, and in turn offered smart advice, are too numerous to appropriately list, but their generosity in providing this feedback undoubtedly played a major role in sharpening my ideas. Finally, I want to highlight the contributions of my editor at *The New Yorker*, Joshua Rothman, who commissioned me to write two articles during this period on topics also covered in this book. These overlapping efforts helped accelerate the pace at which I was able to gather relevant research, and his editorial guidance helped improve both my thinking and writing on these topics.

Notes

Introduction: The Hyperactive Hive Mind

1. Chris Anderson, *Free: The Future of a Radical Price* (New York: Hyperion, 2009), 4.
2. Radicati Group, Inc., *Email Statistics Report*, 2015–2019, Palo Alto, CA, March 2015.
3. Jory MacKay, "Communication Overload: Our Research Shows Most Workers Can't Go 6 Minutes without Checking Email or IM," *RescueTime* (blog), July 11, 2018, https://blog.rescuetime.com/communication-multitasking -switches/.
4. Gloria Mark et al., "Email Duration, Batching and Self-Interruption: Patterns of Email Use on Productivity and Stress," *Proceedings of the 2016 CHI Conference on Human Factors in Computing Systems*, May 2016, 1717–28. See table 2.
5. Adobe, "2018 Consumer Email Survey," August 17, 2018, www.slideshare .net/adobe/2018-adobe-consumer-email-survey.

Chapter 1: Email Reduces Productivity

1. Victor M. González and Gloria Mark, "'Constant, Constant, Multi-tasking Craziness': Managing Multiple Working Spheres," *Proceedings of the 2004*

SIGCHI Conference on Human Factors in Computing Systems, April 2004, 113–20. I call this paper "famous" because it has been cited more than seven hundred times and is almost universally mentioned in articles and studies about distraction and attention in the modern workplace.

2. González and Mark, "'Constant, Constant.'" Table 1 of this paper captures an early form of the data indicating this swap. During my interviews with Mark, she elaborated and clarified this data, including pointing out some outlying data points. The portrayal of the data described in my text matches her updated explanation provided in this personal correspondence.

3. Judy Wajcman and Emily Rose, "Constant Connectivity: Rethinking Interruptions at Work," *Organization Studies* 32, no. 7 (July 2011): 941–61.

4. Gloria Mark et al., "Email Duration, Batching and Self-Interruption: Patterns of Email Use on Productivity and Stress," *Proceedings of the 2016 CHI Conference on Human Factors in Computing Systems*, May 2016, 1717–28.

5. Victoria Bellotti et al., "Quality Versus Quantity: E-mail–Centric Task Management and Its Relation with Overload," *Human-Computer Interaction* 20 (2005): 89–138.

6. Gail Fann Thomas et al., "Reconceptualizing E-mail Overload," *Journal of Business and Technical Communication* 20, no. 3 (July 2006): 252–87.

7. Stephen R. Barley, Debra E. Meyerson, and Stine Grodal, "E-mail as a Source and Symbol of Stress," *Organization Science* 22, no. 4 (July–August 2011): 887–906.

8. Radicati Group, Inc., *Email Statistics Report*, 2015–2019, Palo Alto, CA, March 2015.

9. Jory MacKay, "Communication Overload: Our Research Shows Most Workers Can't Go 6 Minutes without Checking Email or IM," *RescueTime* (blog), July 11, 2018, https://blog.rescuetime.com/communication-multitasking -switches/.

10. Jory MacKay, "The True Cost of Email and IM: You Only Have 1 Hour and 12 Minutes of Uninterrupted Productive Time a Day," *RescueTime* (blog), May 10, 2018, https://blog.rescuetime.com/communication-multitasking/.

11. Deirdre Boden, *The Business of Talk: Organizations in Action* (Cambridge, UK: Polity Press, 1994), 211. It should be noted that Boden was not unreservedly positive about this development in knowledge work. She also predicted that these "interactive" workplaces would be "technologically complex" and "interpersonally demanding."

12. See, for example, this classic paper on the prefrontal cortex and attention, which has been cited more than ten thousand times since its 2001 publication: Earl K. Miller and Jonathan D. Cohen, "An Integrative Theory of Prefrontal Cortex Function," *Annual Review of Neuroscience* 24 (March 2001): 167–202.

13. Adam Gazzaley and Larry D. Rosen, *The Distracted Mind: Ancient Brains in a High-Tech World* (Cambridge, MA: MIT Press, 2016), 77.

14. A. T. Jersild, "Mental Set and Shift," *Archives of Psychology* 14, no. 89 (1927): 1–81. This paper, along with other key papers on executive control functions that I consulted, was brought to my attention by the useful literature review included in the following paper: Joshua S. Rubinstein, David E. Meyer, and Jeffrey E. Evans, "Executive Control of Cognitive Processes in Task Switching," *Journal of Experimental Psychology* 27, no. 4 (2001): 763–97.

15. Gazzaley and Rosen note that these experiments are easy to try on yourself at home. They suggest the following version: Time how long it takes to go through the alphabet from A to J, and then through the numbers from 1 to 10. Next, time how long it takes for you to combine these tasks by dual counting: i.e., A1, B2, C3, and so on. You should notice a difference, as the letter and number counting draw on two different networks.

16. Sophie Leroy, "Why Is It So Hard to Do My Work? The Challenge of Attention Residue When Switching between Work Tasks," *Organizational Behavior and Human Decision Processes* 109, no. 2 (July 2009): 168–81.

17. Paul Graham, "Maker's Schedule, Manager's Schedule," July 2009, www.paulgraham.com/makersschedule.html.

18. "Marshall Retires as Chief of Staff," George C. Marshall Foundation, November 17, 2017, www.marshallfoundation.org/blog/marshall-retires-chief-staff/.

19. For more on George Marshall's career timeline, see "George C. Marshall: Timeline & Chronology," George C. Marshall Foundation, www.marshallfoundation.org/marshall/timeline-chronology/.

20. Lt. Col. Paul G. Munch, "General George C. Marshall and the Army Staff: A Study in Effective Staff Leadership" (research paper, National War College, Washington, DC, March 19, 1992), https://apps.dtic.mil/sti/citations/ADA437156.

21. Christopher C. Rosen et al., "Boxed In by Your Inbox: Implications of Daily E-mail Demands for Managers' Leadership Behaviors," *Journal of Applied Psychology* 104, no. 1 (2019): 19–33.

22. For more on the history of help-desk software, see, for example, Arthur Zuckerman, "History of Help Desk Software: Evolution and Future Trends," CompareCamp.com, February 2015, https://comparecamp.com/history-of-help-desk-software-evolution-and-future-trends/.

23. The primary source for this quote is a 1983 interview of Angelou conducted by Claudia Tate (in *Conversations with Maya Angelou*, ed. Jeffrey M. Elliot [Jackson: University Press of Mississippi, 1989], 146–56). As with many compelling anecdotes about artists' creative habits, I first came across this

quote in Mason Currey's underground classic book *Daily Rituals: How Artists Work* (New York: Knopf, 2013).

24. An addendum to this tale: When I followed up with Sean in 2019, three years after my initial interviews, his company had by then dissolved—for personal reasons unrelated to productivity, I hasten to add—preventing me from reporting on how his shift from the hyperactive hive mind evolved over time. In more recent correspondence, however, Sean assured me that if he ends up once again leading a large team, he plans to put in place similar alternatives to the hive mind—the sound of Slack notifications still makes him shiver.

Chapter 2: Email Makes Us Miserable

1. Harry Cooper, "French Workers Gain 'Right to Disconnect,'" *Politico*, December 31, 2016, www.politico.eu/article/french-workers-gain-right-to-disconnect-workers-rights-labor-law/.

2. Gloria Mark et al., "Email Duration, Batching and Self-Interruption: Patterns of Email Use on Productivity and Stress," *Proceedings of the 2016 CHI Conference on Human Factors in Computing Systems*, May 2016, 1717–28.

3. Fatema Akbar et al., "Email Makes You Sweat: Examining Email Interruptions and Stress Using Thermal Imaging," *Proceedings of the 2019 CHI Conference on Human Factors in Computing Systems*, May 2019, 1–14.

4. These concluding remarks come from Mark et al., "Email Duration."

5. Magdalena Stadin et al., "Repeated Exposure to High ICT Demands at Work, and Development of Suboptimal Self-Rated Health: Findings from a 4-Year Follow-Up of the SLOSH Study," *International Archives of Occupational and Environmental Health* 92, no. 5 (2019): 717–28.

6. Leslie A. Perlow, *Sleeping with Your Smartphone: How to Break the 24/7 Habit and Change the Way You Work* (Boston: Harvard Business Review Press, 2012), 5.

7. Perlow, *Sleeping with Your Smartphone*, 5. We'll revisit Perlow's answer to this question in more detail in the next chapter, but the short version is as follows: no one ever did decide that this workflow was a good idea; instead, in Perlow's estimation, it emerged somewhat haphazardly from an uncontrolled behavioral feedback loop.

8. John Freeman, *The Tyranny of E-mail: The Four-Thousand-Year Journey to Your Inbox* (New York: Scribner, 2011), 12.

9. Douglas Rushkoff, *Present Shock: When Everything Happens Now* (New York: Current, 2013), 95.

10. James Manyika et al., "Disruptive Technologies: Advances That Will Transform Life, Business, and the Global Economy," McKinsey Global Institute,

May 1, 2013, www.mckinsey.com/business-functions/mckinsey-digital/our-insights/disruptive-technologies.

11. This report from the Federal Reserve estimates more than sixty million "nonroutine cognitive" jobs in 2016: "Job Polarization," *FRED Blog*, April 28, 2016, https://fredblog.stlouisfed.org/2016/04/job-polarization/. In 2016, the size of the US labor force was approximately 156 million: Erin Duffin, "Civilian Labor Force in the United States from 1990 to 2019," Statista, January 30, 2020, www.statista.com/statistics/191750/civilian-labor-force-in-the-us-since-1990/.

12. As the researchers who study extant hunter-gatherer groups are careful to emphasize, it's a fallacy to portray these tribes as somehow existing *unchanged* from our Paleolithic past—these are cognitively modern humans with regular interactions with modern society. As Yuval Noah Harari points out in the opening of his book *Sapiens: A Brief History of Humankind* (New York: HarperCollins, 2015), it's also worth remembering that the very fact that such tribes still exist underscores that there must be something remarkable about them as compared with the countless other groups that shifted their lifestyles (e.g., perhaps they exist in environments too harsh to support farming-based lifestyles). All that being said, they do provide insight into hunter-gatherer social dynamics. To avoid falling into the trap of evolutionary *just so* stories, when I do later extrapolate from those dynamics to forces that affect our modern brain, I do so with care, marshaling other, more contemporary strains of evidence to support the claims.

13. Nikhil Chaudhary et al., "Competition for Cooperation: Variability, Benefits and Heritability of Relational Wealth in Hunter-Gatherers," *Scientific Reports* 6, no. 29120 (July 2016): 1–7.

14. Abigail E. Page et al., "Hunter-Gatherer Social Networks and Reproductive Success," *Scientific Reports* 7, no. 1153 (April 2017): 1–10.

15. The definitions of what makes someone robustly connected to a social network are interesting but also somewhat technical. Certainly, the number of strong connections you have to other people in the social network matters, but so do other metrics, like *centrality*, *closeness*, and *betweenness*, which, roughly speaking, all describe how well you are indirectly connected to the network through friends, friends of friends, and so on. If you're only a few short and strong hops away from most people in your tribe—the BaYaka equivalent of Kevin Bacon—you're likely quite popular.

16. Matthew D. Lieberman, *Social: Why Our Brains Are Wired to Connect* (New York: Broadway Books, 2014), 9.

17. King James Version, Leviticus 19:16.

18. William Shakespeare, *Richard II*, act 3, scene 2. Quote from MIT's public

domain Shakespeare website: http://shakespeare.mit.edu/richardii/richardii
.3.2.html. Emphasis mine.

19. Russell B. Clayton, Glenn Leshner, and Anthony Almond, "The Extended iSelf: The Impact of iPhone Separation on Cognition, Emotion, and Physiology," *Journal of Computer-Mediated Communication* 20, no. 2 (March 2015): 119–35.

20. Arianna Huffington, "How to Keep Email from Ruining Your Vacation," *Harvard Business Review*, August 23, 2017, https://hbr.org/2017/08/how-to-keep-email-from-ruining-your-vacation.

21. Richard W. Byrne, "How Monkeys Find Their Way: Leadership, Coordination, and Cognitive Maps of African Baboons," in *On the Move: How and Why Animals Travel in Groups*, ed. Sue Boinski and Paul A. Garber (Chicago: University of Chicago Press, 2000), 501. I encountered this quote in the paper cited in the next note.

22. Ariana Strandburg-Peshkin et al., "Shared Decision-Making Drives Collective Movement in Wild Baboons," *Science* 348, no. 6241 (June 2015): 1358–61.

23. The use of script for accounting purposes dates back as far as ten thousand years, but it's commonly accepted that the more general use of script that we associate today with written expression didn't begin to emerge until around 3000 BCE in Mesopotamia. Here is a good source on this history: Denise Schmandt-Besserat, "The Evolution of Writing," January 25, 2014, https://sites.utexas.edu/dsb/tokens/the-evolution-of-writing/.

24. This experiment is described here: Alex (Sandy) Pentland, *Honest Signals: How They Shape Our World* (Cambridge, MA: MIT Press, 2010), vii–viii. Some of the details of the sociometers in this description come from this magazine profile of Pentland: Maria Konnikova, "Meet the Godfather of Wearables," *The Verge*, May 6, 2014, www.theverge.com/2014/5/6/5661318/the-wizard-alex-pentland-father-of-the-wearable-computer.

25. Pentland, *Honest Signals*, x.

26. Pentland, *Honest Signals*, x.

27. Pentland, *Honest Signals*, 5.

28. Pentland, *Honest Signals*, viii–ix.

29. Pentland, *Honest Signals*, 82.

30. Elizabeth Louise Newton, "Overconfidence in the Communication of Intent: Heard and Unheard Melodies" [original title, "The Rocky Road from Actions to Intentions"] (unpublished PhD diss., Stanford University, 1990). Details on this unpublished dissertation, including Newton's interpretation and the 3 percent number, come from a summary of this work found in Justin Kruger et al., "Egocentrism over E-mail: Can We Communicate as

Well as We Think?," *Journal of Personality and Social Psychology* 89, no. 6 (December 2005): 925–36.

31. Kruger et al., "Egocentrism over E-mail."
32. Sherry Turkle, *Reclaiming Conversation: The Power of Talk in a Digital Age* (New York: Penguin, 2016), 261–62.
33. Gloria J. Mark, Stephen Voida, and Armand V. Cardello, "'A Pace Not Dictated by Electrons': An Empirical Study of Work without Email," *Proceedings of the SIGCHI Conference on Human Factors in Computing Systems*, May 2012, 555–64.
34. David Allen, *Getting Things Done: The Art of Stress-Free Productivity*, rev. ed. (New York: Penguin, 2015), 8.
35. Allen, *Getting Things Done*, 87–88.
36. Victor M. González and Gloria Mark, "'Constant, Constant, Multi-tasking Craziness': Managing Multiple Working Spheres," *Proceedings of the 2004 SIGCHI Conference on Human Factors in Computing Systems*, April 2004, 113–20.
37. Gloria Mark, Victor M. González, and Justin Harris, "No Task Left Behind?: Examining the Nature of Fragmented Work," *Proceedings of the SIGCHI Conference on Human Factors in Computing Systems*, April 2005, 321–30.
38. Brigid Schulte, *Overwhelmed: How to Work, Love, and Play When No One Has the Time* (New York: Picador, 2015), 5.
39. Sheila Dodge, Don Kieffer, and Nelson P. Repenning, "Breaking Logjams in Knowledge Work: How Organizations Can Improve Task Flow and Prevent Overload," *MIT Sloan Management Review*, September 6, 2018, https://sloanreview.mit.edu/article/breaking-logjams-in-knowledge-work/.

Chapter 3: Email Has a Mind of Its Own

1. The story of the CIA's pneumatic tubes and the general push for practical asynchrony is adapted from my 2019 *New Yorker* article on the history of email: Cal Newport, "Was E-mail a Mistake?," Annals of Technology, *New Yorker*, August 6, 2019, www.newyorker.com/tech/annals-of-technology/was-e-mail-a-mistake.
2. According to the CIA historians I consulted during my research, office networking technology was a big part of the reason the tube system was not expanded during the headquarters renovation. It was clear by the 1980s that pneumatic tubes were quite old-fashioned compared with the newly arrived ability to communicate with electrons through wires.
3. Erik Sandberg-Diment, "Personal Computers: Refinements for 'E-mail,'" *New York Times*, May 26, 1987.

4. Anne Thompson, "The Executive Life: Forget Doing Lunch—Hollywood's on E-mail," *New York Times*, September 6, 1992.

5. John Markoff, "Computer Mail Gaining a Market," *New York Times*, December 26, 1989.

6. Stephen C. Miller, "Networking: Now Software Giants Are Targeting E-mail," *New York Times*, May 31, 1992.

7. Peter H. Lewis, "Personal Computers: The Good, the Bad and the Truly Ugly Faces of Electronic Mail," *New York Times*, September 6, 1994.

8. The value of the fact that email is easy to learn shouldn't be underestimated. As Gloria Mark explained to me, during the 1980s and 1990s, as computer networks became more widespread, there was a lot of academic research on how best to leverage this technology to support workplace collaboration. Much of this research focused on advanced multiuser network applications that were customized for specific purposes—like collaboratively editing a certain type of document. As Mark told me, email dominated where these bespoke solutions faltered because it was so easy to learn and could be applied to many different types of work. A onetime investment in an email server could simplify collaboration in all aspects of your business.

9. The story and quote come from this Quora thread: www.quora.com/What-was-it-like-to-work-in-an-office-before-the-birth-of-personal-computers-email-and-fax-machines. I also interviewed Stone to confirm and elaborate some of these points.

10. For a discussion and summary of Brunner's arguments, including relevant citations, see Lynn White Jr., *Medieval Technology and Social Change* (Oxford: Oxford University Press, 1966), 3.

11. White, *Medieval Technology*, 5.

12. White, *Medieval Technology*, 13.

13. White, *Medieval Technology*, 13.

14. As Lynn White Jr. elaborates, though Benedictine monks were trying to stop the practice, around this period many Frankish warriors were being buried with their horses, allowing modern archaeologists to dig up evidence about how these horses were equipped in battle. Also around this time, the words used to describe mounting and dismounting horses shifted from verbs that captured the action of leaping up on a horse to verbs that captured more of a stepping behavior.

15. White, *Medieval Technology*, 2.

16. Neil Postman, *Amusing Ourselves to Death: Public Discourse in the Age of Show Business* (New York: Penguin, 1985), 51.

17. For more on this history, see chapter 1 of my previous book: Cal Newport, *Digital Minimalism: Choosing a Focused Life in a Noisy World* (New York: Portfolio/Penguin, 2019).

18. Blake Thorne, "Asynchronous Communication Is the Future of Work," *I Done This* (blog), June 30, 2020, http://blog.idonethis.com/asynchronous -communication/.

19. Radicati Group, Inc., *Email Statistics Report*, 2015–2019, Palo Alto, CA, March 2015.

20. Michael J. Fischer, Nancy A. Lynch, and Michael S. Paterson, "Impossibility of Distributed Consensus with One Faulty Process," *Journal of the ACM* 32, no. 2 (April 1985): 374–82.

21. For the interested reader, the high-level summary of this impossibility proof unfolds as follows. Every consensus algorithm must, at some point, have each machine look at the messages it has received so far and determine whether to proceed or abort. Regardless of what rule you use to make this decision, there must be some boundary between proceed and abort, where changing just a single message pushes you from one decision to the other. The proof essentially brings a lot of machines right up against this boundary, then crashes the machine that sends the key message halfway through its sending, meaning that some machines receive the message and some don't—leading to conflicting decisions. Interestingly, if you're allowed to flip coins and are satisfied with an algorithm that solves the problem with high probability, then it is solvable. Similarly, if you assume any sort of reasonable time-out on how long to wait for a machine before you know for sure it has crashed, you can also solve the problem.

22. I was at the ceremony in Paris where Lamport was awarded his prize. In typical French fashion, the government officials in attendance wore impeccable suits. In typical computer scientist fashion, Lamport wore shorts and a T-shirt.

23. Leslie A. Perlow, *Sleeping with Your Smartphone: How to Break the 24/7 Habit and Change the Way You Work* (Boston: Harvard Business Review Press, 2012), 2.

24. Perlow, *Sleeping with Your Smartphone*, 8.

25. Perlow, *Sleeping with Your Smartphone*, 5.

26. Douglas Rushkoff, *Present Shock: When Everything Happens Now* (New York: Current, 2013), 100.

27. Aviad Agam and Ran Barkai, "Elephant and Mammoth Hunting during the Paleolithic: A Review of the Relevant Archaeological, Ethnographic and Ethno-historical Records," *Quaternary* 1, no. 3 (February 2018): 1–28.

28. "Is Your Team Too Big? Too Small? What's the Right Number?," *Knowledge@ Wharton*, June 14, 2006, https://knowledge.wharton.upenn.edu/article/is -your-team-too-big-too-small-whats-the-right-number-2/. This article is also the source of the information about Ringelmann's research summarized in the discussion that follows.

29. Information on Drucker's early life, including his parents' salons, can be found at the Drucker Institute's bio of its namesake: www.drucker.insti tute/perspective/about-peter-drucker/.

30. One of many places where this epithet is bestowed: Steve Denning, "The Best of Peter Drucker," *Forbes*, July 29, 2014, www.forbes.com/sites/steve denning/2014/07/29/the-best-of-peter-drucker.

31. Peter F. Drucker, *The Future of Industrial Man* (Rutgers, NJ: Transaction Publishers, 2011), 13.

32. For more on Drucker's GM engagement, see the following account: "How Drucker 'Invented' Management at GM," Drucker Society of Austria, 2009, www.druckersociety.at/index.php/peterdruckerhome/biography/how -drucker-invented-management-at-general-motors.

33. This quote is reproduced in the Drucker Institute's timeline of Drucker's life, www.drucker.institute/perspective/about-peter-drucker/. It also appears in the April 14 entry of Peter F. Drucker, *The Daily Drucker: 366 Days of Insight and Motivation for Getting the Right Things Done* (New York: Harper Business, 2004).

34. Peter F. Drucker, *The Effective Executive: The Definitive Guide to Getting the Right Things Done*, rev. ed. (New York: Harper Business, 2006), 4.

35. Peter F. Drucker, "Knowledge-Worker Productivity: The Biggest Challenge," *California Management Review* 41, no. 2 (Winter 1999): 79–94. Italics in the original.

36. Lloyd didn't use the phrase "tragedy of the commons." This label was introduced later in a now famous article that rigorously analyzes the scenario: Garrett Hardin, "The Tragedy of the Commons," *Science* 162, no. 3859 (December 1968): 1243–48.

Chapter 4: The Attention Capital Principle

1. Joshua B. Freeman, *Behemoth: A History of the Factory and the Making of the Modern World* (New York: W. W. Norton, 2019), 124.

2. The details of the development of the assembly line, including the specific numbers cited in this discussion, come from two excellent secondary sources: Freeman, *Behemoth*, 119–26; and Simon Winchester, *The Perfectionists: How Precision Engineers Created the Modern World* (New York: Harper, 2018), 159–66.

3. As Simon Winchester points out in *The Perfectionists* (see preceding note), at the same time as the Model T's rise, Henry Royce's ultra-luxury vehicles, such as the Rolls-Royce Silver Ghost, which were hand-built by skilled craftsmen, were marketed as the height of precision engineering. In reality, however, the pieces of the lowly Model T were manufactured with considerably

more exactitude—the high price of the Rolls-Royce afforded its manufacturer the labor required to hand-adjust looser parts into a tight fit.

4. Freeman, *Behemoth*, 123.

5. As Simon Winchester points out, American armories had geared up mass production lines years earlier. By 1913, sewing machine, bicycle, and typewriter manufacturers had also begun taking advantage of the interchangeable parts revolution to experiment with fast-moving assembly lines. Ford claims, however, that his main inspiration was actually the *disassembly* of animal carcasses that he had witnessed at the nearby Chicago meatpacking plants, where the knife-wielding meatpackers stood in place while the animals moved by, hanging from chains.

6. Cal Newport, "5-Hour Workdays? 4-Day Workweeks? Yes, Please," *New York Times*, November 6, 2019.

7. Winchester, *Perfectionists*, 160.

8. Peter F. Drucker, "Knowledge-Worker Productivity: The Biggest Challenge," *California Management Review* 41, no. 2 (Winter 1999): 79–94. Italics in the original.

9. Drucker, "Knowledge-Worker Productivity."

10. In industrial economics, the workers were considered more dispensable: a sort of generic force used to activate your main capital resources into motion. This mindset was the foundation of worker dehumanization. As I'll elaborate, one of the benefits of knowledge work versus the industrial alternatives is that the workers are no longer dispensable, but are actually now at the core of an organization's value, enabling the potential for much more human-centric working environments.

11. Peter F. Drucker, *The Effective Executive: The Definitive Guide to Getting the Right Things Done*, rev. ed. (New York: Harper Business, 2006), 4.

12. Freeman, *Behemoth*, 123.

13. Peter F. Drucker, *Landmarks of Tomorrow: A Report on the New "Post-Modern" World* (New York: Harper Colophon, 1965), 31.

14. James T. McCay, *The Management of Time* (Englewood Cliffs, NJ: Prentice-Hall, 1959), ix.

15. Freeman, *Behemoth*, 126.

16. Freeman, *Behemoth*, 127.

17. These details, and the connection of *Modern Times* to Ford's plant, come from David E. Nye, *America's Assembly Line* (Cambridge, MA: MIT Press, 2013), 97.

18. To explain to the younger reader born after a time when these services were more common: A telephone answering service played the role of a live voicemail system. If you needed to reach a doctor after hours, for example, you would call the practice's answering service, where a live operator would

answer and pass along your information to the doctor on call. It is much cheaper to have one service implement this for many clients than to have each of those clients staff their own phone lines twenty-four hours a day.

19. Sam Carpenter, *Work the System: The Simple Mechanics of Making More and Working Less*, 3rd ed. (Austin, TX: Greenleaf Book Group Press, 2011), chapter 2. I had access to only an electronic version of this book on my Kindle, so I am unable to cite specific page numbers for quotes taken from this source.

20. Carpenter, *Work the System*, chapter 3.

21. Carpenter, *Work the System*, chapter 4.

22. The income quote and notes on being number one of 1,500 in some categories come from the official website for *Work the System*: Sam Carpenter, "Synopsis—For Your Business: Breaking Loose," July 1, 2015, www.workthe system.com/book/synopsis/.

23. All quotes in this paragraph are from Carpenter, *Work the System*, chapter 11.

24. The specific version of the autoresponder reproduced here comes from this site: https://tim.blog/autoresponse/.

25. See, for example, Adam Grant, "In the Company of Givers and Takers," *Harvard Business Review*, April 2013, https://hbr.org/2013/04/in-the-company -of-givers-and-takers.

Chapter 5: The Process Principle

1. An interesting aside for fans of David Allen's Getting Things Done methodology: the "tickler" file, a mainstay of Allen's modern system, comes up as a standard tool in these early twentieth-century industrial productivity discussions.

2. Joseph Husband, "What a New System of Management Did for Us," ed. John S. Runnells, *System: The Magazine of Business* 29, no. 4 (April 1916).

3. Andrew S. Grove, *High Output Management* (New York: Vintage, 2015), 33.

4. Kent Beck et al., "Manifesto for Agile Software Development," 2001, agilemanifesto.org.

5. Modus Cooperandi website, https://moduscooperandi.com, accessed September 22, 2020.

6. *Thrive*, the official blog of Personal Kanban, http://personalkanban.com/pk/.

7. Alexie Zheglov and Gerry Kirk, "Lean Coffee or an Introduction to Personal Kanban," Agile Tour Toronto 2012 session, YouTube video, 1:40, https ://youtu.be/aOrfRhcD6ms.

8. Bradley Miller, "Personal Kanban Scheduling Board," March 4, 2018, YouTube video, 7:46, https://youtu.be/tTdbcoTlljQ.

9. I long ago realized that trying to generate complex numerical grades for my problem sets—e.g., scoring a problem on a scale of 1 to 15—wasn't worth the effort, and made it very hard to grade consistently. I've since shifted to a scale with three possibilities (check plus, check, or zero), which lets me and my TAs quickly and consistently assess the degree to which the student understands each concept.

10. If my TAs are undergraduates, I'll add an extra step in which we have a prescheduled thirty-minute meeting to look through the problem sets and update the grading notes together. When I use graduate TAs, however, I trust them to figure this out on their own, saving me this extra thirty minutes. When Georgetown's campus was closed due to COVID-19, we used a software tool called Canvas to make all the paper handling virtual; students submitted digital copies of their assignments, and the TAs graded them online. The process was easily adapted to this new fully electronic setup.

11. Rory Vaden, "The 30x Rule: How Great Managers Multiply Performance," American Management Association, February 3, 2015, https://playbook.amanet.org/30x-rule-great-managers-multiply-performance/.

Chapter 6: The Protocol Principle

1. When I was writing my master's thesis at MIT in the electrical engineering and computer science department (the field Shannon created from scratch with his 1937 work), we heard about Shannon's spectacular student efforts. In retrospect, I'm not sure if this was supposed to motivate us or demoralize us.

2. For a more complete treatment of Claude Shannon, I recommend Jimmy Soni and Rob Goodman's fascinating 2017 biography, which was the source for much of the summary that follows: *A Mind at Play: How Claude Shannon Invented the Information Age* (New York: Simon & Schuster, 2017).

3. Information theorists would traditionally use the word *code* instead of *protocol* in this instance, but for the sake of clarity in the discussion we're having here, I'm going to use *protocol*—as in a set of communication rules agreed on in advance—as it sidesteps the colloquial associations people hold with respect to the word *code*.

4. Though he didn't have the mathematical framework required to quantify what he was doing, Samuel Morse assigned the shortest possible encoding, a single dot, to "e," the most common letter in written English, in his famed telegraph communication protocol, Morse code.

5. Prior to Shannon, communication engineers dealt with interference on channels such as telegraph or telephone wires by trying to make the signal stronger to overcome the noise. Shannon showed the power of a *digital*

approach, where you encode a single bit using multiple bits, deployed using a clever code that allows you to reconstruct the original bit even if many of those transmitted are corrupted with noise. This is how all digital communication and storage mediums now work.

6. More on the investment rounds of x.ai can be found in Kyle Wiggers, "X.ai's AI Meeting Scheduler Now Costs $8 per Month," *VentureBeat*, October 10, 2018, https://venturebeat.com/2018/10/10/x-ai-introduces-calendar-view-and-new-plans-starting-at-8-per-month/. The specific $26 million figure comes from my personal conversations with Mortensen. Interestingly, as detailed in this article, Mortensen eventually realized that having Amy communicate with natural language wasn't actually that important. The latest version of the product offers more structured interfaces for meeting planning.

7. Leslie A. Perlow, Constance Noonan Hadley, and Eunice Eun, "Stop the Meeting Madness," *Harvard Business Review*, July–August 2017, https://hbr.org/2017/07/stop-the-meeting-madness.

8. To elaborate on my use of part-time assistants, I do not, at the moment, have a permanent assistant. I tend instead to bring on assistants temporarily to help during particularly busy periods, such as those surrounding book launches. This would not have been possible in an age before web-based part-time remote work platforms.

9. Cal Newport, "A Modest Proposal: Eliminate Email," *Harvard Business Review*, February 18, 2016, https://hbr.org/2016/02/a-modest-proposal-eliminate-email.

10. Jason Fried and David Heinemeier Hansson, *It Doesn't Have to Be Crazy at Work* (New York: Harper Business, 2018).

11. Fried and Hansson, *Crazy at Work*, 56.

12. Fried and Hansson, *Crazy at Work*, 57.

13. Scott Kirsner, "I'm Joining the Open Office Hours Movement, November 24th," Boston.com, November 20, 2009, http://archive.boston.com/business/technology/innoeco/2009/11/im_joining_the_open_office_hou.html.

14. Cal Newport, *So Good They Can't Ignore You: Why Skills Trump Passion in the Quest for Work You Love* (New York: Business Plus, 2012), 73.

15. The original name of the company was Princeton Internet Solutions. Michael and I soon realized, however, that the resulting acronym was less than optimal.

16. Tom Foster, "Tim Ferriss's 4-Hour Reality Check," *Inc.*, April 2, 2013, www.inc.com/magazine/201304/tom-foster/tim-ferriss-four-hour-reality-check.html.

17. Here are the relevant histories from which the different aspects of the email story were pulled: Samuel Gibbs, "How Did Email Grow from Messages between Academics to a Global Epidemic?," *The Guardian*, March 7, 2016,

www.theguardian.com/technology/2016/mar/07/email-ray-tomlinson -history; and Ray Tomlinson, "Frequently Asked Questions," http://open map.bbn.com/~tomlinso/ray/firstemailframe.html.

18. C. L. Max Nikias, "Why All My Emails Are the Lengths of Texts," *Wall Street Journal*, September 19, 2017, https://www.wsj.com/articles/why-all -my-emails-are-the-lengths-of-texts-1505829919. It's worth noting that a year after the publication of the 2017 op-ed cited here, Nikias resigned from his position as president of USC. As subsequent reporting revealed, the outward successes of his presidency had been mirrored by an erosion of trust between Nikias and the faculty at the university, leading to unhappiness. It's probably safe to assume, however, that this ouster had nothing to do with his email habits (faculty do not have direct email access to the president at large universities), so we can still learn from his tactics for remaining productive with an overfilled inbox.

19. Mike Davidson, "A Low-Fi Solution to E-Mail Overload: Sentenc.es," MikeIndustries.com, July 17, 2007, https://mikeindustries.com/blog/archive /2007/07/fight-email-overload-with-sentences.

20. Michael Hicks and Jeffrey S. Foster, "Adapting Scrum to Managing a Research Group" (Department of Computer Science Technical Report #CS-TR-4966, University of Maryland, College Park, September 18, 2010), https ://drum.lib.umd.edu/handle/1903/10743.

Chapter 7: The Specialization Principle

1. Edward Tenner, *Why Things Bite Back: Technology and the Revenge of Unintended Consequences* (New York: Vintage, 1997), 238–39.

2. Tenner, *Why Things Bite Back*, 240.

3. Peter G. Sassone, "Survey Finds Low Office Productivity Linked to Staffing Imbalances," *National Productivity Review* 11, no. 2 (Spring 1992): 147–58. This study was also cited and summarized by Edward Tenner in *Why Things Bite Back* (cited in the preceding two notes), which is how I first came across it.

4. Cal Newport, "Is Email Making Professors Stupid?," *Chronicle of Higher Education*, February 12, 2019, www.chronicle.com/interactives/is-email-making -professors-stupid.

5. Greg McKeown, *Essentialism: The Disciplined Pursuit of Less* (New York: Crown Business, 2014), 1–3.

6. Readers of my book *Deep Work* might identify this phenomenon as what I called the *whiteboard effect*. Generally speaking, using a common screen or board to work collaboratively with a small group on a hard problem will intensify the depth of concentration you achieve compared with working

alone. Cal Newport, *Deep Work: Rules for Focused Success in a Distracted World* (New York: Grand Central Publishing, 2016).

7. Anne Lamott, "Time Lost and Found," *Sunset*, April 5, 2010, www.sunset .com/travel/anne-lamott-how-to-find-time.

8. Pat Flynn, "SPI 115: 9000 Unread Emails to Inbox Zero: My Executive Assistant Shares How We Did It (and How You Can Too!)," June 28, 2014, in *Smart Passive Income Podcast with Pat Flynn*, 35:22, www.smartpassivein come.com/podcasts/email-management/.

9. Laura Vanderkam, "Can You Really Spend Just 20 Hours a Week on Core Production?," LauraVanderkam.com, October 15, 2015, https://lauravander kam.com/2015/10/can-you-really-spend-just-20-hours-a-week-on-core -production/.

10. For more on Scrum sprints and the timing of this methodology's formation, see Ken Schwaber and Jeff Sutherland, *The Scrum Guide: The Definitive Guide to Scrum: The Rules of the Game*, November 2017, www.scrumguides .org/docs/scrumguide/v2017/2017-Scrum-Guide-US.pdf.

11. The timeline and details of Google Ventures cited come from its website: www.gv.com/.

12. My summary of the sprint methodology comes from Jake Knapp, with John Zeratsky and Braden Kowitz, *Sprint: How to Solve Big Problems and Test New Ideas in Just Five Days* (New York: Simon & Schuster, 2016).

13. Bruce Janz, "Is Email Making Professors Stupid? That's Not the Issue," Department of Philosophy, University of Central Florida, February 12, 2019, https://faculty.cah.ucf.edu/bbjanz/is-email-making-professors-stupid -thats-not-the-issue/.

14. Laura Vanderkam recommends that individual knowledge workers start by figuring out how much time to invest in different activities, and then work backward to hit these targets, implementing a self-imposed activity budget: Laura Vanderkam, "How to Craft a Perfect, Productive 40-Hour Workweek," *Fast Company*, October 13, 2015, www.fastcompany.com/3052051 /how-to-craft-a-perfect-productive-40-hour-work-week.

15. Linda Babcock, Maria P. Recalde, and Lise Vesterlund, "Why Women Volunteer for Tasks That Don't Lead to Promotions," *Harvard Business Review*, July 16, 2018, https://hbr.org/2018/07/why-women-volunteer-for-tasks-that -dont-lead-to-promotions.

16. Around the time I was writing this chapter, Georgetown began putting into place an impressive, invisible UI–style service to help professors work on academic research more effectively. The university is appointing "research coordinators" for each of the major research areas. If a professor has any questions about the administrative infrastructure surrounding their work

(e.g., grant issues), they can just ask the coordinator, who will then find the right support units to get the needed information or resolve the issue.

Conclusion: The Twenty-First-Century Moonshot

1. Neil Postman, "Five Things We Need to Know about Technological Change" (talk delivered in Denver, CO, March 28, 1998), https://web.cs.ucdavis.edu /~rogaway/classes/188/materials/postman.pdf.

Index

About the Author

Cal Newport is an associate professor of computer science at Georgetown University, where he specializes in the theory of distributed systems, as well as a *New York Times* bestselling author who writes for a broader audience about the intersection of technology and culture. He's the author of seven books, including *Digital Minimalism* and *Deep Work*, which have been published in over thirty languages. He's also a regular contributor on these topics to national publications such as *The New Yorker*, *The New York Times*, and *Wired*, and is a frequent guest on NPR. His blog, *Study Hacks*, which he's been publishing since 2007, attracts over three million visits a year. He lives with his wife and three sons in Takoma Park, Maryland.